TO SERVE OTHER GODS

An Evangelical History Of Religion

Michael A. Harbin

UNIVERSITY
PRESS OF
AMERICA

Lanham • New York • London

Copyright © 1994 by
University Press of America,® Inc.
4720 Boston Way
Lanham, Maryland 20706

3 Henrietta Street
London WC2E 8LU England

Library of Congress Cataloging-in-Publication Data
Harbin, Michael A.
To serve other gods : an evangelical history of religion /
Michael A. Harbin.
p.   cm.
Includes bibliographical references and indexes.
1. Religions.   2. Evangelicalism.   I. Title.
BL85.H24   1994   291—dc20   94-29677 CIP

ISBN 0–8191–9717–3 (cloth : alk. paper)
ISBN 0–8191–9718–1 (pbk. : alk. paper)

 The paper used in this publication meets the minimum requirements of
American National Standard for Information Sciences—Permanence
of Paper for Printed Library Materials, ANSI Z39.48–1984.

I wish to dedicate this work to my wife, Esther, with thanks for her patience, her encouragement, and her careful, critical reading of the various revisions of the manuscript. Likewise, I would like to thank my Pastor, Dr. Michael Kempainen, who read the original manuscript and strongly encouraged me to continue.

Contents

Preface

This study surveys the development of world religion. The arguments are forthright and twofold. History shows a universal trend from monotheism to polytheism. The Biblical record provides adequate insight to explain the apparent chaos on the world religious scene. As an introductory study, this work is necessarily limited in its scope. There are many religious issues which have not been covered. This is not to say that they are unimportant, but that they are beyond the limits of this introductory study. It is hoped that this work will precipitate further studies to explore those issues.

Because of the complexity of the material the main body covers very broad brush stroke themes. Extended footnotes amplify many issues which, while important, could not be explored in the main survey. This includes much of the substantiating detail. This allows the reader the opportunity to evaluate the overall argument separately from all the data which support it, while at the same time provides that detail for those who desire to explore further.

Since this work covers a number of religious systems, each must be developed with the barest amount of detail--focusing on the *history* and process of development to the detriment of current beliefs and related issues. In many cases there are a number of works which cover individual religions or issues. An annotated bibliography points the interested reader to some of the many works available which cover those areas in more detail.

As the material was surveyed, judgment calls were made on what to include and what to omit. The decisions were entirely my own, as I attempted to draw together in a concise manner extensive research. Recognizing that my judgment is not infallible, I accept the blame if the decisions on certain particulars do not bear up. I trust and pray that the overall work points in the right direction, solely for the glory of God.

Introduction

Man is a religious creature. This is one of the factors which sets him apart from the animal kingdom. But, it is obvious that we do not agree on the religion we follow. In fact, we are surrounded by a plethora of religions, religion substitutes, and even supposed anti-religious groups.

How do we chose what religion we should follow? Most of us adopt the religion our parents and grand-parents held. It was part of the culture we grew up in, much like the food we ate, or the language we spoke. As such, it now feels comfortable like a well worn coat. Usually, we are hard-pressed to identify the particulars that appeal to us. Philosophers label these values our "presuppositions"--values we hold on a sub-conscious level.

True, we often question our backgrounds as we grow older. This questioning normally coincides with exposure to other values, sometimes in high school, sometimes in college. It is a part of developing our personal self-identity. The type and intensity of our questioning varies and somewhat depends on individual security and the pressures we experience growing up.

Historically, most people have matured in a more or less homogeneous sub-culture, such as a rural community where the young people inherited and stayed on the family farm. Or where they continued the family business. There the questioning experience is less intense. Cosmopolitan communities such as trade centers or large cities have promoted more intense questioning. The American society has from its outset promoted a more intense value questioning due to its juxtaposing of various sub-cultures in close proximity. Still, for the first one hundred and fifty years or so, the preponderance of these replanted sub-cultures were of a similar strain--different aspects of the Judeo-Christian tradition.

From the initial settlements on the East Coast during the 1600's until the Civil War, the predominant force was the Protestant aspect of that stream. From the Civil War forward, the Catholic and Jewish portions of that stream increased drastically. Even-so Protestantism held sway, at least in the key power positions. Other religious heritages showed up as distinct minorities, usually confined to narrow geographical locations.

During the past half-century that picture has changed radically as the U.S. has become an increasingly multi-cultural society. As a result, we are challenged by people from vastly different backgrounds with very diverse beliefs. In the give and take of the market-place of ideas, we are challenged to examine our beliefs critically to discover why we believe what we believe.

World War II irrevocably changed our society. Prior to the war, the U.S. was predominantly rural and agricultural. After the war, it became predominantly urban and industrial. Prior to the war, a college education was the exception, usually preserved for an elite. After the war, with the G.I. Bill, it became a norm. More critically, we became a dynamic society. It has been estimated that by the 1960's the average family moved every three years.

As a result, the post war generation (whatever its religious background) grew up without a solid foundation for its faith. As it hit the university in the 1960's, for the first time there was a wholesale questioning of the entire inherited value system as an entire generation began searching for meaning. Alternative sources of meaning were explored. Many individuals tried drugs, eastern religions, or abandoned religion all together.

But no-one ever really abandons religion. Instead we substitute one creed for another. It may be Zen. It may be humanism. It may be Marxism. It may be materialism. It may be self. Every man is religious in some sense. Modern man finds this hard to swallow and attempts to deny it, refusing to accept his own religiosity. Still, we all have something that we hold of ultimate importance, a standard by which we evaluate all other things. This is our religious foundation. Or, as Webster defines religious:

> 1. relating to that which is acknowledged as ultimate reality: manifesting devotion to and reflecting the nature of the divine or that which one holds to be of ultimate importance.[1]

Introduction

It is for this reason that the U.S. Supreme Court has held historically that even secular humanism fits the criteria for a religion. Miceli found in his in depth study of atheism that even atheists do not "merely deny God," but rather prefer "some other Being above God." In other words, they "create mythical gods in place of the true God."[2]

If it is true I serve some god, how do I determine the validity of the god I serve? Is there a "true God?" If so, how do I know Him? How we answer these questions determines how we view religion in general.

When I entered college in the turbulent 60's, I was afraid to examine my faith. I was secure in it and didn't want my security stripped from me. I was afraid that under close scrutiny, the religion I had accepted as a boy might be found wanting. As I worked on my engineering degree in a secular college, I didn't think I had to deal with the issue; not even when I changed my major from nuclear physics to history to make sure I graduated. I kept my religion in its little closet reserved for Sundays. I studied, rowed crew, and tried to go along with the crowd.

But by the end of my junior year I had discovered I couldn't avoid the issue. If I dated girls from different backgrounds, religious questions arose. As I talked to friends in the dorm late at night, I was struck by differences in background--and beliefs. Finally, I realized that I could not be satisfied with a religion that could not be tested. I needed one that satisfied intellectually. Ultimately that is where this study began.

As I applied the rigid principles of examination learned in my engineering program and my history major, I found only one "religion" met those standards, historic Christianity. The first question I had to answer was, "was Jesus really who he claimed to be?" To answer that question, I examined critically the book that contained those claims. As a result, I came back to the Bible as containing ultimate truth and revelation, and attempted to apply it to my life. I then asked the question, "if Jesus was really who He claimed to be, what did that mean to me as an individual?" The answer to that question changed the entire course of my life.

Still, one question bothered me. If there is one true God, why are there so many religions?

Since the time of Darwin[3] and Wellhausen,[4] the popular answer has been that religion has developed evolutionally. The evolutional view argues that since primitive tribes (i.e., not civilized) today have a multitude of gods and pagan beliefs, likewise early man (also not civilized) had similar beliefs. The idea is that technological simplicity denotes intellectual simplicity and "primitiveness." So, it is argued that man made gods in his image. As man became civilized, so did his religion, and as there are different civilizations, there are different religions. By the time I graduated from college, I had accepted this answer--but solely because I had never examined it.

Over the subsequent years, I have found serious problems with this view. From a scientific perspective, more and more evidence suggests that it is inaccurate, simplistic, and misleading. Religious systems tend to divide, creating different sects and concepts of God. The number of Christian denominations easily illustrates that. There are similar divisions in Judaism, Islam, Hinduism, and Buddhism. Religions tend to multiply even the number of gods. The trend historically has been increasingly toward polytheism, rather than toward monotheism.[5]

From an individual perspective, Darwin's view does not give me any reason to esteem any being higher than myself. If I am the product of chance and change, who is the being that is worthy of my worship? Evolution substitutes the god of chance for the God Who creates. Why then should I even seek out any religion in the organized sense of the word at all? Yet, I have an almost intuitive realization that I need to do so. I crave to find a god.

If religion is merely man's attempt to explain the inexplicable, what difference does it make which religion I choose? Why should I even limit my religious perspective, if there is no value in picking any one religion over another. In fact, according to this view, the highest religion might be the one which can encompass the most of conflicting views. Several religions in recent years have tried to do just that.

Are there similarities in all religions? Yes, because they all try to answer the same basic questions. Do they all have the same answers? No.

Are their answers compatible? Some are, and some aren't. The basic concepts of morality are similar. The procedures for functioning best in society are similar. After all men are basically the same. But the question of how man should approach God appears to be a great water-shed. Some religions claim it doesn't matter. Others claim exclusivity.

But if there is true truth, there must be an explanation for the world as we see it. The Judeo-Christian tradition proposes such an explanation.[6] My premise is Paul's--man was made in God's image and originally worshipped the one true God. That true worship has been carried on throughout history by a minority as the majority has abandoned God and His revelation. Paul states that Jesus demonstrated the reality of His claims with power through the resurrection (Romans 1:4). Throughout the centuries fallen men have substituted the created for the Creator as Paul asserted in Romans 1.

This book begins with the following premises. There is a logical explanation for the world as we know it. Jesus was Who He claimed to be. The Bible is the inspired Word of God, inerrant wherein it speaks.

We recognize that the Biblical record is incomplete. Its purpose is not to write an exhaustive, or even a complete history of man. Still, where the Biblical record interacts with others records, there should be correlation. I believe that these assertions can be demonstrated through history, and especially through the history of religion. And that is the purpose of this book.

Notes

[1] *Webster's Third New International Dictionary of the English Language, Unabridged*, 1971 edition. A number of scholars in the field have developed similar working definitions. For instance, John A. Hutchison (*Paths of Faith*, p. 4) opts for "ultimate value" after rejecting Paul Tillich's "ultimate concern" and R. B. Perry's "ultimate interest."

[2] Vincent P. Miceli, *The Gods of Atheism*, p. xiv. Miceli's work is a "must" for the study of modern philosophy because of his insightful examination of modern "atheistic" thinkers.

[3] Charles Darwin expounded this view merely in an outline sense in *The Descent of Man* published in 1871, 12 years after his *Origin of Species*. He states:

> But until the faculties of imagination, curiosity, reason, &c., had been fairly well developed in the mind of man, his dreams would not have led him to believe in spirits, any more than in the case of a dog. . . .
> The belief in spiritual agencies would easily pass into the belief

in the existence of one or more gods.

. . . then in fetishism, polytheism, and ultimately in monotheism (*Great Books of the Western World*, vol. 49, pp. 320-3).

[4] Julius Wellhausen published his *Prolegomena to the History of Ancient Israel* in 1878. He had two premises, one stated, one unstated. The stated premise is that the Old Testament developed from several documents all written during the late kingdom and exile time-frame (p. 13). From this he attempts to show a development of Judaism from a loosely related collection of tribal rites centering around local altars to a unified religion during the period of about 600 to 300 BC. The unstated premise is that before this time a certain amount of evolutionary development occurred. He does state:

> It was not as if Jehovah had originally been regarded as the God of the universe who subsequently became the God of Israel . . . . Whatever Jehovah may have been conceived to be in His essential nature--God of the thunderstorm or the like--this fell more and more into the background as mysterious and transcendental . . . (p. 437).

[5] Arthur C. Custance covers the issue quickly in his monograph "From Monotheism to Polytheism," (pages 113-131) in *Evolution or Creation*, volume 4 of The Doorway Papers, published by Zondervan, 1971.

[6] The premise of traditional Christianity is that Jesus Christ is the Messiah who was promised to the Jewish nation, and thus Christianity is considered the fulfillment of Judaism. Modern Judaism denies this claim and looks for another Messiah. Initially, this issue alone divided the two groups. Up to this point they claim a common heritage and worship the same God, follow the same ethic, and even follow the same Scripture (as far as the Old Testament is concerned--Christianity puts the New Testament on an equal footing with the Old since it is viewed as the fulfillment and explanation of the Old).

PART I

Early Religion

The origins of religion are lost in the "pre-history" of man--that period of his existence on earth prior to our earliest historical records. Still, there are hints in the data we have that are suggestive. If our premises are true, there should be strong evidence, not only substantiating the premises, but indicating the development process.

Chapter 1

The Beginnings

The first question of any history of religion is, "Where did it all begin?" Prior to the age of discovery, our ancestors did not discuss the issue, at least on what we would call a scholarly level. Some writers did mention the subject, but in these cases history of religion equated to a history of the Judeo-Christian tradition, with some mention of the early Greek and Roman cults.

Few Europeans encountered religions beyond their own because few traveled beyond their local circles. Even then, encounters were essentially limited to adherents of Judaism or Islam. As explorers began expanding the European horizons in the 15th century, the picture changed. This larger world contained a plethora of other religions.

Theories of Origins

It has only been during the past two centuries, however, that history of religion has become a subject of study. Almost as soon as the subject was recognized, different theories began to arise to explain the phenomenon.

Fetishism. The age of exploration began with the Portuguese. Early explorers noted worship in African tribes centering around physical items such as shells or stones. The shell or stone was viewed as the dwelling place of the spirit worshipped. Outside observers perceived them as objects of worship (in many cases, perhaps a very subtle distinction). The Portuguese called these objects *fetiches*, which can be translated as "charms." Some scholars saw these objects as primitive precursors of idol worship, and thus the first form of religious worship.[1]

Animism. In 1872, Ed. B. Tylor postulated that primitive man had become aware of the concept of soul through comparing the body in death and sleep (when the body appeared abandoned), and dreams, where figures appeared without the actual body. By analogy, he argued, these primitives applied the soul principle to all nature---e.g., beasts, plants, rocks, etc., possessed a body and a soul.

Several subsidiary schools of thought sprang out of animism. One was the idea that religion began with ancestor worship, which is the worship of the souls of men who had died and no longer had the physical body. Another suggested that it began with nature worship, which is the worship of a soul which indwells all the physical world. Animism was displaced as further studies in various ancient near eastern inscriptions revealed the "advanced nature" of those early religions, although aspects still survive today.[2]

Totemism. As explorers encountered various primitive tribes, they noticed that different tribes worshipped animals which were closely associated with the tribal ancestors. This theory proposed that a given culture would postulate that an ancestor of the tribe was an animal which possessed traits which the tribe valued. In the totem, these traits were purified--e.g., if the "bear" tribe esteemed strength, then the totem bear was a paradigm of strength. "Real" bears were portrayed as mere shadows of this totem.[3]

Totemism is closely associated with the work of Sir James Frazer (*The Golden Bough*), who exhaustively collected details of primitive religious beliefs. Frazer made an important distinction between magic (man's direct control of natural phenomena) and religion (man's use of superior powers or beings to control natural phenomena). Later studies, notably those of Emile Durkheim, have shown that totemism is a sociological system rather than religious.[4]

Fableism. Some scholars postulated that primitive man looked around and began to ask what caused different natural events that man could not copy, e.g., rain, winds, etc. These observers then postulated beings more powerful behind the events. These postulated beings were man-like by projection or anthropomorphism, and became the first gods. As man became more sophisticated, so did his conception of the beings behind the natural phenomena. This school is also called *nature-myth*.[5]

Variations of this school probably represent most current thinking.

Joseph Campbell builds on these premises in his popular "The Power of Myth" series on the Public Broadcasting System (and the associated book). Campbell, however, includes the intermediary of a shaman who has had a mystical experience.[6]

Shift From The Biblical View

While other theories have been postulated, these four have provided the key elements of the debate over the past century. In the process, the view expounded by the Bible has been shunted aside and forgotten. Three factors produced this shift.

A Logical Development. From the start, scholars had the problem of accommodating the, to us, rather repulsive, polytheistic beliefs discovered in the primitive tribes the European explorers were finding in their quests. The logic was disarmingly simple. Technologically, these tribes were primitive. Their weapons were simple and antiquated. They lacked "culture." Their world view was extremely limited. Therefore, their religion must have been "primitive." If that is the case, then it must have prefigured the "more advanced, revealed" religions.

By the end of the 19th century, the adjective "revealed" was being thrown off in many circles as religious development was integrated into a comprehensive evolutionary theory. Thus, the argument ran, primitive people had primitive ways, and primitive religions.[7] As man evolved [i.e., advanced], his technology advanced, and so did his religion.[8]

Of course, every one of these "advanced" religions had been founded almost 1500 to 2000 years earlier, in much simpler, less technologically advanced periods. In fact, there had been no religious development that correlated to the technological development of Western Europe. Religious discussion, whether in Western Europe or the Far East, was all refinement and application of ideas written down centuries earlier.

But many reports were already emerging that challenged these assumptions. A.W. Howitt reported by 1884 that certain tribes in Australia worshipped what he called "primitive high gods," i.e., a Supreme Being.[9] More reports came in from other quarters presenting similar data. By the turn of the century, Andrew Lang was able to gather reports that tribes in Africa, and both North and South Americas shared a primitive belief in a Supreme Being with the Australian tribes.[10]

Lang's reports were acknowledged briefly, but solely in British journals. On the continent and in America, his conclusions were received "with the deepest silence."[11] Even when Lang was discussed, however, his conclusions were dismissed without evaluation of his data. Schmidt states: "The other point has been left almost as completely unnoticed. It is the universal distribution of a Supreme Being over the whole earth."[12] The conclusion is that by the early 20th century, the evolutionary school of thought had taken root so strongly it was ignoring evidence to the contrary, and was able to do so with impunity.

Biblical View of History. A second problem is that the Bible does not give us world history of the type we would like. We would like a detailed outline of every generation from the beginning. We would like to see the political decisions, the conflicts, the great discoveries--who did what to whom and when. Oh yes, and included in that picture, we would like to see specifically how God intervened and directed history to His purpose.

Rather, we have received a book that focuses on one relatively insignificant tribe that enjoyed but a brief moment or two of fame in the sweep of history. Even there, the history is erratic, with large gaps in coverage.

The Nature of Man. The third, and probably the real reason that the biblical view has been ignored is that man from the time of the fall has not seen fit to honor God as God, as Paul states in Romans 2:1-2. Christianity has mandated from its beginning that its validity stands on the historically verifiable resurrection of Christ. If Christianity is valid, then there must be an explanation for how all these religions fit together. That is the purpose of this study--to explore that explanation.

Divine Purposes

The Bible has another purpose. Its focus is man (as a whole) and his relationship to God. The purpose is to show how the world got into its current predicament, and how God has worked in human history to bring forth a Messiah who would redeem a world estranged from God. At the same time, God allows sinful man to chose to reject Him, His program, and His Messiah.[13] The story of how man attempts to run his own show is given only in so far as it relates to God's purpose.

This is shown from the start. The book of Genesis focuses primarily on Abraham, one man that God called out to develop a nation, and not with Adam, the first man. Genesis tells about Adam only sufficiently to explain man's plight. It then quickly rushes on through the succeeding generations, the flood, and the dispersion of man. Suddenly at chapter 12, the book shifts gears, and tells in detail of Abraham, his son Isaac, and his grandson Jacob (or Israel). Eleven chapters to cover all families and generations from the beginning of time to the time of Abraham, and then thirty-nine chapters to cover three generations of one family (four if we include Joseph, but the story of Joseph is a transition--it serves to show how Jacob moved to Egypt--the story actually ends with the death of Jacob). Genesis ends with the nation in embryo form having descended to Egypt.

Exodus skips 400 years to pick up that embryo nation still in Egypt, but now needing to be transplanted to the land where God would mature it. The rest of the Old Testament relates portions of God's dealings with that nation over the next 1000 years. The Old Testament finishes with the promise of the Messiah, seemingly coming soon.

Four hundred years later, the New Testament continues the story. Its focus is the man Jesus, who claimed to be that Messiah,[14] and the proofs he offered. Presenting himself as the Servant who suffered for his people, Jesus was crucified. The book goes on to explain how by the resurrection, He proved His claims. After Jesus was crucified and resurrected, the rest of the New Testament discusses the implications of his claims, culminating in a promised second coming as a ruling king.

From the pages of these two testaments come three of the world's "great" religions, and numerous sects and cults. Judaism began after the exodus as God revealed a system of worship, sacrifice, and ritual to Moses. Judaism continues today, although the forms of worship and ritual have modified over the centuries. The sacrifice system awaits the rebuilding of the temple. Judaism rejects Jesus' claims to be the Messiah.

Christianity began with Jesus. It accepts his claims to fulfill prophecy and thus be the Messiah as correct. Christianity viewed the crucifixion of Jesus as the fulfillment of the Jewish sacrifice system. Because of this and the rapid expansion of Christianity into non-Jewish cultures, the Christian system of worship and ritual quickly diverged from the Jewish system in which it began.

Islam began when Mohammed tried to reconcile Judaism with a distorted form of Christianity. He did not recognize Jesus as the Messiah, but saw him as a great man. A number of visions assisted Mohammed in this process. Over the centuries, similar efforts to interpret the Bible without accepting the claims Jesus which made have resulted in a number of movements which are usually termed cults.[15]

But these all came much later. Abraham lived approximately 2166-1991 B.C. Moses was several centuries later, about 1526-1406 B.C.[16] By any view of the origin of man, these founders of the Jewish nation and religion came relatively late. How did man worship before then? If the Bible was correct that God called Abraham out of a pagan culture, how do we explain the origin of those pagan cults?

Notes

[1] Salmon Reinach (*Orpheus: A History of Religion*, p. 12) notes that Charles de Brosses, [*Du Culte des dieux fetiches*, published 1760] originated this school of thought. A. Comte adopted fetishism as the first of his three stages of religion: fetishism, polytheism, and monotheism, [*Cours de philosophive positive*, 6 vol., 1830-42].

[2] Wilhelm Schmidt, *The Origin and Growth of Religion*, p. 103. This school of thought developed from concepts proposed by J. F. M'Lennan in *Primitive Marriage*, 1866, and "On the Worship of Animals and Plants," *Fortnightly Review*, 1869-70. Bronislaw Malinowski (*Magic,Science, and Religion*, p. 18) observes that Tylor's view was "based on too narrow a range of facts."

[3] Schmidt, pp. 74-75. The term "totem" derives from the Ojibwa Indians. Sir James Frazer's totemism actually was more a form of animism which tied in sympathetic magic. He derived the origin of the priestly class from a group of users of a form of magic (*The Golden Bough*, pp. 52-55), but based the magical concept on animistic principles (pp. 206-208).

[4] The concept advocated by sociologists is actually a construct derived from various related characteristics observed around the world, since no culture exhibits "ideal totemism." The key trait that the totem denotes an expanded blood related group and members must marry outside that group is the reason Schmidt and others see the issue as sociological rather than religious.

[5] Reinach (p. 13) traces this school back to Fontenelle who wrote a treatise on myths in 1694. Andrew Lang resurrected the idea in the late 19th century (*The Making of Religion*, 1898). Actually, Lang turned against his earlier support of animism as a result of further observation. He pointed out several

primitive tribes that worship a Supreme Being without any ancestor or spirit worship. He noticed that all these tribes include both what are called higher religious elements and lower mythical elements, without any indication of which came first (cf. Schmidt, pp. 172-84, who analyzes Lang's theories in detail).

⁶ Campbell's views are also set forth in his books, e.g., *The Power of Myth*, pp. 37-40, 100. Campbell eclectically picks bits of "myths" from a multitude of traditions to prove his point (cf. pp. 43-45 where he "parallels" the Genesis creation account with pieces of myths from Asia, Africa, and North America). Campbell argues that there are two explanations to these similarities, one of which is a similar human psyche all over the world which he accepts and develops (p. 51). He then ignores the other possibility that they derive from a common source. The problem with Campbell's view, however, is that he provides no authority or explanation as to why his understanding of the "metaphor" is more valid than anyone else's (pp. 56-57). Mircea Eliade (*A History of Religious Ideas*, Vol. 1, "From the Stone Age to the Eleusinian Mysteries") comes to similar conclusions (pp. 37-51) although he also seems to hint at an animistic foundation (pp. 5-28). He does stress a magico-religious relationship similar to Frazer (pp. 206-208).

⁷ Interestingly, Malinowski observes "the problem of primitive knowledge has been singularly neglected by anthropology (p. 25)." He continues to demonstrate that primitive man has a broad understanding of the natural world and its processes, as well as an acute understanding of his own limitations.

⁸ It was only in the Judeo-Christian tradition (including Islam) that true monotheism has appeared. Joseph Campbell (p. 101) terms the exclusivity principle of Ex. 20:3 ("You shall have no other gods before Me") a purely Hebraic idea found in no other culture. When Bill Moyers asked him why, Campbell stated, "This I do not understand."

⁹ Schmidt, pp. 87-89. Howitt's articles, "On Some Australian Beliefs," and "On Some Australian Ceremonies of Initiation," were published in the *Journal of the Anthropological Institute* (Vol. 13, 1884, pp. 185-99 and 432-59).

¹⁰ Ibid., pp. 174-75. These were the same Australian tribes that sociologists have characterized as having the most complete form of totemism, supposedly the most primitive form of religion.

¹¹ Ibid., p. 173. William F. Albright (*From The Stone Age To Christianity*, p. 171) makes the interesting observation: "It has been particularly interesting to see the reaction of American anthropologists, nearly all of whom oppose Schmidt in his main thesis, though accepting many of his ideas in detail." Popularists such as Joseph Campbell ignore it.

¹² Ibid., p. 184. Schmidt later (p. 186) quotes E.W. Mayer who reviewed Schmidt's earlier book *Der Urspringe des Gottes idee.*" Mayer stated, "I know no recent work which denies such views as those of Lang and Schmidt and at the same time takes the trouble to sift, quite quietly, the evidence, which grows

more abundant every day, of the existence of a faded and ineffective belief in a Supreme Being among numerous savage peoples, and to do so with the requisite thoroughness." Many comparative religion studies do mention him in passing. John A. Hutchison (*Paths of Faith*, p. 29) casually observes "if the theories of Wilhelm Schmidt and Andrew Lang are correct, a high god is one of humankind's most ancient memories." Geoffrey Parrinder (*World Religions: From Ancient History to the Present*, p. 14) denigrates the idea stating "Schmidt was "probably influenced by the story of Adam's knowledge of God in Genesis." Parrinder never evaluates the *evidence*, however.

[13] One of the great tension points of Christianity is why God, who claims absolute sovereignty, would willingly allow created beings to make choices contrary to their best interests, and God's real desires. This is a theological question which lies outside the scope of this book. We begin with the premise that the resurrection demonstrates the validity of the claims of Christ. As a result, the other statements of Scripture about God are deemed validated. Basically, we must accept that God makes inscrutable choices, and God loves without condition. God decided (knowing the outcome) to create beings who could choose, and God desired that these beings love Him--and love is a product of the will, not called up on command from another.

[14] Throughout this book, the term Messiah (the Anointed One) will be used understanding the dual aspect of the Suffering Servant who would die for his people, and the Triumphant King who would lead his nation to glory. The New Testament presentation is that Jesus, the God-Man fulfilled the first aspect at the turn of the millennia, and will fulfill the second when he returns. The Jewish people for the most part were looking for the second aspect, and presently are still looking the Messiah in this sense.

[15] The term "cult" is considered pejorative and often avoided. The definition of the word shows it to be a valid term, since each of these groups coalesce around a distinguishing issue which separates that group from historic Christianity. Normally, this issue is the teaching of a leader who claims the ability to "correctly" interpret Scripture in a way that no-one else can. Usually this involves a reinterpretation of who Jesus was (away from the straight-forward presentation already cited), and the meaning of his crucifixion and resurrection. These reinterpretations distinguish these groups from Christianity since the various branches of historic Christianity are agreed on this point, although they may disagree on many of the implications of this event.

[16] This follows the dating of Eugene H. Merrill, *Kingdom of Priests*, pp. 25-79.

Chapter 2

The Source

It All Started In Eden

The creation account of Genesis 1-3 makes it clear that the first man and woman worshipped the one true God. There is no record of when the descendants of Adam and Eve first began to worship other gods. It is evident, however, that the process began in the temptation and fall of that first couple.

Man was created to have dominion over the world. This is clear from God's declaration of purpose in Genesis 1:26--

> Let us make man in our image, according to our likeness; and let them rule over the fish of the sea and over the birds of the sky and over the cattle and over all the earth, and over every creeping things that creeps on the earth.

God declared the same principle in His initial guidance to this newly created man--

> Be fruitful and multiply, and fill the earth, and subdue it; and rule over the fish of the sea and over the birds of the sky, and over every living thing that moves on the earth (Gen. 1:28).

He amplified this declaration in Genesis 2, where Adam is authorized to name the various creatures. Throughout early history (and in many respects, even today), the right to name represents authority.

Perhaps the most significant event in world history occurs in Genesis 3 where Adam and Eve sin and set in motion a chain of events which culminates in the crucifixion of Christ. Without a clear understanding of that event and its consequences, virtually nothing about the world today makes sense.

God had created a perfect world. God had created a perfect man and perfect woman to rule this world. The animals came up to Adam without fear. They lived in a garden where every plant that produced fruit was good and nourishing. Adam cultivated it, and never had to worry about weeds. Even the climate was perfect; not too hot, not too cold--and it never rained.

But God also gave man the freedom to make choices. When God created angels and man, He allowed them to chose to obey, to love, and to have fellowship with God, or to disobey and lose that fellowship. Satan had already made his choice. He wanted to be in charge and challenged God. Satan, a created being, lost, but still felt that he could ultimately triumph--if he could gather enough allies. In the process, he took one third of the angels in heaven with him (cf. Ezek 28:11-15, Is 14:12-14, and Rev 12). Satan viewed the special relationship man had with God as a challenge.

In the midst of their Edenic perfection, Adam and Eve had but one key responsibility--obey God by respecting one restriction: don't eat from one tree, the tree of knowledge of good and evil. The command was clear, and the consequences were clear. Satan used a key tactic to challenge this command. He did not deny the command, but questioned the consequences and challenged the motives for it. As a result, he made Eve doubt. With doubt came deceit, then disobedience. Adam was not deceived, but just flatly disobeyed (cf. 1 Tim 2:14). As a result, evil was given sway, and man has suffered the consequences since.

The results of that chain of events still reverberate through the world, and will not be finished until the creation of a new heaven and earth as related in Revelation 21-22. One key result is that in the process Satan usurped dominion over the world. Jesus observed this in John 12:31 where he calls Satan the ruler of this world, who will be cast out by the completion of Christ's work.

This fact cannot be emphasized enough. The world we live in is not in the shape God created it. The evil of this world is a result of the current world ruler who is still in direct rebellion against God. The battle is still ongoing, and man is caught up in the midst of it. Created in the image of God, he is bound by sin and rebellion.

Fortunately, God still sets limits as to how far Satan can go. The case of Job demonstrates this. Job worshipped God with pure allegiance. Satan challenged Job, but *had to ask permission* to do so. Even when he was given authorization, it was within certain limits. But Satan would not have even this much authority, if Adam had not given it to him in the garden.

A Campaign of Deceit

Satan's goal is to deceive each person in the world. Whether this is because misery loves company, or whether he thinks that by doing so he can show God as being unjust in his justice is uncertain. The net effect has been a campaign of deceit throughout history. There is every reason to believe that Satan continued his deceitful ways immediately after the fall recorded in Genesis 3, although it is not documented.

We do see later examples. When Satan confronted Jesus in the wilderness, he offered world power and dominion if Jesus would worship him (Matthew 4:8-9). This is an overt challenge to the worship of God and true religion. While it is true that Satan had the power to offer dominion, what he offered to Jesus would have been a subsidiary role--first after Satan.

It is unlikely that Jesus was the first one given that offer of world dominion. While we are not told exactly who that first person was, it is certain that within one generation of the creation of man, Adam's sons began tinkering with religious forms.

What Is A Sacrifice?

In Genesis 4, Cain and Abel, Adam and Eve's first two sons, brought sacrifices to God. God never says why He accepted Abel's sacrifice but not Cain's, and scholars looking at the evidence disagree. There *are* two clear distinctions between the sacrifices which have focused the discussion.

First, the nature of the sacrifices differed. Cain brought fruit of the ground as opposed to Abel's offering from the flock. Some have inferred that the issue is blood sacrifice as opposed to grain. This view correlates with God's requirement for a blood sacrifice to atone for sins. The blood requirement is very evident in the Old Testament law and in the need for Jesus to die.[1] Also, the patriarchs commonly offered animal sacrifices. Noah offered an animal sacrifice right after

the flood (Gen. 8:20). Abraham offered several (e.g., Gen. 15:9 and
Gen. 22:13). Even the garments of skin which God made for Adam
and Eve before driving them from the garden imply killed animals,
suggesting blood sacrifices.

But not all Old Testament sacrifices required animals. Leviticus 2
details how to present a grain offering. A key sacrifice of the Old
Testament law was that of the first fruits. As outlined in Leviticus 23
and Deuteronomy 26, the first fruits sacrifice reminded the farmer of
God's role bringing the nation to the land and providing the harvest.
It was part of the tithe system for the nation. The violation of this
overall system precipitated God's judgment and the exile.

Cain and Abel's sacrifices fit this pattern. Their choices reflect their
different careers--Abel kept flocks, and Cain tilled the ground. But we
are not told about the sacrifices themselves, i.e., how were they
offered?[2]

We see a hint that there is a second difference between the two
sacrifices. Abel brought the firstlings. Cain brought an offering. I.e.,
he brought something, as opposed to the "firstlings." This is a
distinction of attitude.[3] Abel placed God first. Cain viewed Him as an
afterthought. Abel worshipped God out of love, Cain because he had
to. God told Cain that he too could do well, if he had the right attitude
(Gen. 4:7). Instead, Cain murdered his brother.

Before The Flood

The rest of the history of man before the flood is problematic. We
have no secular records. Chapters 4-6 in Genesis only hint at world
affairs but they point to one dominant trait: man in his pride became
more evil. Lamech boasted of his murder (Gen. 4:23) and told how he
would be avenged 77 times as opposed to Cain's 7 times.

This increasing evilness culminates in Genesis 6. The inter-marriage
of the sons of God and the daughters of men was the deciding factor
which brought God's judgment of the great flood. While this segment
occurs before the flood, and the destruction of virtually all humankind,
some of the concepts involved are highly enlightening on post-flood
events. This section is also difficult and highly controversial. Who
were the sons of God as opposed to the daughters of men? The two
primary views are that they were fallen angels or that they were the
line of Seth (Adam's third son) as opposed to the line of Cain.

Several factors suggest that most likely the issue is the inter-marriage of fallen angels with men. First is the term "sons of God" itself. In verse 1 the writer tells us that men began to multiply on the earth and have daughters. Logically, he is referring to the human race, which must make the sons of God something other than the human race. Likewise, when the term "sons of God" is used elsewhere in Scripture, it refers to angels.[4]

In Jude 1:6 the writer tells of angels who did not keep their own domain. By itself, this verse seems to speak of angels falling from their original pure state. But the context of verse 7 throws the sexual perversions of Sodom and Gomorrah into the same category: "since they [Sodom and Gomorrah] in the same way as these [the angels of verse 6] indulged in gross immorality and went after strange flesh."

Two other New Testament passages support this interpretation. 2 Peter 2 mentions fallen angels who were cast into hell almost in the same breath with the judgment of the flood. Peter also includes Sodom and Gomorrah as a third example of judgment because of sensuality and greed. 1 Corinthians 11 states that woman's long hair is her glory, and so she needs to cover her head while praying or prophesying "because of the angels (v. 11)." We are not told why this is the case unless angelic beings can be enticed by women in this manner.[5]

Satan's Hierarchy

How one interprets this issue can affect his understanding of pagan mythology and other religions. Two views of pagan gods are presented throughout the Bible. Some are idols, i.e., man-made creations without any power. But at least some are supernormal creatures who arrogate to themselves the authority and power that belong to God. Paul specifically states that when the Gentiles sacrifice to their idols, they sacrifice to demons (1 Corinthians 10:20).[6] If demons are part of the fallen angel hierarchy, the concept then is that these pagan gods are fallen angels.

This would be just part of a behind the scenes spiritual hierarchy headed by Satan. This hierarchy manifests itself in the various gods worshipped within the nations.

Daniel 10 is a fascinating chapter of a fascinating book. As Daniel tells us about his efforts to understand what was going to happen to his people, he reveals a couple of items that are easily overlooked. In this chapter, he tells of three supernormal beings, the prince of Persia, the prince of Greece, and the prince of Israel, who is identified as Michael the archangel.

The prince of Persia stands against and holds back the messenger from God who is sent to answer Daniel's prayers. Later, Michael is sent to hold off this being, so God's angel can carry out his assigned task.

In this brief comment, we are given a hint at a struggle going on behind the scenes. The prince of Persia is apparently the real power behind the throne, the one who keeps things going.[7] This is indicated where Daniel is told that prince of Greece is about to come and replace him. The prince of Israel is responsible for preserving the nation despite the fact that it is in exile.

These princes have real authority and power. Their authority is subsidiary to that of Satan who is the prince of the world (except for Michael, who is not in that hierarchy). God allows Satan and thus his underlings to exercise that authority only up to certain limits (cf. 2 Thes 2:6-7, where the Holy Spirit is identified as the One Who restrains evil). Thus, by veto and intervention, God exercises ultimate control in a world that is poorly run by Satan.

Beyond this, there are super-normal beings who focus on individuals. In the gospels, they are characterized as demons. Their position would be below that of the princes. Paul seems to indicate several layers in the hierarchy when he warns that our struggle is "against the rulers [the princes?], against the powers, against the world-forces of this darkness, against the spiritual forces of wickedness in the heavenly places [false gods?](Ephesians 6:12)." Unfortunately, we are not told the exact structure of this hierarchy.

If many of the gods of the nations are actually fallen angels, then it would not be surprising if we saw similar characteristics between the fallen angels and the pagan gods.[8] For example, throughout pagan mythology, gods are presented as having off-spring from human women. This trend is suggestive with respect to the situation in Genesis. Greek mythology is a prime example.[9]

Genesis 6, relates that "giants" or *nephilim* were in the land. Actually, "giants" is a translation of the Septuagint's *gigantes*. The Hebrew word means "the fallen." This passage calls them the mighty ones of old, men of renown. While these *nephilim* were destroyed by the flood, the passage states that others were on the earth later.

The suggestion then is two fold. Various fallen angels assumed the prerogatives of God as objects of worship,[10] and became the gods of pagan mythologies, or at least the prototypes for these gods. Also, through "inter-marriage" with human women, they gave birth to the early super-heroes of pagan mythology.[11]

This action brought judgment on the evil world. This world-wide judgment reduced the world population to 8; Noah, his wife, his three sons and their wives. While the rest of the population was destroyed in judgment, the passage goes on to say in Gen 6:4 that *nephilim* also appeared after the flood. This is another reason to view the reference to fallen angels. If the problem had been the inter-mingling of the Seth and Cain lines, there would be no more Cain line to mingle at this point. However, there would still be fallen angels, who could still violate God's law, producing the *nephilim* who appeared in later times. Modern fiction, such as *Rosemary's Baby*, keeps the idea alive. But is it all fiction?

After the Flood

According to the Biblical accounts, as Noah and his family came off the ark they worshipped the one true God. Noah built an altar to God, and God made a covenant with Noah and his three sons. When we begin to examine apostasy here, a critical question would be, when was the flood?

Mathematically, it should be easy to add up the dates in the genealogies and establish the date. Archbishop Usher did that in 1650 and arrived at a date of 2348 BC. More recent evaluations of the genealogies of Abraham and his descendants (such as have been done by Edwin Thiele and Eugene Merrill[12]) would move that date back to about 2459 BC. This still gives problems when we compare archaeological data and the extremely long times hypothesized by some geologists and anthropologists.

There are indications that this genealogy is not a strict chronology. For example, in Luke 3:36, Cainan appears between Shelah and Arphaxad while the Hebrew text of Genesis 11 omits Cainan. Clearly, the purpose of the genealogy is not to give a detailed history of events, but to show how God guarded the Messianic line. This suggests that there is some uncertainty as far as dates are concern. Still there are limits to our uncertainty. It is probably safe to limit Babel to less than a millennium after the flood, although a shorter time is likely. Likewise there is a practical limit of about two millennia between Babel and Abraham, although here, a shorter period is even more probable.[13]

The reverse side of the issue is the accuracy of archaeology's dating systems. Scientists give old dates with extreme confidence--far more than deserved.[14] It is extremely interesting that many if not most historians put the earliest dates of historical civilization at no earlier than approximately 3100 BC, or approximately 1000 years before Abraham. This is well within the limits we have just established. From the data we have at hand, this is far more time than needed to allow the development of the multitudes of religious systems which permeated the ancient near east.

Confusion at Babel

Four generations after the flood, the dispersion from Babel occurred.[15] The cause of the dispersal was man's sin in not spreading out to repopulate the world as God commanded.[16] The symptom of this sin was the attempt to build a great city and tower to prevent being scattered. The pride evident in this decision is conquerable to that of Satan noted above.

God judged this group by "confusing their language." The product was the rise of linguistic and national groups as we know them today.[17] As a result man spread throughout the world.

We are not told where and how man began worshiping other gods, but there is no reason to suppose that Satan had cut back on his deceptive ways. Certainly, the idea that man could build a tower which reached to heaven came from deceit. In fact, it might be safely posited that post-flood man, united in civilization and language, was also basically united in religion, a false religion based on man's ability to substitute for God (of course we maintain that in each generation God retained those who were faithful to Him--in Genesis 6 we are told of Noah in the last generation before the flood). In that case, Genesis 11:6 becomes a conditional statement of irony. *If* men are able to stay united as one people with one language, they can do anything. But God showed His sovereignty by removing the unifying factors. The result was that man stopped building the city which inspired his hopes and scattered in many directions. Shortly after this we find our first secular records, already showing a dispersed world population with differing religious systems.

Notes

[1] Cf. Hebrews 9:22 which states "without shedding of blood there is no forgiveness," and Leviticus 17:11 which states "For the life of the flesh is in the blood and I have given it to you on the altar to make atonement for your souls; for it is the blood by reason of the life that makes atonement."

[2] This episode does not represent confrontation between the agricultural and nomadic portions of society (as per Joseph Campbell, *The Power of Myth*, p. 109). The context of the account gives a no-win situation—one son is killed and the other cursed. If this account was developed to represent an early struggle, we would expect a polemic victor. This victor would be the ancestor of the nation of Israel, representing and vindicating the purported pastoral occupation of the nation.

Furthermore, the text is clear that neither son is the ancestor of the nation of Israel. That line came from their brother Seth. While the nation of Israel descended from herders (Abraham and sons), by the time of the creation of the nation, a large segment was agricultural as indicated by the law and the promises given to the nation, e.g., the firstfruits law.

[3] The writer of the Letter to the Hebrews makes this point when he declares that "Abel offered unto God a more excellent sacrifice than Cain *by faith* (Heb 11:4)."

[4] U. Cassuto, *A Commentary on the Book of Genesis, Part I: From Adam to Noah*, pp. 291-2. Specific passages which use the term in that sense include: Ps. 29:1, 89:6, Job 1:6, 2:1, 38:7 and Deut 32:8. Isaiah 43:6 uses a different term, "sons of Jehovah," when it talks about the regathering of Israel. Merrill F. Unger, (*Biblical Demonology*, p. 46) notes that some manuscripts of the Septuagint, the Greek translation of the Old Testament translate this phrase in Genesis 6 as "the angels of God."

[5] The primary argument against this view comes from Matthew 22:29-30. There Jesus tells the Sadducees (who did not believe in a resurrection) that resurrected men and women do not marry, but are like the angels in heaven. The conclusion that is drawn from this is that angels are *unable* to marry, and thus are *unable* to have sexual relationships. This is a non sequitur since Jesus talks about state, not ability. Since Jesus specifically notes the angels in heaven, this leaves open the possibility that fallen angels, not being in heaven, might be different in their actions. While angels are spiritual beings, they can appear to men and emulate many human activities. Whether a fallen angel could chose to appear as a man, marry, and produce offspring is extremely problematic. While the question of how they would be able to procreate is a

mystery, in many respects it is not much more mysterious than how life is conceived in a "normal" manner. The fact is that we just do not know enough about the nature of angels to be dogmatic either way.

[6] Merrill F. Unger, *Biblical Demonology*, hesitates to follow this interpretation of Genesis 6 because he sees the off-spring as demons (based on the passage in *The Book of Enoch*, chapter 14). He determines that demons are fallen angels, and seems to support the view that Genesis 6 refers to fallen angels, but never puts the two points together (pp. 45-61).

[7] The struggle between the prince of Persia and God's messenger which delayed Daniel's answer, militates against an allegorical interpretation of these figures. The evidence suggests personal beings, who struggle in a realm we are not normally privy to.

[8] We do not use pagan mythology to "prove" Scripture. However, we would expect Scripture to provide a framework of truth in which to understand and interpret pagan mythology. In the issue of demonic forces, there seems to be no question but that pagan mythology unitedly proclaims the presence of demonic super-normal forces in the world. The overwhelming evidence is that these forces are adversaries of men. While on one hand our scientific age purports to laugh at such ideas, the spate of horror films and books over the past decade or two suggests that most of us still accept the possibility. As such, we see a deeper meaning to mythology than a fictionalized account of historical forces (cf. Robert Graves, *The Greek Myths*, p. 17 who states "a large part of Greek myth is politico-religious history").

[9] Zeus, "the father of heaven" is represented in Greek mythology as the key perpetrator (cf. Robert Graves, *The Greek Myths*, p. 55). Unger notes that the Septuagint translates the Hebrew word *nephilim* ("fallen") as *gigantes* ("giants") as indicating that the translators viewed the progeny in this passage as half angel, half mortal (p. 48). The Greek Titans were beings who are half celestial and half terrestrial, but who were termed *gegenes*, "earth-born," because of their origin. The origin of the Titans, like much of Greek mythology, is obscure deriving from a number of different, even contradictory tales. Graves compares the Titans ('lords') with early Babylonian astrological deities who ruled the seven days of the sacred week (pp. 28-29). They are viewed as off-spring of air and earth (Uranus and "Mother-earth"--pp. 35-37). In general, however, they are viewed as having come into existence prior to man (cf. p. 27).

[10] In this sense they emulated their leader Satan, who stated "I will ascend to heaven; I will raise my throne above the stars of God, and I will sit on the mount of assembly in the recesses of the north. I will ascend above the heights of the clouds; I will make myself like the Most High" (Isaiah 14:13-14).

[11] The hierarchy of pagan gods and semi-gods is much more complex than this represents. For example, Zeus, the head Greek-god, fathered several of the other gods, fathered children through female Titans (see footnote 10

above), and mortal women. At this point it would be impossible, and probably not even desirable to attempt to sort out what aspects of these mythologies relate actual spiritual battles fought of old, and which are story-tellers' accretions.

[12] Edwin R. Thiele (*The Mysterious Numbers of the Hebrew Kings*) examined the dating of the Old Testament kings noting the differing use of ascension years (whether the year of ascension counted as the first year of the reign or not), calendars, and co-regencies. As a result, he produced a coherent whole of this somewhat confusing material. Eugene H. Merrill (*An Historical Survey of the Old Testament*) shows how this coherent whole fits well within the known history of the Ancient Near East.

[13] Morris and Whitcomb examine this issue is some detail in *The Genesis Flood*, Appendix II, pp. 474-89. They present several of the indications that this genealogy is not a strict chronology, and explain that the purpose of the genealogy is not to give a detailed history of events, but to show how God guarded the Messianic line (p. 477). We would also add that the genealogies show how worship of the true God continued through the entire period, which could explain why some generations are skipped. Morris and Whitcomb place the elastic limits of the chronological data to place Babel less than a millennium after the flood, and Abraham less than about two millennia after Babel. They admit, however, that these limits really stretch the genealogies, suggesting a shorter period.

[14] Morris and Whitcomb's *The Genesis Flood* examines each of these dating systems in detail and evaluates the assumptions which lie behind them, as well as the accuracy that might be expected. Less technical evaluations might be found in John C. Whitcomb's *The World That Perished* and James F. Coppedge's *Evolution: Possible or Impossible*. Information is also available from the Creation Research Society (San Diego), the Biblical Science Association (Minneapolis), and Probe Ministries (Dallas).

[15] Not only is the exact date for this dispersal uncertain, we can only approximately place it in the overall historical accounts. Gen. 10:25 notes that Peleg was given his name because in his days, "the earth was divided." This is usually taken as a reference to the dispersal from Babel. This suggests a reference to Peleg's birth, which would give us minimum limits, placing Babel at least 101 years after the flood, and 191 years before Abraham, according to the genealogy in Genesis 11.

[16] Cf. Allen P. Ross, *Creation and Blessing*, p. 233.

[17] The Genesis account is the only account which adequately explains the available data regarding language families and their development (cf. Michael A. Harbin, "Language Was Created, Not Evolved," *Creation Research Society Quarterly*, June 1982).

Chapter 3

Polytheism Runs Rampant

History begins at Sumer. Sumer was the early civilization in the delta region of the Tigris-Euphrates rivers--the southern portion of modern Iraq and Kuwait. By this, scholars mean that the earliest written documents have been found in ruins from this area. But it is also generally accepted that Sumer was the first civilization, and the other civilizations probably developed as a result of its influences.[1]

We have already observed how Satan used his campaign of deception against man from the beginning. We saw how it affected Adam and Eve who disobeyed and how it affected Cain who murdered his brother. We also saw how the earth was divided and then judged as a result of Satan establishing his spiritual hierarchy and setting into effect his program of world dominion.

Satan has used that hierarchy to set up false religions which not only counterfeit true worship, but which seek to displace the true God. As a result (coupled with man's ego-centric perception of the universe after the fall), man has continually faced the problem of discerning true religion from false.

Paul warned of this problem in a number of places. For example, he cautioned the Corinthians to be on guard against false apostles (men who purported to be followers of Jesus, but who really taught other teachings, i.e., they served other gods). More critically, he noted how even Satan disguised himself as an angel of light--a messenger of truth (2 Cor 11:14). Paul had observed and was critically concerned that true religion was (and is) constantly being counterfeited by a spectrum of false religions established by leaders flying false colors.[2]

We cannot assume that this confusion was a peculiarity of Paul's age. Nor can we assume that it was a problem associated solely with the faith centered around the recently resurrected Christ.

Unfortunately, this confusion campaign was well entrenched long before any historical records we have available. Thus, the normal

interpretation and translation problems of the few early records we have
are complicated by this spiritual blindness so prevalent in the world--
blindness which eagerly seeks any explanation for man's plight other
than man's sin.

Since Satan's campaign was well underway before the dispersion of
Babel, it would be highly surprising if Satan had not taken advantage
of the confusion of Babel to advance his own program. Now that man
was divided by linguistic differences religious confusion was even
easier to cultivate.

Initially, each culture probably still retained a remnant which served
the true God. Even within this minority of true worshippers, the newly
created languages produced different names of address. While these
differing terminologies would by themselves affect the tribal concepts
of the nature of God, it would appear that counterfeits were already in
place, although perhaps not so entrenched as we might expect.

Even for those who still served the true God, cultural differences of
concern and understanding developed as the dispersing tribes with their
distinctive languages moved into different climatic conditions.[3] A tribe
moving into a mountainous region would have different concerns, and
thus focus on different aspects of God, than a tribe living in a river
valley, or along an ocean coast. Likewise they would develop different
metaphors to describe these attributes.

Even in the same climatic conditions, individual finite men would
focus on one attribute of an infinite, multi-faceted God, producing a
plethora of lesser, more limited god-concepts centered on single
attributes. For example, one man might be drawn to the power of God
and his neighbor to God's wisdom.[4] Lookers-on could conclude that
their discussions actually involved two gods--a god of power, and a god
of wisdom.[5]

As these tribes began to re-meet and intermingle, these concepts met
in the forms of differing gods. This would be true after the passage of
even a couple of generations.

But the actual situation is much more complex. The key element in
the development of new gods was the displacement of the true God by
various members of the Satanic hierarchy. It is probable that it was
here that Satan instituted the national princes that Daniel saw in Daniel
10.[6] Since these spiritual figures also possessed limited super-normal
powers, one must also posit that they used their powers as they
assumed their position as gods.

Obviously, this is a reconstruction of a process which occurred primarily in the spiritual realm, and much of which occurred before the institution of writing and secular history.[7] However, if valid, one would expect to find hints in the evidence at hand. We have already noted some indications in the religious traditions of non-technologically advanced tribes. As we look at man's earliest cultures, we find further evidence.

Sumer

The Biblical accounts essentially skip the period from the time of the dispersion from Babel to the time of Abraham. Yet during this period of several hundred years, the earliest civilizations emerged. The Biblical record picks up with Abraham, as he leaves the city of Ur of the Chaldeans along with his father, his nephew, and his wife.

Presently, the site labeled Ur lies about halfway between modern Baghdad and the head of the Persian Gulf. The archaeological site was excavated by Sir Leonard Woolley between 1922 and 1934. Geological studies suggest that at the time that Ur flourished, it was much closer to, if not on the coast of the Gulf. Most archaeologists agree that it was in this region that "civilization" began.[8]

By the time of Abraham (2166-1991 BC), Ur was a great city under the dynasty of Akkad (approx. 2300-2100 BC).[9] It was a cosmopolitan center with a population of as much as a quarter of a million people.[10] As part of Sumer, it was also part of the source of many elements of early civilization.[11]

It is also one of the sources of the many clay tablets we have recovered in the Sumerian language--the oldest written documents in the world. While museums and private collections contain several hundred thousand tablets from Sumer, we still know little of its culture and especially of its religion. The vast majority of the material we have is economic, e.g., receipts and sales contracts. The literary material includes only a few thousand tablets and fragments in varying states of repair. Of these only a few cover religious issues.[12]

Beyond the paucity of material is the problem of correlating these tablets which come from different sites and span a several century period. Many of the documents we have are late copies of earlier stories. Some are remarkably consistent. Others change drastically.[13]

For example, the Akkadian Gilgamesh epic dates from about 1600 BC, the end of the Old Babylonian period. Gilgamesh was a king who lived about 2600 BC in Uruk, an early city-state in Sumer (the Biblical Erech, about 60 miles up river from Ur). His story is still vivid and challenging as Gilgamesh the man encounters mortality and human finiteness.[14] The first fragments which mention Gilgamesh date from about 2100 BC. The fullest documents date from about 1600 BC. As a result, we can piece the various fragments and texts together to show a trend in the development of the story of Gilgamesh over a 500 year period.[15] As the layers unfold, different tales found in various forms throughout the Middle East are attributed to Gilgamesh to the point that he becomes a super-hero who can challenge the gods.[16] By his interaction with the gods, we can learn much about the gods and religious thought. Although the actual man lived long before the earliest documents extant, a reasonable picture can be still be put together through the available data.

Even the earliest references suggest that Gilgamesh had a special relationship with the gods. Can we assume that Gilgamesh as a mortal king lived a life totally devoid of what we might call super-normal elements?[17] Only by totally ruling out any form of interference in our physical realm from the spiritual realm, which is a presuppositional determination. The evidence for that type of interference is too wide-spread and diverse to decide so arbitrarily. It is true that in our western culture, we have struggled to piece together this evidence eliminating the spiritual aspects. Unfortunately the result does not satisfy, since there is no framework to tie the elements together.

Our premise of a spiritual hierarchy provides just such a framework in that it allows for super-normal manifestations as the behind-the-scenes spiritual rulers use their powers to manipulate human events. Even so, we recognize that not all reports of the super-normal are valid. But, we argue, neither can they be arbitrarily dismissed.

Our real question is whether changes can be seen in religious thought over this millennium of literature? The answer is yes, but the process is not that which has been put forth as the way religion developed.

First, the changes in copies of the stories were not as radical as we have been led to believe. While there are different "editions" of the stories, the main themes are not only recognizable, but many of the details are the same.[18]

Second, rather than an initial polytheism which slowly evolved towards monotheism, we see just the opposite. Sumerian religious documents *imply a initial one god*, with an early expansion to include many. While some of this multiplication of deities occurred prior to our written documents, it is evident from the available evidence. Some of our earliest documents come from Uruk and are dated approximately 3300-3100 BC. They focused on the heaven god An.[19]

There is other evidence that at the earliest historical times the Sumerians were still working with a very limited number of deities. For example, the tale "Gilgamesh, Enkidu and the Nether-world," revolves around An (the heaven god, who was male), Ki (the earth god, who was female), and Enlil (the air-god, male, reportedly from the union of An and Ki).[20] There is further evidence that even though the pantheon was becoming somewhat complex fairly early, it was still with a limited number of gods. The problem is that the entire early picture is deduced from later material.[21]

Later, however, it is clear the number of gods proliferated. By about 2500 BC, several hundred deities could be listed.[22] Later lists of gods include "two to three thousand names."[23] Final lists (from about 1500 BC) include almost 15,000 names.[24]

This increase in the number of gods is striking.

Even more striking was the displacement of the original heaven-god, An by the air god Enlil. While there is strong evidence of this event, the data that we have is after the fact, when Enlil already enjoyed his position of prominence.[25] It would appear that the challenge of An occurred at about the same time that the initial Sumerian pantheon appeared. With this displacement, Enlil became the head of the Sumerian pantheon, or in effect, the leader of their spiritual hierarchy.

This event is highly suggestive that An is a late pre-historical interpolation of the true Creator God who allowed Satan to rebel and claim godly prerogatives as the ruler of this world. Early historical evidence supports this.[26] In the later literature, Enlil also lays claim to having created the heavens and the earth, and even the other gods, although his powers are limited.

An interesting side light is the fact that the literature of both Sumer and later Mesopotamia view all the gods as created beings, although the nature of the creator and the method of creation are inconsistent through the various sources. Likewise, the gods are always limited in their powers, and prone to competition between one another. This probably reflects attempts to correlate dimly recollected bits of the truth with the situation of spiritual beings presenting themselves as gods.

The history of Sumer, as we have been able to reconstruct it, is one

of competition between various city-states. Each city-state had its
patron god who looked out for its welfare in the spiritual realm, and
who helped it when it competed or fought against another group.[27]
During the third millennium (ca. 2900 to 2300 BC), the political
hegemony of the region moved from one city to another--with the
exception of Nippur. Never a political capital, Nippur was recognized
by all as a religious center sacred to Enlil. While the other gods in the
pantheon[28] enjoyed greater or lesser adulation as a result of the political
and military successes of their human proteges, Enlil maintained his
position at the head of the pantheon, and Nippur enjoyed a special
position.

At this point, it is clear that we lack sufficient evidence to develop
with any clarity a comprehensive picture of the religious situation of
Mesopotamia. Still, even with the limited evidence at hand, with the
complex sociopolitical situation, it would be extremely naïve to assume
that even any city-state possessed one cohesive "cult." We would
argue, moreover, that there were still some who followed the true God
as passed down from their ancestors.

Babylon and Assyria

About 2300 BC, Sargon, the ruler of Akkad became the first ruler
to join Sumer and the more northern reaches of the Tigris-Euphrates
valley. From a humble Semitic background, Sargon probably was able
to advance by some form of an alliance with a priestess of Ishtar, the
Babylonian equivalent of Inanna. By this time, Nanna (the mother of
Inanna) was the key goddess of Ur, the future birthplace of Abraham.

Sargon's empire shifted the cultural center north from Sumer, and
increased the already strong Semitic influence. In the process, the
early Akkadians continued to assume Sumerian culture, including many
Sumerian religious beliefs. Actually, many of the Sumerian religious
beliefs had already amalgamated Semitic influences as the Semites had
settled in the area.

It is not surprising then that Sargon placed his daughter, Enheduanna
as the head priestess of the temple to the moon goddess Nanna in Ur.
What is surprising is the role in which Enheduanna played in advancing
the cult of Inanna, or Ishtar. Certainly, part of the reason she did so
was associated with her father's conquest of both Sumer and Akkad.[29]
Throughout the accounts which relate his elevation to the throne is a

strain giving Ishtar the credit.[30] It is clear that Sargon and his daughter both saw a direct correlation between events within the spiritual hierarchy behind the scenes, and events which occurred in the spiritual realm.[31]

Sargon's empire waxed and waned over the next 200 years, finally to be lost by his great-grandson (Shar-Kali-Sharri). After a twenty-five year reign, he was defeated and killed about 2100 BC by the Gutians who probably swept out of present day Turkey. This was the time-frame that Abraham and his father left Ur for Haran, en route to Palestine.

Abraham's personal beliefs before he was called out of Ur are problematic. Joshua 24:2 states that Abraham and Terah served other gods when God called them. The assumption then is that since Abraham was a pagan, that knowledge of the true God had died out.[32] Genesis 31:53, however, declares that both Abraham and his father Terah (as well as Abraham's brother, Nahor) worshipped the true God.

The probable solution is that Abraham and Terah were of a family that retained knowledge and some worship of the true God even while becoming involved in the pagan worship of their Sumerian culture.[33] It would be in this situation that the true God appeared to Abraham drawing him out of Mesopotamia (cf. Acts 7:2 ff). As such, Abraham and his family are a realistic portrayal of the problem of following the true God in a world ruled by a pretender.[34]

The calling of Abraham is the first significant step in God's preparation for the Messiah who was to reconcile man to God. We see here God's counter-move to Satan's attempt to draw the entire world to worship him. Just as Satan was approaching his goal, God chose one man to make a nation. That is why Genesis 12 suddenly changes gears and begins to examine the life of Abraham in a detail far beyond virtually any other Biblical character.

After Abraham left Mesopotamia, more than a 1000 years would pass before that region would again play a significant role in Israel's religious development, even though it would produce several major empires. During that period, Babylon and Assyria continued to develop along the polytheistic lines already noted. Still, even during these times, hints of a long ago, almost forgotten, monotheistic past appear in the documents which we have found.

Certainly one of those hints must lie in the person of Melchizedek. The king/priest of Salem, Melchizedek is recognized by Abraham as serving the same God--"God Most High" (Gen. 14:18-22). Although we know virtually nothing about him, he appears to have received his knowledge of God through different means than Abraham, although both recognized that they served the same God. As King of Salem (now Jerusalem), he was probably a native of the area as opposed to Abraham who had recently immigrated. This would suggest a separate line preserving the memory of the true God.

As the Semitic elements of Akkad, Babylon, and Nineveh successively ruled the Mesopotamian region, they appropriated the Sumerian writing system. At first their documents were in Sumerian, the language of learning (much as Latin was in Europe in the medieval period). Gradually, they began to use the same script for their own language. Still, earlier stories were recopied and handed down to new generations.

While we do not have Sumerian copies of many of the stories, the Babylonian copies which have been recovered contain names known to be in the Sumerian pantheon. Some of these contain the names of new gods substituted for key Sumerian counterparts.

One such story is *Enuma Elish*.[35] This account of the creation of the world contains certain parallels to the Old Testament. As a result, it has received considerable attention since its first discovery. There are also considerable differences between it and the Biblical accounts. Scholars suggest that *Enuma Elish* was originally composed sometime during the First Babylonian Dynasty (1894-1595 BC) as a propaganda piece to justify replacing Enlil by Marduk, the key Babylonian god.

Because this proposed date predates the writing of the Biblical account (by Moses, circa 1446 BC), some have been quick to charge that the Biblical account is drawn from the Babylonian story. A comparison of the two accounts reveals that there are actually few points where the two accounts really compare. The Genesis account focuses on the creation of the physical universe, and covers it in a few broad strokes. *Enuma Elish* focuses on the creation of the gods, and a war between the created gods and Ti'amat and Apsu, their source.[36]

Enuma Elish does reveal many points of the Babylonian view of the spiritual realm. It embroiders the creation of the gods in a manner not seen in other material. It also highlights the limitations of the gods. In their war against Ti'amat, Marduk volunteers to do battle, but demands as a price to be made head of the pantheon. One aspect of this demand is that he desires the power to determine fate through the spoken word, a power which apparently previously resided in the pantheon as a whole.

The Mesopotamians retained their polytheistic spiritual hierarchy on through the conquest of the Neo-Babylonian Empire by Cyrus the Persian in 539 BC. The fact that the structure of the hierarchy changed from time to time points out the dynamic nature of Satan's hierarchy. This is evident from Daniel 10, where the spiritual princes fight not only with God's messengers, but with each other. This type of infighting might well be expected within a hierarchy ruled by a rebel.

Egypt

The available evidence suggests that Egyptian civilization began shortly after that of Sumer. There is some evidence that early Egypt developed through a series of migrations, at least one of which carried elements of Sumerian culture and religion.[37]

The key historical event was the unification of Upper and Lower Egypt under Menes about 3100-2900 BC. By this time, the Egyptians already served a number of gods. However, there never seemed to be as many as developed in Mesopotamia, perhaps a few hundred.[38] As in Mesopotamia, most of these were secondary deities, filling subservient roles in a hierarchy. Also, as in Mesopotamia, key cities championed singular gods, although the Egyptians viewed them more singularly than merely as heads of pantheons. There is also evidence that these deities go back to a single creator god.

Shortly after the union of the two Egypts, during the "Old Kingdom" (approximately 2686 to 2181 BC), we have evidence of the so-called Memphis Theology which focused on Ptah as the head and source of all other gods. While there are derived or created forms of this god, Ptah himself was considered a self-existent, eternal, spirit.[39]

At a very early point (approximately 2500 BC), however, Ptah was displaced by Ra (or Re), the sun-god (the great god of Heliopolis). While the period is in the earliest phases of our documentation, the implication is that Ra appealed more to the baser elements than the spiritual Ptah.[40] Later, Ra was merged with Amun (or Amen), the great god of Thebes. Other gods, such as Osiris, Horus, Isis and Seth assumed significant positions, especially with regard to the pharaoh by the time of Abraham.

Thus, the situation was complex by the time Joseph was sold into slavery in Egypt about 1899 BC.[41] While Joseph clearly followed the true God that his father worshipped, the Biblical evidence is mixed regarding his brothers. Clearly they functioned as a family/tribe. Likewise, several unsavory deeds are recorded, not the least of which was selling their younger brother into slavery as opposed to murdering him. Joseph married an Egyptian woman. His brothers married a mixed group, including Canaanites (Gen. 38:2 and 46:10). Settled in Goshen, the northeast corner of Egypt, it is amazing that they not only kept their identity, but kept alive the tradition of serving the true God.

Shortly after the time of Moses,[42] Akhenatan (1370-1362 BC) tried to force worship of the sun-disc Aten. Since Akhenatan tried to concentrate all worship in Aten, his efforts are often viewed as an attempt at monotheism, although the significance is debated.[43] His efforts were unsuccessful, although he moved his capital from Thebes to Akhetaten (Tell el-Armarna). After his reign, his religion and capital both were abandoned, and Egypt continued with its historic polytheism.

Summary

Throughout the ancient near east, we see a picture of developing polytheism. Behind the scenes, we see evidence of an earlier monotheism. Further, we see a widespread understanding of the inter-relationship between the physical and spiritual realms. Through all of this, we see God working with certain individuals as He prepares to create a nation.

Notes

[1] History is said to begin at Summer because it is the location of our oldest writing and written documents. The Sumerian writing system was adopted for the writing of Akkadian, the written language used by both the Babylonian and Assyrian empires. Gelb (I.J. Gelb, *A Study of Writing*) proposes that it also was the impetus for all other writing systems, each of which developed at a later date in a culture open to foreign influence (pp. 212-220). Gelb states that while the evidence is not conclusive, it is neither more nor less compelling than the evidence for the spread of other aspects of civilization, such as astronomy, which are accepted without question.

[2] This was not a new concern for Paul. Some time earlier (about AD 54-56), he had warned the same Corinthians that there was a lot of confusion

about the spiritual realm because many people did not have the means to discern truth from falsehood in that arena (1 Cor 2:4-16). His concern was that many, failing to discern the truth would ignore God's truths, or perhaps more critically, denigrate them to the same level of any other religious declaration. The fact that this amount of confusion could already be present less than 25 years after the crucifixion and resurrection illustrates how effective Satan's campaign was and is. That is why Paul was so careful to point out the objective validity of the historical events which demonstrated God's program. This is undoubtedly the key area of confusion for comparative religious studies today. Man (created in the image of God) has an innate sense of right and wrong. To be an effective counterfeit, a religion must appeal to that sense, and *appear* to stand for "truth," "justice," and "goodness." To effectively differentiate, we must look at much broader spectrum, specifically noting the verification of various claims.

³ A critical misconception prevalent today is how long these cultures require to develop. We think in terms of centuries, when in reality cultures change in a matter of a couple of generations, or even in a few years. The noted historian Eric Hobsbawm notes that many of the traditions we assume to be rooted deeply in a culture can be shown to have been "invented" and instituted over a short period of time, often very recently (*The Invention of Tradition*, pp. 1-5). Hobsbawm's observations are especially valid in cultures which undergo significant social upheaval. We recognize the upheaval our world has undergone in the past century, where we have people who can remember when man could not fly, watching men go to the moon. Even as I write this, those who follow evolutionary premises are arriving at similar conclusions. Derek Bickerton (*Language and Species*, reviewed in *The Dallas Morning News*, January 28, 1991) has advanced the argument that true language "evolved" suddenly from what he calls "protolanguage"--"in a single generation." Our premise is that the social upheaval after the dispersion at Babel was at least as great as any we have seen since, including during the past century. We also have every reason to believe that ancient cultures were as flexible and adaptive in this sense as those of the current century.

⁴ This is a practice commonly observable today as we compete with one another. One child soon learns that he is stronger than his playmates. He then uses force to get his way, and strength become the criteria by which he measures value. Another child is not as strong, but finds school comes easily to him. For him, intelligence becomes the measure of value. Because these become psychological measurements of value, if God (or any god) is valued, it is because he is superlative in the area of value.

⁵ While we might view this process with disbelief, even renowned scholars of today have fallen into the same trap. For example, Albrecht Alt, a reputable Old Testament scholar (*Essays on Old Testament History and Religion*, p. 10) declares that the various titles given to God in the Old

Testament are each distinct gods whose worship was fused into Judaism. His conclusions are predicated on a view that Judaism evolved from primitive polytheistic forms, and as a result, he must find the "primitive gods" behind the monotheistic religion as reported in the Old Testament. This process of deifying attributes has been observed in virtually every known religious tradition.

[6] What constitutes a national grouping in this sense is unknown. Most likely, Daniel was not speaking in terms of nation states as we observe them today, although Psalm 86:9 observes that God created the nations. One suggestion would be that there are levels of spiritual leaders based on various ethnic groupings, but these do not account for apparent empire rulers as in the case of Persia and Greece. It is even more complex today with the amount of ethnic movement involved in the colonization of the new world and multi-ethnic nations such as the U.S., Canada, Mexico, and the U.S.S.R. (now defunct).

[7] Again, we must point out the dating problem for these early cultures. Gelb (pp. 62-63) discusses the earliest dates for writing and remarks that "the dating of all early remains in the Near East is still in the realm of fantasy, with the extreme dates differing by as much as one thousand years." He would put the earliest Sumerian writing at about 3100 B.C., but hastens to add that he bases that by comparison with Egyptian dating, which is also open (cf. John A. Wilson, *The Culture of Ancient Egypt*, p. 319). A date as late as 2500 B.C. is still possible (and perhaps preferable). Even then, the first documents were economic–religious and other extensive documents date somewhat later, perhaps several centuries.

[8] This definition of the beginning of civilization omits the role of pre-tower Babel. Landsberger notes that Sumerian documents place human culture as a legacy from pre-flood times (Benno Landsberger, "Three Essays on the Sumerians," *Monographs on the Ancient Near East* [*MANE*], Vol. 1, p. 8). Samuel Noah Kramer (*The Sumerians*, p. 123) echoes Landsberger citing moral and ethical virtues as key ingredients to this legacy which was given by the gods. While our records (including the Biblical records) only hint at the content of this legacy, we can suggest that it included at a minimum agriculture and husbandry (Gen. 4:2), music (Gen. 4:21), metallurgy (Gen. 4:22), carpentry (Gen. 6:14), and probably writing (Jude 14). Both A. Leo Oppenheim (*Ancient Mesopotamia*, p. 49) and Gelb (p. 63) deem it likely that the Sumerians adapted an already existing writing system. Implied in the records are several other skills including weaving (from the making of tents), stonework (from early altars), mathematics (dimensions of the ark), and astronomy (the use of the stars to measure seasons [Gen. 1:14-16]).

[9] These dates are from William W. Hallo and William K. Simpson (*The Ancient Near East: A History*). Cf. Sir Leonard Woolley, *Ur 'of the Chaldees'*, p. 15, who places the dates approximately 2334-2154 BC. Eugene

Merrill (*Kingdom of Priests*) observes that the birth date of Abraham (about 2166 B.C.) probably occurred after the fall of Ur to the Gutians from the northeast, between about 2240 to 2115 BC.

[10] The Sumerians were a distinct non-Semitic group living at the head of the Persian Gulf. Because they refer to themselves as "the black heads," some scholars propose with good reason that they were a black race (cf. Arthur C. Custance, *Noah's Three Sons*, pp. 72-76). There is evidence that they had regular trade routes to Africa, and the advanced Indus Valley civilization which was Negroid. By 2000 B.C., the region was mixed with many Semitic elements, as is evident by the Semitic words which show up in Sumerian documents. The region was also heavily populated with several large cities, of which Ur was but one. Kramer (*The Sumerians*, pp. 88-89) estimated the population of Ur at approximately 200,000 (although 20 years later, he had become more conservative and lowered that number to 50,000 with a disclaimer of any accuracy [Diane Wolkstein and Samuel Noah Kramer, *Inanna: Queen of Heaven and Earth*, p. 121]). C.L. Woolley estimated 360,000. I.M. Diakanoff, with a more conservative estimate, posited a "free" population of 100,000. There was also a significant slave population, many of whom were prisoners of war, an added cosmopolitan influence.

[11] Samuel Noah Kramer (*History Begins At Sumer*) records approximately twenty-five "firsts" which the Sumerian culture recorded, which includes writing. Custance records the astounding record of the contributions to civilization of the various ethnic groups, which, while it includes the contributions of the Sumerians, goes far beyond.

[12] Kramer (*Inanna: Queen of Heaven and Earth*) observes that the 5-6000 Sumerian literary tablets and fragments contain about 20 myths, 9 epic tales, and some 200 hymns, along with various laments and other texts (p. 125). Most of the religious information that we have gleaned from these texts is incidental to the purpose of the text itself. As A. Leo Oppenheim (*Ancient Mesopotamia*, pp. 172-83) carefully points out, we are given a lot of details which had accumulated over more than a thousand years regarding rituals. He warns that we should be very careful in putting these bits together. Religion in Mesopotamia was a dynamic affair changing drastically over the 1500 years of records we have, and we should be cautious in attempting to pigeon-hole it. Unfortunately, most scholars are not so cautious.

[13] Cf. Thorkild Jacobsen, *The Treasures of Darkness*, pp. 195-215. This process is familiar and traceable in American folk-lore. We cannot necessarily conclude, however, that every story that involves "super-normal" episodes falls into the genre of tall tale or myth. To do so commits the logical fallacy of *petitio principii* (begging the question)--assuming as a premise the intended conclusion. In this case, we can only place the story in the tall tale category by demonstrating that the "super-normal" episode did not occur. To argue that "super-normal" events *cannot* occur is presuppositional, and again begs the

question. We must also be careful not to use circular reasoning in the process.
For example, while Jacobsen notes that "it is often difficult to say with
certainty whether a document originated in the period from which it seems to
come, or whether it was in fact from other times (p. 20)," he then reconstructs
a development process based on a presumed sequence of change. He uses the
resulting outline to show the characteristics and changes of religion for the
Sumerian culture through three different eras, two of which *predate* the written
documents.

[14] The well-known science-fiction writer, Robert Silverberg recently took this
story and converted it to the form of a modern novel with very little change to
its plot or structure (Robert Silverberg, *Gilgamesh the King*, Bantam Books,
1985).

[15] It would similar to the situation if our knowledge of the great emperor
Charlemagne (742-814) came from a few scraps dated from the time of
Chaucer (about 1340-1400), and a novel written by Charles Dickens (1812-
1870).

[16] This process is also not to be confused with Biblical "higher" criticism.
Here the layers are evident in the different documents, and most of the super-
normal attributes are ascribed well after we have record of the man. In the so-
called Biblical higher criticism the layers are relegated to theoretical verbal
histories which antedate all the written documents. In this school of thought,
these hypothetical histories have a greater authority than the actual documents.
The available documents date back to at least to 100 BC and although they
have been copied through the generations, have remained essentially unchanged. Kenneth Kitchen, (in "Ancient Orient, 'Deuteronism,' and the Old
Testament," in *New Perspectives on the Old Testament*) demonstrates that in
the context of the Near Eastern culture of the Hebrews, the Biblical text fits
into the 13th/14th centuries BC. Thus, it is a part of the era it describes,
rather than an attempt to describe something written centuries earlier (cf. pp.
3 and 14).

[17] We prefer the term super-normal to supernatural, since the latter term
implies an unwarranted absoluteness to so-called "natural law." "Natural law"
is a summation of observed data of the physical universe. As such, beings
which transcend the physical (e.g., spiritual beings) have the ability to
transcend these so-called limits. Still, there are a number of ways that super-
normal tales get started. We recognize that man has a fertile imagination and
records his wishes and hopes in the forms of super-normal abilities. Sometimes, he embellishes good tales. The fact that these ideas persist (even in the
"scientific" guise of psychic powers) in a age of rationalism, suggests that there
is more to their origin than mere wish projection.

[18] Kramer (*Inanna: Queen of Heaven and Earth*) observes that his
restoration of "The Descent of Inanna" is pieced together from more than 30
tablets and fragments to produce "more than four hundred lines of text in

almost perfect condition (p. 127)." It is because many of the texts overlap that gaps and breaks can be filled in.

[19] The most important contribution to this knowledge was the approximately 30,000 tablets uncovered during four excavation campaigns through the period 1889-1900 (Kramer, *Sumerian Mythology*, p. 9). Kramer dates the library contents from about 2500 BC up to about 1500 BC, but places the most significant material at about the time of Hammurabi, the Babylonian ruler, circa 1750 BC. William Foxwell Albright, (*From the Stone Age to Christianity*, p. 190) states that the initial tablets from Erech focus on the sky god An and his consort Inanna. It is unclear whether Albright sees this mention as a singular worship, or whether he sees An merely as the singular head of a pantheon of gods. Cf. Arthur C. Custance, *Evolution or Creation?* The Doorway Papers, vol. iv. p. 114.

[20] Kramer (*Sumerian Mythology*, pp. viii and 40-41 and p. 74) argues that Nammu was the first goddess who created everything, although she is relatively unknown elsewhere. He arrives at this conclusion from the use of the ideogram "sea" in the name of Nammu, who is also described as "the mother who gave birth to heaven and earth." The confusion derives from Kramer's identification of the god who has control of an aspect of nature with that force. E.g., Nammu gave birth to the heaven and the earth. Since An is the god of heaven, and Ki is the god of the earth, therefore, Nammu gave birth to An and Ki. Also, since Nammu is written with the ideogram for sea, she has to be some primeval physical sea which produced the physical heaven and the physical earth. This is a confusion of the spiritual and physical realms. While the Sumerians saw an inter-relationship between the spiritual and physical realms, they also tended to keep the two distinct.

[21] Again, we must emphasize the difficulty of piecing together the evidence of this culture. As Jacobsen (p. 19) observes "we find among these materials religious documents, myths, epics, laments, which have been handed down almost unchanged in copy after copy for as much as a thousand or fifteen hundred years, and it is often difficult to say with certainty whether a document originated in the period from which it seems to come, or whether it was in fact from earlier times." For this reason, Oppenheim warns against trying to synthesize a systematic presentation of Mesopotamian religion. He postulates that much of what we have used to develop comprehensive theologies are the works of "court poets" who were "bent on exploiting the artistic possibilities of a new literary language (p. 177)."

[22] Kramer, *The Sumerians*, p. 118.

[23] Oppenheim, *Ancient Mesopotamia*, p. 194.

[24] Benno Landsberger, "Three Essays on the Sumerians," *MANE*, p. 14.

[25] Samuel Noah Kramer (*The Sumerians*, p. 118-19) lists three items which support this argument. Early tablets (dated to 3000 BC) from Erech show An to have a preeminent political role. Later documents (2500 BC or later) give

this position to Enlil. Although An is worshipped throughout the history of Sumer, it is usually as a shadowy figure in the pantheon with Enlil wielding the actual power. Even as late as the Neo-Babylonian period (sixth century BC), a toothache incantation begins with a declaration of Anu (the Akkadian form of An) having created the heaven and earth. Other evidence from Akkadian material supports this view, especially from the Akkadian "creation myth," *Enuma Elish*.

[26] For example, in "Enlil and the Creation of the Pickax," he is viewed as the god who separated heaven from earth, which could be an interesting way of expressing the fall, although in the past it has usually been interpreted as an aspect of the creation of the physical universe (cf. Samuel Noah Kramer, *Sumerian Mythology*, pp. 37-41). Similarly, the introduction from "Gilgamesh, Enkidu, and the Nether World" suggests a territorial division between the two gods, rather than a creation description:

After An had carried off heaven,
After Enlil had carried off earth,
After Ereshkigal had been carried off into Kur as its prize.

[27] We see here an early understanding of the inter-relationship between the physical and spiritual realms. This understanding still exists today in a number of societies who have not arbitrarily ruled out spiritual forces. Bronislaw Malinowski (*Magic, Science and Religion*, p. 29) observed that the "primitive" Melanesians perceived distinct physical and spiritual realms. He noticed that they clearly understood physical cause and effect (the basis of our modern science and technology), but also saw a spiritual realm acting behind the scenes.

[28] Kramer (*The Sumerians*, pp. 122-23) distinguishes three levels in the hierarchy. First were the 7 great gods who "decree the fates." They included An, Enlil, Enki (god in charge of the abyss), Ninhursag (also known as [aka] Ninmah or Nimmu, the mother-goddess), Nanna (aka Sin, the moon god), Utu (aka Shamesh, the sun god), and Inanna (the Semitic Ishtar, daughter of Nanna). The second level were fifty "great gods," referred to as the Anunnaki (the children of An [cf. chapter 2). We currently do not know which of the gods mentioned belong to this group. The third level were those remaining, often referred to as the Igigi.

[29] Sargon viewed his success as a divine intervention on the part of goddess Ishtar. How this success worked is problematic. We are fortunate in that we have recovered a number of tablets which tell Sargon's story, but are unable to determine how much was written after the fact to defend his position (e.g., that his birth name was Sharru-ken(u), meaning "the legitimate king").

[30] One suggestion is that Sargon used a priestess of Ishtar (probably as a lover) to land him in his initial position as cup-bearer to the king of Kish, which he then used to spring-board to later success (William W. Hallo and J. J. A. Van Dijk, *The Exaltation of Inanna*, pp. 6-7).

[31] Current scholarship, at best, argues that this is a projection of physical events. For example, Hallo and Van Dijk state "we can go further and suggest that the constantly changing status of the different gods in Mesopotamian theogony and theology may have at times reflected the actual fortunes of their priestly counterparts on earth (p. 6)." Our argument is that the situation was reversed.

[32] So Eugene Merrill, *Kingdom of Priests*, p. 28. Many scholars use this background as a springboard to the idea that worship of the God of Israel was totally new (e.g., Albrecht Alt, *Essays on Old Testament History and Religion*, p. 59 ff). However, we know that at least one contemporary of Abraham, Melchizedek, also served the true God.

[33] Ur was originally a Sumerian city which attracted a number of Semitic elements. We are not given any further guidelines regarding when Abraham's ancestors moved to the area. The Biblical record merely links Abraham to his ancestors Noah and Shem by a perfunctory genealogy listing the 8 generations between Shem and Abraham. The details we would like to see are totally missing.

[34] A demonstration of the problem is the stop in Haran. The Genesis passage suggests (but does not state) that God originally called Terah who took his family with him (Gen. 11:27). In Acts, Stephen states specifically that Abraham was called in Ur. The goal was Canaan, but they stopped in Haran, a city in northern Syria. It is possible that the original call was to both, but that Terah lost his confidence in Haran. Regardless, it was not until after Terah died, that Abraham was told again to go to Canaan. By now, the Canaanites were in the land, and Abraham was given a promise for future generations. His descendants would not be able to inherit the land until the Canaanite (or Amorite) inhabitants had been allowed to carry their iniquity to the point that it demanded judgment (Gen. 15:13-16). God allowed Terah to stop in Haran, which apparently lost him his role in the promise. He also allowed the Canaanites to move into the land during this layover, which delayed the subsequent possession for four hundred years. These actions demonstrate that God does not force man to do His will, but show how He works around man's decisions to still achieve His goals. Mordecai visualized the same power when he warned Esther that the Jews would be delivered, whether she had a part in it or not (Esther 4:14).

[35] This "title," the first phrase of the story, means "when above." The story is inscribed on seven clay tablets. Several copies have been found in varying states of deterioration which has allowed a virtually complete restoration. No copy predates 1000 BC, and most date from the Neo-Babylonian period, the time of Nebuchadnezzar (James B. Pritchard, *Ancient Near Eastern Texts*, p. 60).

[36] Alexander Heidel (*The Babylonian Genesis*, p. 14) gives an excellent discussion of both similarities with and differences between the Babylonian tale

and the Biblical creation account. The similarities lie primarily in the order of some events, and etymologies of certain terms. He concludes that there is "no incontrovertible evidence" that can be produced to show that either account is dependent upon the other. Differences include the entire process (one of fashioning rather than creating), purpose, and a polytheistic pantheon as opposed the one God.

[37] A.H. Sayce (*The Religions of Ancient Egypt and Babylonia*, pp. 85-86) draws several parallels between the cosmology of early Egypt and that of Babylonia. One of the more significant ones would be a correlation (under the Heliopolis theology) of Atum with Anu as the creator god who brought forth the other gods. Sayce emphasizes that both cultures saw this creator god as originating in a primeval abyss of waters, which he argues must derive from the Sumerian environment on the Persian Gulf, rather than along the Nile River.

[38] Henri Frankfort (*Ancient Egyptian Religion*, p. 4) states that the number is unknown, then cites a "small handbook" listing "more than eighty." However, Frankfort, like most writers about the ancient near east, surveys the entire period of Egyptian history as if it were a single, clearly delineated religious system. E. A. Wallis Budge (*From Fetish to God in Ancient Egypt*, p. 9) places the number of gods at several hundred, but he notes the problem of reconciling "Egyptian monotheistic belief."

[39] Budge, p. 16. The primary document covering Ptah and Memphis theology is an inscription of Shabaka dating from about 712 BC. Budge, however, refers to K. Sethe, the German Egyptologist, who published an earlier archetypal text from the early Old Kingdom. This text places the spirit god Ptah right at the beginning of Egyptian history.

[40] Budge (p. 17) states: "Men preferred the worship of anthropomorphized fetishes whose attributes could be easily understood, and whose natures and habits were believed to be very like their own." However, as Alan Gardiner (*Egypt of the Pharaohs*, p. 84) points out, inter-city competition played a factor. Some records suggest that Userkaf, the first pharaoh of the fifth dynasty, had been foretold to become the high priest of Ra. This recalls the close tie-in of the spiritual and physical realms.

[41] Eugene Merrill (*Kingdom of Priests*, pp. 30-55). Merrill shows clearly how the Biblical chronology fits well with what is known of Egypt in this period. John J. Bimson (*Redating the Exodus and the Conquest*) shows how the traditional "early" date for the Exodus (1446 BC, according to the Biblical chronology, and as developed by Merrill) fits in with the archaeological evidence.

[42] Akhenatan was the third pharaoh *after* the Exodus, which took place approximately 67 years before his reign under this earlier chronology. His father, Amenhotep III, ruled 1417-1379 BC. The conquest of Joshua was concentrated between 1406-1399 BC, although Joshua points out that the

invading Israelites did not take the entire land, but a number of the original inhabitants still lived in their midst (Joshua 23:1-13). In the ruins of Tell el-Amarna, a number of letters from Canaanite princes addressed to Amenhotep III and Akhenatan have been found. These letters ask for assistance against invaders in the land (cf. Merrill, pp. 98-108 who demonstrates the correlation between these invasions and the Israelite settlement).

[43] It has been viewed either as the effort of a visionary before his time, or a cold calculation on the part of a weak ruler attempting to overcome the entrenched Amun priesthood. The problem is that these scholars date Moses about 200 years later (see chapter 4), and then try to understand how the two fit together. It is more likely that Akhenatan tried to implement a dimly understood religion that was responsible for the Exodus in the days of his great-grandfather. In this light, the comments of Charles F. Pfeiffer (*Tell el Amarna and the Bible*) are important. He observes that the worship of Aten first appears in the reign of Thutmose IV (reigned 1414-1406 BC). Thutmose IV was the younger son of Amenhotep II, the pharaoh of the Exodus. As younger son, he assumed the throne unexpectedly (as evidenced by a stela found at the base of the Great Sphinx near Memphis). Aten's position improved during the reign of Thutmose IV's son Amenhotep III. From this period inscriptions have been found describing him as the god who holds sway over all the peoples and lands. His son, Amenhotep IV, changed his name to Akhenatan and demanded sole worship for his god. This process suggests a family that misidentified the God of the Exodus, and then unsuccessfully tried to shift national allegiances towards the misidentified god.

PART II

THE SURVIVAL OF
MONOTHEISM

Judaism and Christianity are unique in their relationship among all the major religions of the world. They share a common heritage, and a common book, the Old Testament. They worship the same God, and agree on the nature of man's problem. They both look for the Messiah as the solution to that problem, and that is where they differ. Jesus Christ claimed to be that Messiah. The Christians accepted that. The Jews did not.

Chapter 4

The World's Oldest Organized Religion: Judaism

Abraham was not a Jew. In fact, neither was Jacob, his grandson (whom God gave the new name of Israel). Jacob founded the nation of Israel through his twelve sons.[1] Judaism was instituted by Moses approximately 400 years after Jacob (or Israel) died. Judaism is based on the Torah, the five books of the Law which Moses wrote. However, Judaism, as we know it today, is the product of centuries of evaluation as the leaders attempted to apply that Law to every aspect of daily life, especially after the return from exile.

Spiritually, a direct line can be drawn from Abraham to his distant descendant some 500 years later. This is evident by the leap from the end of Genesis, where Jacob died, to the beginning of Exodus where Moses was born.[2] While in many Bibles these two events are but a page apart, historically they were about as far apart as Columbus and the Spanish-American War in American history.

Making A Nation

Jacob descended to Egypt with his family, some seventy strong approximately 1875 BC. About four hundred years later, his descendants left Egypt some one to two million strong.[3] In the interim, the people had been transformed from a small group of herders to a large group of herders, farmers, builders, and skilled artisans in a number of areas. They retained the tradition of the God who had met with and guided their ancestors. But the tradition was dimming in the allure of splendiferous pagan temples round about them. And the people themselves were in slavery. They certainly did not have an organized religion in any sense. And the God of their fathers had not spoken nor revealed Himself for centuries.

It would not be surprising then, if a number of the Israelites had

begun to participate in the religious activities around them. That they
did so is evident in their quick return to idolatry with the golden calf
while Moses was up on Mount Sinai.[4]

This explains the dramatic Exodus. The purpose of the nation was
to prepare the way for the Messiah who was to reconcile man to God.[5]
To do so, the nation had to focus solely on the true God and turn away
from any counterfeits. The stage was set by allowing the Egyptians
virtually absolute authority over the embryo nation. It was when the
nation finally cried out to the God of their fathers that God sent Moses.

Moses had been raised in the house of pharaoh but fled to the
wilderness after killing an Egyptian. At God's direction, he returned
to confront the ruler on part of his people. He had two messages. To
pharaoh, he cried out, "Let the Israelites go." To the Israelites, he
declared, "The God of our fathers has spoken again."

The confrontation with pharaoh has been the subject of many books,
novels, and even movies. The process of deliverance was orderly and
designed to prove a key theological point: the God who delivered the
Israelites was mightier than any and all the gods of Egypt.[6] But it was
necessary to prove this to the Israelites as much as to pharaoh. Finally,
on the night of the first Passover in 1446 BC Moses led the Israelites
out of Egypt.[7]

God gave the people one more powerful lesson regarding His
position as He led the people to the shore of the Red Sea. When
pharaoh led his army out after the Israelites, God led the nation through
the sea itself, and then drowned pharaoh's army behind it. From there,
He led the fledgling nation to Mt. Sinai, where He gave it a national
charter. This national charter became the foundation for Judaism.

Establishing A Religion

The nation had two functions. The immediate function was that it
was to serve as a nation of priests to the Most High God. As such, the
entire political, social and economic organization would reflect the
national position. This is demonstrated in the structure of the covenant
given on Mt. Sinai, which was patterned after standard suzerain-vassal
treaties of the period.[8] There was to be no king for God was their
suzerain. As His vassals, the people had social, economic, and
religious responsibilities. These were spelled out in detail. If these
responsibilities were faithfully executed, then God on His part would

prosper the nation. These responsibilities are the heart of the Torah or Law.

If these responsibilities were disregarded, then God swore to punish the people to bring them around. Their vassalhood was not voluntary, but part of the other national function. The other function, the *long term* function of the nation was to prepare the way for the Messiah, the "sent-one" from God who was to reconcile the entire human race to God. But reconciliation required that man recognize the God to whom he was being reconciled.

We have already seen the insidious nature of the counterfeits thrown before man. How could he distinguish between the true God and false gods? That was the role of the nation of Israel, to point to this true God. As such, its history was to be unique. And there were to be distinctives in its society, most critically in the area of worship.

That was also the area where the nation faced the most problems. Historically, as demonstrated throughout Old Testament, the people struggled with the question of which god they were going to serve-- whether the God who made them a nation and demanded their allegiance, or the gods of the nations around them. Time and again, they chose to serve other gods.

True to His word, God disciplined His people to remind them where their allegiance was supposed to lie. There are three distinct periods in the history of the nation of Israel. All reflect the same trends.

Fighting Idols

First, the nation struggled in the theocracy. Also known as the period of the judges, the people struggled with the temptation to serve the local gods of the pagan inhabitants of the land.[9] At least six times the land was oppressed by a pagan enemy because the people turned to other gods.[10] When the people cried to God for deliverance, He raised up a leader who delivered the nation, and guided it back to the true God. The upshot of the situation was that the people struggled in their attempts to follow the true God.[11]

The same held true as the nation asked for and received a monarchy. Each of the kings who ruled over the nation exhibited serious character flaws. Even Solomon in all of his wisdom allowed the introduction of syncretistic religious practices.[12] He married heathen wives and then allowed them to erect altars to their pagan gods in Jerusalem even as he built a temple to the true God, and centralized worship for the nation in Jerusalem. As a result, the nation was divided between the north and the south.

Jeroboam, the first king of the Northern Kingdom, immediately set up a rival religious center to counter the temple in Jerusalem. Politically motivated, it is reminiscent of the situation in the wilderness. Jeroboam made two calves and declared them to be the gods which brought Israel up out of Egypt. Over the next two centuries God sent prophets to both halves of this divided nation to warn of future judgments.

It was a time of spiritual sorting out among the people. The kings of the north without exception followed Jeroboam. The southern report was mixed. Periodically, the kings in the south would lead a return to the true God. Some tried to sway the nation away.[13] Some people in the north moved south to serve the true God (2 Chron 11:16). Still others remained in the north, and remained faithful to the true God (2 Chron 30:1).

Still, as is evident throughout both Kings and Chronicles, both kingdoms suffered from attempting to serve two masters. The severity of the situation should have been apparent when the Northern Kingdom was carried off into exile in 722 BC. Indeed, Hezekiah made a tremendous effort to pull the Southern Kingdom in the right direction. He is the first king of Judah for whom there is no criticism in the books of the Kings (cf. 2 Kings 18:3-6).[14] But the nation as a whole still was mixed in its allegiance and under Manasseh, his son, just as wholeheartedly went in the opposite direction. As a result, the Southern Kingdom was exiled to Babylon in 605-586.[15]

The Samaritans

Following the exile of the Northern Kingdom, the Assyrians further syncretized Jeroboam's hybrid northern religion. After Samaria, the northern capital was captured by the Assyrians in 721 BC, Sargon exported many of the Israelites, and imported natives from several Mesopotamian cities.[16] When attacked by lions (sent by God), they sent back to Sargon asking for Israelite priests to teach them "the custom of the god of the land (2 Kings 17:27)." Sargon sent a priest from the group he had carried often into exile, who "taught them how they should fear the Lord." However, it was a syncretistic religion as is evident from the report, "so while these nations feared the Lord, they also served their idols (2 Kings 17:41)."

This group as a whole became known as the Samaritans and their region Samaria after the city of Samaria. When the southern exiles were rebuilding the temple in Jerusalem, the Samaritans offered to help, but were refused because of their syncretism (Ezra 4:2). By the time of Jesus, they had become monotheistic, professing belief in the one true God, and Moses as the only prophet (cf. John 4:1-26). They retained the Pentateuch (or Torah) with some differences (e.g., in Deuteronomy 27:4, the altar of God is to be built on Mt. Gerizim).[17] They looked for a messiah, a man like Moses to show them the truth.[18] Between the time of Nehemiah and Jesus, they built their own temple at Mount Gerizim which completed the schism.

The Babylonian Exile and Return

God had sent prophets as His spokesmen for various purposes throughout the history of the nation. After the exile of the Northern Kingdom, however, they increased both in number and intensity, as God prepared the Southern Kingdom for its exile. They exhorted the nation to turn to the true God as they warned of God's coming judgment and future restoration. As a result of the declarations of the prophets there was to be no question in the mind of the people that the exile was a result of God's direction, not Nebuchadnezzar's whims.[19]

When the remains of the once proud nation[20] began to return from exile following Cyrus' decree in 538, it was a sober group. In the 70 year interim, most of the syncretistic elements had been purged.[21] But as the people rebuilt the temple, they wept to realize what they had lost in the process (Ezra 3:12 and Haggai 2:3). God sent three more prophets (Haggai, Zechariah, and later, Malachi) to encourage the people, reinforcing His promise for the still to come Messiah. Based on the accounts of the prophets, that Messiah was to be more than four hundred years in the future,[22] but the people were to be faithful and wait.

After Malachi, there were no more prophets.[23] Facing this period of silence, the Jews concluded that God had nothing more to say. Therefore, they reasoned, they had all the revelation from God they needed. However, they needed to interpret what He had already said in order to apply it to the new environment, especially after the time of

Alexander, when the issue of Hellenization arose.

Oral Tradition

The roots lay in Ezra and Nehemiah, who read the Law aloud, and then had to translate (from Hebrew to Aramaic, the common post-exilic spoken tongue) and explain it (cf. Neh 8:8). The return also changed the social and religious structure of Judaism. As a result of the destruction of the temple and the exile, the Jewish people organized around the synagogue for the purpose of worship and instruction. The leaders acquired the title, Rabbi, meaning "my superior." With the return, this new institution developed alongside the newly restored temple worship.

Alexander the Great swept through Judea in 332 BC, after taking Sidon and Tyre on his way to Egypt. Thus, Judea was incorporated into Alexander's empire which was divided among his four generals after his death in 323 BC. After the infighting concluded, Judea was included in the section ruled by the Seleucids (descendants of Antiochus, one of Alexander's generals), who retained control until the Romans annexed Syria in 64 BC. Since the ruling class was from a Greek (or Hellene) culture, Hellenizing influences soon began to filter through the society.

In this environment, several groups arose within Judaism as the people responded in different ways. The first were the Sopherim, or scribes. Actually, the Sopherim were interpreters who explained how the law of Moses should be applied in periods of change.[24] The Sopherim began with Simeon the Just the high priest about 300 BC. Their understandings of the Law were passed along orally as "Midrash," coming from the verb "to search." Midrash began to be committed to writing in the 2nd century BC, the period of the Maccabean revolt.[25]

After harsh and blasphemous actions by the Syrian King, Antiochus Epiphanes,[26] the Jews revolted in 167 BC under the leadership of Mattathius, a pious priest who refused to follow the command to sacrifice on an heathen alter. His sons, Judas Maccabee and his brothers took up the leadership when Mattathius died in 166 BC. The Maccabeans won a series of brilliant battles, and retook the temple in 165 BC. The cleansing of the temple is celebrated at Hanukkah.[27] As a result of these wars, the Jews won the right to worship God according to their traditions.[28]

Pharisees

Soon, the leadership divided into two key schools of thought: the Pharisees[29] and the Sadducees. They differed primarily on the method of interpreting Torah (or Law) and how to apply its precepts to the current situation. Underlying these differences were varying understandings of God's nature and reactions to the Hellenization process.

The Pharisees deplored what they perceived as concessions to Hellenization. Passionately devoted to God, the Pharisees held to a Jewish cultural spirit of the law, which attempted to apply it to all of life. If a law seemed inappropriate in a different culture, they sought to interpret this through oral tradition. Men of devout piety, they sought to follow the law *in all of its details*, often getting bogged down in the details.

In time, this oral tradition came to occupy a place equal to the written law.[30]   During the period of 200 BC to AD 200, these oral traditions were written down and compiled in a work called the Mishnah. The traditional Rabbinic system gradually evolved out of the Pharisaic party and its traditions after the destruction of Jerusalem in AD 70.

Sadducees

The Sadducees[31] were note as opponents of the Pharisees, although they actually tended to outnumber their rivals. Being the party of the elite, and a majority, they managed to rule the Sanhedrin, the ruling Jewish council.

The Sadducees claimed to refuse to accept any authority unless it was based directly on the Torah, thus they disdained oral tradition. Rather, they stressed a greater freedom of the will, and were less concerned about the details of the Law. More importantly, they began with more Hellenistic values which they attempted to integrate into Judaism (which profoundly affected the understanding of the Torah. The Sadducees denied the existence of angels, resurrection from the dead, and the immortality of the soul. They have been termed the secularists of their day.

Since the Sadducees focused on the present world, they saw God as

a God of the nation. When Jerusalem was destroyed, they lost support
and quickly disappeared.

Essenes

Meanwhile, in the background of our history were the Essenes.
Noted recently because their association with the Dead Sea Scrolls, the
Essenes were the mystics of the period.[32] The Essenes differed from
the other two major sects primarily in their monasticism and penchant
for ritual cleansing and purity. They could be characterized as ascetics
and legalists.

Jesus, the Messiah

It was into this environment that Jesus appeared. He claimed to be
the Messiah which the prophets had foretold. To substantiate this
claim, He claimed to have fulfilled prophecy, and He performed
miracles. Even His opponents did not deny His claims to fulfill
prophecy. While His miracles were acknowledged, their source was
disputed.[33] When pressed to make a final decision, the Jewish
leadership decided that Jesus was not the Messiah they were looking
for, so they gave Him over to the Romans for crucifixion on Friday,
April 3, AD 33.[34]

By Sunday, April 5, the grave in which Jesus had been buried was
empty, and the Jesus who had been crucified and verified dead by the
Roman military was appearing to His followers again. On May 14, the
Apostles reported His ascension. On the 24th, 3000 Jews from all over
the Roman Empire concluded that He was their Messiah. A short time
later, another 2000-5000 (it is not clear whether the 5000 is an addition
or a total) joined in that group, although the Jewish leadership as a
whole still refused to recognize claims of Jesus. There were exceptions
such as Nicodemus and Joseph of Arimathea. One of the most noted
was the student of Gamaliel (one of the most distinguished leaders of
the Pharisees), Saul. Confronted with the risen Jesus, Saul recognized
Him as his Messiah, and became more widely known as Paul the
Apostle.

Another Revolt

While many of the Jews had remained abroad following the exile (the Diaspora), Judea was still considered a homeland, even though the Jews chaffed under the Roman rule. Amid increasing unrest, they rose in rebellion once again in AD 66, drawing the wrath of Rome down on the province and city. Jerusalem was destroyed in AD 70 and the temple burned to the ground. The last of the defenders (Zealots) retreated to the hilltop fortress of Masada, where they committed mass suicide in AD 73 just prior to the Romans' breaking through the walls.

During the siege of Jerusalem, Rabbi Jochanan ben Zakkai slipped out of the city to meet with the Roman general Vespasian. After prophesying that he would become the next emperor of Rome, he requested and received permission to found a school at Jabneh (or Jamnia). Here, the Mishnah was continued and the school of Jamnia began to codify the traditions of the fathers by subject matter.

In the interim, after yet another revolt (under Bar-Cochba), the Romans put Jerusalem off-limits to all Jews.[35] Christians (except Christians of Jewish ancestry) were allowed to come and go freely. This declaration is considered by some to have marked a final schism between the Jews and the Christians.[36]

The Talmud

By the early third century, under the leadership of Rabbi Judah ha-Nasi, the Jewish community in Palestine had collated the traditions of the fathers into a closed, systematized work, the Mishnah.[37]

The Mishnah quickly became the Jewish standard for interpreting Torah. However, it was compiled in Palestine and reflected life there. The sizable community in Babylon, and Jews throughout the Diaspora had questions regarding legal applications in other areas of life. This produced endless discussion among the rabbis both in Babylon and in Palestine. These discussions and their conclusions were written down as Gemara. The Mishnah and Gemara placed together became the Talmud. Historically there are two Talmuds, the Babylonian and the Palestinian. The Talmuds were completed and closed by about 500.[38] The Babylonian Talmud became the glue that held the Jewish people together as they spread throughout the world in the Diaspora--the scattering of the Jewish people after the Babylonian captivity.

The Diaspora

The Jewish people spread throughout the Roman Empire. When Christianity achieved an official status, the Jews lost many privileges. In practical terms, their situation varied with the whims of the civilian authorities, which usually meant that they fluctuated between being barely tolerated and persecuted outright. The Crusades changed the situation for the worse. In 1096, the Rhineland Jews were caught up in a massacre which set a trend.

As the persecutions of the Jews increased in the medieval period, many Jews retreated into a form of mysticism. Supposedly based on the oral tradition aspect of the Torah (see footnote 30) Jewish mysticism flowered in the thirteenth century in the form of Cabalism.[39] Cabalism had appeared in a gnostic form at the turn of the millennia, and in various forms through the centuries. One of the key contributions was the *Zohar* ("Book of Splendor"), which first appeared in Spain in the 1280's. With the expulsion of the Jews from Spain in 1492, Cabalism spread throughout Europe and contributed to the rise of Hasidism in the 17th century.

Sephardic Jews

Spain had been the home of Sephardic Judaism. Sephardic comes from the from Hebrew name for a nation mentioned in Obadiah 20, which has traditionally been identified as Spain. Sephardic Judaism had blended Torah and Talmud along with the Greek and Islamic influences on the Jews in Spain. Taking advantage of Muslim tolerance, they had entered the mainstream of Spanish life rising to positions of wealth and power. A key Sephardic leader was Moses Maimonides of Cordoba (1135-1204) who wrote several commentaries on the Mishnah based on Aristotelian logic. His works also influenced Christian scholasticism. When the Spaniards evicted the Jews,[40] many Shephardics moved into Eastern Europe, where the Ashkenazi Jews had retreated as they had progressively expelled from Western Europe. Others moved into more tolerant Muslim areas, notably Turkey.

Ashkenazi Jews

Western Europe began moving against the Jews when Edward I

expelled them from England in 1290. Even there they were banished into ghettos, walled off enclosures where the Jew was required by law to live. The name Ashkenazi comes from the Hebrew word for German. Bound by law to the ghetto, the Ashkenazis contented themselves with the study of Talmud.

Hasidism

In this drear environment in the 18th century sprang up a strong pietistic movement called Hasidism. Its founder, Israel ben Eliezar was a student of the Cabala who had a very charismatic personality. Emphasizing emotional response, he declared that true religion covered all aspects of life, derived from an understanding of God's immanence.

Hasidism won many followers and fierce opposition. The learned Talmudists attempted to outlaw it, especially in Lithuania, a key Jewish center. In Poland, it spread like wildfire. By the 19th century, perhaps half of Eastern European Jews embraced Hasidism. Like many charismatic movements, it began faltering through a lack of overall leadership and organization. Still, Hasidism remained a strong element of Orthodox Judaism in Eastern Europe until World War II. Today, there are a number of small Hasidic groups following different leaders.[41]

With the French Revolution and the Enlightenment, the Jewish position in Western Europe alleviated greatly. The French national assembly opened the way by enfranchising the Jews on Sept. 28, 1791.[42]

Modern Jewish Movements

The key Jewish religious reformer was the German hunchback, Moses Mendelssohn (1729-1786). Raised in the ghetto in Dessau, he studied Torah, Talmud, and Maimonides. As a young man he moved to Berlin where he studied German, Latin, French, and English. He won fame as a philosopher. He realized that the ghetto would eventually suffocate his people, but also realized that the Jews were not prepared to be flung headlong into European society.

He devised a means of drawing out the people by translating the Torah into German, using Hebrew characters. While many Rabbis saw Mendelssohn's translation as a threat, others saw it as a means of modernizing Judaism. Following Mendelssohn, a series of Reformed Jewish writers succeeded in producing a new movement. Spearheaded by David Friedlander, Reformed Judaism discarded phylacteries and many of the old rituals, got rid of Aramaic prayers which no longer were meaningful to the reader, updated synagogue services, and took the Talmud out of the divinely inspired category. Many Reformed Jews began emigrating to the United States at the turn of the 20th century, where the movement took root readily.

At the same time, Jews from Eastern Europe were migrating to the U.S., and the two groups clashed. The older generation naturally perceived the Reformed Jews as apostate, but also saw how the new environment drew the younger men and women.

A third movement, called Conservative Judaism, was founded in the 1890's by a group of moderates. It followed some of the Reformed ritual changes (e.g., not segregating the sexes during worship) and relaxed some of the dietary laws, while retaining rabbinic traditions. Conservative Judaism permits reinterpretation of those traditions based on modern needs. Both Reformed and Conservative Judaism reject the concept of resurrection still accepted by the Orthodox tradition.

In response to increasing assimilation in Western culture and persecution in other areas, Zionism, the return of a Jewish nation to the land of Israel, arose in the late 1800's.[43] It also fed on the tradition of Hebrew Messianism. The first Jewish colony in Palestine was established in 1878 as Jews around the world contributed to the Jewish National Fund. By World War II, more than 500 square miles of Palestine were owned by the Jews. After the Balfour declaration of 1917,[44] the number of immigrants increased.

After World War II, the victorious allies surveying the murder of six million Jews in Germany, promised to provide the Jews a homeland in Israel, which had been wrenched from them by the Romans, 1800 years earlier. The story of the modern Israel[45] is totally outside the scope of this survey, except to say that many Christians see this return as a fulfillment of Jesus' prophecy regarding His people. The Jews are still looking for their Messiah.

Notes

[1] Technically, there were thirteen tribes of Israel. Jacob had twelve sons, but

God gave his next to youngest son, Joseph, a double portion in the inheritance through Joseph's two sons Ephraim and Manasseh. As the nation was organized after the Exodus, the descendants of the third son, Levi, were not given a region of the territory, but were assigned a priestly role. With this role went certain lands dispersed throughout the forthcoming kingdom, specifically certain cities with supporting farm land.

[2] When God met Moses in the wilderness at the burning bush, He introduced Himself as "the God of your father, the God of Abraham, the God of Isaac, and the God of Jacob (Ex. 3:6)." The point of this extended identification is that He is the same God from Abraham right down to Moses' own father. That is, He was the God Who called Abraham in Ur and Haran, the God who moved Isaac through Canaan, and Jacob to Egypt and served by Moses' father, Amram, in Egypt. Now, He was appearing in the wilderness. This argues that the God appearing to Moses was more than a local "numen," (as posited by Albrecht Alt in *The God of The Fathers*, and others), but the same God who transcended space and time. As such, this leads up to the later declaration when Moses asks, "who should I say sent me?"

[3] The 70 includes essentially only sons and grandsons with wives and sisters omitted (cf. Gen. 46:7-27). The departure number is based on Exodus 12:37-38 which reports 600,000 men with the addition of children and a "mixed multitude" which went with them. These numbers are not out of line for the period of settlement in Egypt. If the average family had 1.75 male children, and a new generation every 25 years, in 400 years the male population for the *final generation alone* would be over 540,000. John J. Davis (*Biblical Numerology*, p. 73) observes "Scholars have not dismissed the large numbers of the exodus because archaeological or topographical data would absolutely forbid it, but because such a vast number of people would require supernatural assistance which *a priori* they reject."

[4] The seriousness of this sin is accented when we realize that the molding of the golden calf occurred *after* Moses had brought down the God's guidelines against other gods and idols (Ex. 20) and Aaron and the other leaders had seen the theophany on the mountain (Ex. 24). It is clear that the image of the calf was chosen from the Apis bull, which was closely tied to the Memphis Ptah cult. Also, Joshua reminded his people that their ancestors served other gods in Egypt as the nation prepared to settle the land it had just begun occupying (Joshua 24:14-15).

[5] This purpose is extremely evident in the manner by which the Exodus was instituted. Each family sacrificed a lamb, then put the blood of the lamb on the door. When God's angel of death moved through the land, he passed over the houses with the blood. This clarifies a number of New Testament passages, such as John 1:36, where John the Baptist proclaimed that Jesus was the Lamb of God. Paul, in 1 Cor 5:7 refers to Jesus as the Passover. Coulson Shepherd (*Jewish Holy Days*, pp. 23-32) briefly covers the details of the

Passover celebration today, and how Jesus is the fulfillment of its prophetic
aspects.

[6] John J. Davis (*Moses and the Gods of Egypt*, pp. 79-172) gives an
excellent overview of the 10 plagues and their purposes. The plagues and
Exodus not only served to demonstrate the impotency of the Egyptian state
(pharaoh and his army), the Egyptian religious structure, and the Egyptian
gods, but provided it a historical rallying point for the nation of Israel. The
Exodus served as a national birthdate, and a ceremony to look back upon the
super-normal creation of the nation.

[7] Eugene Merrill (*Kingdom of Priests*, pp. 58-64) uses the dates established
in the *Cambridge Ancient History* and Biblical texts to establish the probable
date of the Exodus. His development is logically sound and produces results
which fit well in the known history of Egypt. This places the Exodus in the
reign of Amenhotep II, shortly after he replaced Thutmose III. Thutmose III
reigned 54 years, which accounts for Moses' long exile. Amenhotep II was not
succeeded by his oldest son as a result of "an unforeseen turn of fate such as
the premature death of an elder brother." This would make the domineering
Hatshepsut the daughter of pharaoh and provides a background of palace
intrigue to the Exodus account. John J. Bimson (*Redating the Exodus and
Conquest*) examines the archaeological evidence which has been held by many
to demand a date during the reign of Ramses II (about 1290 BC). He
concludes that an earlier date is valid, although he arrives at a slightly earlier
date (about 1470) by rounding off some of the Biblical periods.

[8] Meredith Kline (*Treaty of the Great King*) examines the structure of the
book of Deuteronomy in detail and concludes that it parallels the structure of
recently translated Hittite suzerain-vassal treaties dating from the period of the
Exodus.

[9] Eugene H. Merrill (*An Historical Survey of the Old Testament*, p. 169)
summarizes the Canaanite religion: "Over all there was a rather shadowy,
nebulous figure known as El. He seems to have been prominent in early
Canaanite theology, but was gradually displaced by his son Baal, though he did
continue to exist as Father God. His wife was Asherah, the aforementioned
goddess of fertility, who was also, strangely enough, thought to be the virgin
goddess." It is evident from even this cursory summary that the Canaanite
religion had developed along lines observed in other parts of the ancient near
east. By the time of the Israelite conquest, the Canaanite worship focused
around Baal and Asherah. It also involved gross immoralities including sacred
prostitution, divination, and child sacrifice to induce the gods to provide
fertility and prosperity (Cf. William F. Albright, *Yahweh and the Gods of
Canaan*, pp. 115-52).

[10] The nation was never uniform in its obedience, nor in its disobedience.
Consequently, many of the judges were local leaders who were raised by God
to deal with local issues. It is clear that some of the judges served at the same

time in different areas (cf. R. K. Harrison, *Introduction to the Old Testament*, p. 692 or Leon Wood, *A Survey of Israel's History*, pp. 206-207).

[11] For example, one of the judges was Gideon. Gideon knew who God was, and seemed to serve Him (Judges 5:13), yet one of his first tasks after being called by God to deliver the Israelites from the Midianites was to tear down his father, Joash's altar to Baal and the sacred grove beside it. When the locals demanded Gideon's death as a result, Joash replied, "If [Baal] is a god, let him contend for himself (Judges 6:31)." This interchange shows that Joash had attempted to serve both Baal and the true God.

[12] When Solomon assumed the throne, the nation still sacrificed on "high places because there was no house built for the name of the Lord (1 Kings 3:1-3)." While he was still building the temple, Solomon married pharaoh's daughter to ally himself with Egypt. This political marriage set the stage for his later apostasy. It led to other political marriages which first diluted, then stole away, his affection for the true God (1 Kings 11:1-10). This is perhaps part of the tragedy of Solomon. At a critical point in history, he had the opportunity to focus the spiritual attention of his people on the true God, but instead allowed himself to be entangled with the worship of the counterfeits. Part of this entanglement resulted from internal pressure as Solomon failed to lead his people in the way they *should* go, but followed the popular trends.

[13] As a whole in the south, the reigns of the evil kings were relatively short compared to the good kings (cf. John Phillips (*Exploring the World of the Jew*, p. 27).

[14] The only other king for which that is true is Josiah who reigned some 45 years after Hezekiah. Between the two was the wicked king Manasseh. Manasseh, coming from so godly a father as Hezekiah, sealed the fate of Judah and Jerusalem as far as God was concerned (2 Kings 21:11-15). However, because Manasseh's grandson, Josiah, instituted a reformation, God postponed the date of judgment (2 Kings 22:18-20).

[15] The exile of the Southern Kingdom took place in several waves. The first was in 605 after the battle of Carchemish where Nebuchadnezzar defeated the Assyrians and Egyptians, and incorporated Judah as a vassal state. On his way back to Babylon he took a number of Jewish captives, including Daniel and his friends. The second wave was in 602 when Jehoiakim rebelled. Nebuchadnezzar carried off more captives and plundered the temple after he forced Jehoiakim to submit. In 597, Nebuchadnezzar took Jerusalem from Jehoiakin, Jehoiakim's successor and set up Zedekiah as a puppet king. After further rebellion (against the advice of Jeremiah), Nebuchadnezzar returned to Jerusalem in 588, and burned the city in 586 after he captured it. All but the very lowest classes were deported to Babylon. See Merrill (*Kingdom of Priests*, pp. 448-96) for a good overview of the political events of this period.

[16] The nature of this exile is problematic. The common understanding is that the Northern Kingdom was taken into exile and ultimately disappeared (i.e.,

the 10 lost tribes of Israel, a foundation belief of Herbert W. Armstrong and the World Wide Church of God, who argued that the descendants of these tribes became the Anglo-Saxon settlers of England). This understanding of the 10 tribes is based on 2 Kings 17:18 which states: "So the Lord was very angry with Israel and removed them from His sight; none was left except the tribe of Judah." However, the Samaritans claim that their ancestors were true Israelites, and the reason for the schism between the two was the moving of the ark to Jerusalem under Eli (of course their religious and historical documents which date from long after this period, reflect their contention). Actually, neither view correlates with the historical data, nor with the later prophets and the New Testament which continue to speak of the 12 tribes. There was an exile. Even Sargon brags of his exile of the Israelites (cf. James B. Pritchard, *Ancient Near Eastern Texts Relating to the Old Testament*, pp. 284 ff). This exile does not seem to be a total removal of the population. In the context of 2 Kings 17, verse 18 is referring to national identity. In actuality, by the time of the exile carried out by Sargon, a large part of what had been the Northern Kingdom had been removed by Tiglath Pilezer. The remains centered around the city of Samaria. Outside of that area, a number of individuals remained including a large number who still worshipped the true God and journeyed to Jerusalem during the reign of Hezekiah for his Passover celebration. Likewise, a number of outsiders were brought in and settled. This was the normal practice of the Assyrians--and it made good political sense. The official religion of the region remained the cult developed by Jeroboam, a syncretized cult which was compromised further during this period.

[17] Throughout this period, some individuals of the Northern Kingdom still retained allegiance to the true God, as is evident by their attending Hezekiah's Passover (2 Chron. 30:1 and 11), and their contribution to Josiah's restoration of the Jerusalem temple (2 Chron. 34:9). The majority, however, had turned away from the true God (2 Chron. 30:10).

[18] Cf. John 4:25. Given the source of the Samaritan religion in Jeroboam's syncretism, supplemented by Sargon's imports, it is amazing that the inhabitants retained as much truth as they did. This suggests that even though they disagreed with Ezra and Nehemiah regarding critical issues, they also learned from them. While the Samaritans rejected the later books of the Old Testament, they did come to adhere to the portion of truth they had (cf. John Bowman, *The Samaritan Problem*, pp. 29-56). It is clear that Jesus built on that when he declared to the Samaritan woman that He was the Messiah that she was looking for. This is also clear in the Great Commission where Samaria is given a special position between Judea and the rest of the nations. The Samaritans have survived the centuries, but at last report, they had become a small, ingrown group with but a handful left.

[19] It is clear throughout Scripture that role of the prophet was more than just to call the people to return to God, or even to reveal hidden things such as

future events. Their function was closely intertwined into the overall function of the nation, which was to reveal the true God as the one Who was Sovereign and in control of history (cf. Hobart E. Freeman, *An Introduction to the Old Testament Prophets*).

[20] John Phillips (*Exploring the World of the Jew*, p. 32) observes that the majority of the Jews remained in exile. Only 42,360 (Nehemiah's count–Neh 7) returned at that time. Phillips states "Most of the Jews were unimpressed at this remarkable fulfillment of prophecy [Cyrus' decree]. Many of them had been born in Babylon and had made it their home."

[21] Even so, Ezra recounts how some of the returnees, including priests and Levites, were still inter-marrying with the pagans around them. When he reminds the leaders of the costs, they re-committed themselves to ensuring the national (and hopefully religious) purity (Ezra 9-10). However, the concept of religious purity stopped at the point of declaring for the one God and following prescribed ritual.

[22] This was the same people who had just seen God tell their ancestors through Jeremiah that the exile would last 70 years (Jeremiah 25:11). Daniel, at least, had taken that number seriously. As the 70 year period neared its conclusion in 538 BC, Daniel (who had come out of Israel with the first wave of exiles in 605 BC), started looking for the fulfillment of Jeremiah's words. In Daniel 9, he asked God, when? God explained to him that the fulfillment was going to occur on time, and by the way, there would be another 490 years after the decree (to rebuild Jerusalem) for Daniel's people and the city. This decree to rebuild the city was given by Artaxerxes in 444 BC. Robert Anderson (*The Coming Prince*) and Harold Hoehner (*Chronological Aspects of the Life of Christ*) go into detail of how the 490 year period works out for the nation of Israel.

[23] Both the method the Israelites used to determine a true prophet and the method by which they determined that prophecy had ceased are unclear. It is clear that in the case of prophetic events, the prophet had to be 100 % correct or face death by stoning (Deut 13:1-5). However, many of the canonical prophets foresaw events which would take place long after the prophet and his contemporaries would die--events for which there was no way to verify fulfillment. This points to the use of short term prophecies and super-normal events to validate the long term prophecies (cf. Freeman, *An Introduction to the Old Testament Prophets*, pp. 16-117). Freeman (p. 130) suggests that several criteria were used to close the canon: 1) Ezra formed the canon and no book after Ezra could be included (this would seem to exclude Malachi, however); 2) Only books written originally in Hebrew could be included (this would seem to exclude Ezra and Daniel [both of which have major sections in Aramaic], however). Whatever the method, it is clear that while a number of books (including the group known today as the Apocrypha) were written during this period, they were never accepted by the Jewish people or leaders as part

of the canon.

[24] After the return from Babylonia, many of the people no longer spoke Hebrew. Initially, Aramaic was the primary means of communication, and many of the books (including the Apocrypha) written during this period were written in Aramaic, although the Mishnah was still written in a Hebrew dialect called Mishnaic Hebrew. Later Greek replaced Aramaic as the lingua franca of the exiles throughout the world. Between 285 and 130 BC, the Old Testament was translated into Greek. This became a prime aid in the struggle against Greek rationalism. Interestingly, the Gemara, the later commentary on the Torah and Mishnah, was written and passed down in Aramaic, which became a key language for Jewish studies. Christian writings were invariably in Greek, until Latin replaced it among the later Church fathers.

[25] It is popularly termed the Maccabean revolt since it was led by Judas Maccabee and his brothers. Judas was the oldest of 5 sons of a priest named Mattathias of the house of Hasmon. The surname for Judas, "Maccabee," is considered by many scholars to be derived from the Hebrew term for hammer. Technically, according to Josephus, the insurrection should be termed the Hasmonaean revolt.

[26] Antiochus pursued a vigorous policy of Hellenization, whereby he attempted to solidify his reign under a common culture, including a syncretistic pagan religion. In the process, he identified himself with the head of the Greek pantheon, Zeus, and set up worship to Zeus in the Jewish temple (in 168 BC). From his perspective, this was merely a local application of his broader Hellenization process. From the Jewish perspective, it was unmitigated blasphemy, although some Jews did seek to compromise.

[27] Hanukkah, like all Jewish holidays, is based on the lunar calendar. It normally falls in late December, giving it a western cultural relationship to Christmas. According to the tradition, when the Jews sought to rededicate the temple to the true God, there was enough oil for one night. Miraculously, the oil lasted for the eight days of dedication. In remembrance, the Jewish people light candles in a menorah each evening of the eight day celebration.

[28] After these initial victories, the Jews faced defeat against the key Syrian general, Lysias. When Lysias had to suddenly return to Syria to put down an internal revolt, Lysias allowed religious freedom. Although the primary goal had been achieved, the war continued and a degree of independence was achieved in 152 BC. Independence and strife continued until the Romans intervened in 63 BC.

[29] The Pharisees were the successors of the Hasidim or "pious ones." They in turn derived from the Sopherim, the spiritual heirs of Ezra and Nehemiah. The Hasidim taught a strict adherence to God's law, and were especially meticulous about the Sabbath. The term Pharisee is thought to derive from the Aramaic "Perishim" meaning "separated ones" (Leah Bronner, *Sects and Separatism During the Second Jewish Commonwealth*, p. 69).

[30] To justify this position, it was argued that Moses was given two laws by God--the written law, i.e., the Torah, and the oral law, which was to be supplemented by the prophets and traditions of the fathers. Of course, when the tradition was set up as the authority to properly interpret the Law (and especially when it was claimed to have a position equal to it), the interpretation became the ultimate authority.

[31] The term Sadducee is either derived from the Hebrew "Tsedukim" meaning "righteous ones," or it denotes descendants (or followers) of Zadok, high priest during the time of David (cf. Isidore Epstein, *Judaism: A Historical Presentation*, pp. 95-109).

[32] The first historical mention of the Essenes is actually by Josephus, the first century historian. The Essenes lived in closed, restrictive communities outside of the mainstream of Jewish culture of the period. From the little we know about them, they attempted to live disciplined lives of ritual purity. It is probable that Qumran was an Essene community, although there are differences between the descriptions of the Essenes (e.g., by Josephus in his *Antiquities of the Jews*) and what we know of Qumran. There has been some conjecture that John the Baptist was from the Essene community, but no real evidence has been presented to demonstrate that (for example, his public baptizing ministry and proclamation of Jesus as the Messiah strong differentiate him from the Essenes). Likewise, Jesus was obviously not an ascetic, being accused by the Pharisees of being just the opposite.

[33] In Matthew 11:4-6 Jesus sent word back to John the Baptist as an illustration of His claim to fulfill prophecy. Shortly after that, the Pharisees accused Him of using Beelzebul (ruler of the demons) to cast out demons. In Matthew 21:23, the High Priest questioned the authority that Jesus had to do His works. Throughout the Gospels, two points are clear. Even His adversaries recognized His record (including no sin), and yet they denied His authority.

[34] This follows Hoehner's chronology developed in *Chronological Aspects of the Life of Christ*.

[35] The Romans also changed the name of the area from Judea to Palestine after the traditional enemies of the Jews, the Philistines. It retained this name until the modern nation of Israel was founded in 1948.

[36] Kenneth Scott Latourette ("A History of the Expansion of Christianity," Vol. 1: *The First Five Centuries*, pp. 336-38) maintains that the early Christian Jews were considered by the rest of the Jews as just another school of Judaism. The primary intolerance they encountered was against their aggressive proselytism. However, he does note an increasing schism after the revolt of AD 70.

[37] Written over the period of about 200 BC to AD 200, this work provides interesting insights into the discussions going on during this important time in the history of Judaism and early Christianity. It records various opinions of

the leaders, and declares which opinions the majority of the leaders followed, and thus were considered binding.

[38] The format of the Talmud has the Mishnah in the center of the page, with the Gemara as commentary around it. Thus the focus of the discussion is on the Mishnah rather than the Torah on which the Mishnah is based. The Gemara is written in Aramaic The Palestinian Talmud was completed about 395. The Babylonian Talmud was completed by about 500. Although missing some of the Mishnah tractates covered by the Palestinian Talmud, the Babylonian is fuller and larger. It became accepted as the standard for the Jews in the Diaspora, and is still the standard today (cf. Herman Wouk, *This Is My God*, pp. 144-185).

[39] Cabala means "tradition." The Mishnah averred that its oral tradition was handed down by Moses along with the written law. Cabala included esoteric learning which predated Moses, some supposedly going back to Enoch and to Adam.

[40] The edict of March 31, 1492 decreed eviction or conversion. Needless to say, the number of nominal conversions was high. Distrusting the majority of conversions, Ferdinand and Isabella gave the Grand Inquisitor, Tomas de Torquemada, almost unlimited authority to interrogate and torture. The Spanish inquisition persecuted the Jews because of the high position they had enjoyed in the Muslim culture, along with a general repugnance the Europeans countenanced, incited by intolerant Popes. It also squelched incipient protestant movements coming out of the reformation, and harassed Muslims who had accepted baptism.

[41] These movements are loosely organized, and poorly documented. The novels of Chaim Potok illustrate some of these groups in the environs of Brooklyn, New York during the mid-twentieth century.

[42] There had been a few earlier efforts in the right direction. For example, Roger Williams, founder of the colony of Rhode Island, encouraged the settlement of Jews in the colonies.

[43] Zionism dates to the Middle Ages when during the persecutions, a number of would be "messiahs" attempted to lead the Jews back to Palestine. With the Enlightenment and a resulting greater tolerance, Zionism subsided. During the early 1800's, the movement was supported predominantly by Christian millennarians who connected the nation of Israel with the Second Coming of Jesus Christ. Ironically, modern Zionism early on encountered stiff opposition from both Orthodox and Reformed elements. Some Orthodox Jews saw it as an affront to God's sovereignty ('a fly in the face of heaven'). On the whole, most Orthodox Jews supported the concept. The Reformed school saw Zionism as a challenge to their position of cultural assimilation.

[44] Arthur James Balfour was the British Foreign Minister in 1917. His declaration stated that Great Britain acknowledged the historical right of the Jews to *a* national home *in* Palestine. This declaration was endorsed by the

League of Nations in 1922.
[45] A couple of salient points are worth noting. After the break-up of the Ottoman Empire following World War I, Palestine was occupied and administered by the British. This occupation was marked by increased Jewish immigration (buying land through the Jewish National Fund) and Arab unrest and rebellion. Before a solution could be found, World War II intervened. After the war, the situation continued. The Arabs feared being ousted from their homes, and the Jews continued to immigrate (often illegally). In 1946, the United Nations voted to partition the land based on land ownership. This gave the eastern portion of Galilee, a strip along the coast between Haifa and Tel Aviv, and the southeastern portion of the Negev to the Jews and the rest to the Arabs. Jerusalem was to be an international city. The Arabs objected, both on principle, and the fact that even in the Jewish areas there would be a sizable minority of Arabs. The United Nations' resolution was never fully carried out because of the Arab objections. When the British pulled out on May 14, 1948, the nation of Israel was declared with the boundaries of the U.N. partition. The next day Syria, Trans-Jordan, Iraq, and Egypt attacked. The United States gave *de facto* recognition of Israel on the 15th and the Soviet Union gave *de jure* recognition on the 17th. Israel successfully fought against the combined Arab forces. The United Nations forced an armistice the following year. On May 11, 1949, Israel was admitted to the United Nations. Three times since, Israel has fought with its Arab neighbors. In 1956, it joined England and France in a war against Egypt over the Suez Canal. In 1967 Israel conducted a preemptive strike against a coalition of foes poised to attack. In 1973, suffering from the sting of criticism over its 1967 actions, it allowed its opponents to strike first on Yom Kippur, the Jewish holy day. Almost defeated in the initial assault, it finally beat back the combined forces of Egypt and Syria. Defending itself, this little country has almost miraculously defeated much stronger opponents on each occasion and expanded its borders as a result.

Chapter 5

Hope Fulfilled: Christianity

Although Christianity is based on the person of Jesus Christ, His life more properly falls under Judaism. He claimed to be the Messiah[1] the Jewish nation was waiting for. He claimed to fulfill prophecies made by the Jewish prophets for the Jewish nation. He performed a number of super-normal signs to validate His claims. The final sign was the empty tomb.[2]

The Apostolic Church

After Jesus ascended as recorded in Acts 1, His disciples suddenly were transformed by the Holy Spirit from a small group cowering in a locked room to bold proponents powerfully declaring His Messiahship to all who would listen. This small group laid the foundations for the organization called the church. During this period (from the ascension of Jesus to the death of the last Apostle, John, about AD 100) the church declared Jesus as the Christ (or Messiah) and Saviour throughout the known world.[3]

Their first declarations were to the Jewish nation on the day of Pentecost (May 24) in AD 33, led by the Apostle Peter. The first 8000 plus who accepted these declarations were Jews. The early leadership of this movement was a group from the inner-circle of Jesus' followers, the Apostles, normally viewed as the remainder of the 12 disciples (Luke 6:13-16). Paul was included in this group after his conversion.[4] All were Jewish. Even when the disciples began leaving Jerusalem to proclaim the Messiahship of Jesus, their first expansions were to Jewish synagogues in the Diaspora.

In fact, it took a special nudging from God to get Peter to approach the first non-Jews (or Gentiles) in Acts 10. His trip to Cornelius is estimated to have happened about AD 40, although it may well have been sooner.[5] Once the Gospel (or good news) was taken to the

Gentiles, the leaders of this movement (still all Jews) held a special
conference in Jerusalem to discuss the issue (Acts 11). They realized
that it demonstrated that Jesus' mission and ministry were of a much
broader scope than merely to the Jewish nation. However, it was not
until some eight years later that these leaders came to grip with the
implications of this fact.[6]

Still, the fact that the first Gentiles were accepted as Gentiles, and
not as proselytes forced the leaders to realize that some changes were
in store. Even so, the movement was still viewed as a fulfilled
Judaism, not a separate religious movement, and the focus of evangelism remained within Judaism. The changes indicated changing
perceptions, although they were not formalized for several years.

A key event of this era was the conversion of a leading Pharisee,
Saul of Tarsus, who later changed his name to Paul.[7] Several years
after his conversion, Paul was sent out from Antioch with Barnabas to
proclaim the Messiahship of Jesus in the synagogues of Cyprus
(showing that the thinking was still essentially Jewish--Acts 13). After
being rejected by key Jewish leaders, Paul and Barnabas followed
Peter's lead and publicly declared that they would go to the Gentiles.
These were eager to hear what they had to say. Although they
continued to visit the synagogues of the Jewish Diaspora first as they
traveled through Asia minor, the focus of expansion was increasingly
towards the Gentiles.

After the work of Paul and Barnabas, a group from Judea created
dissent by mandating circumcision, an aspect of the Old Testament law,
essentially requiring conversion to Judaism in order to follow the
Messiah. Paul (the former Pharisaical Rabbi and student of Gamaliel),
Barnabas, Peter, and several others refuted this position. Their policy
was validated by the second conference in Jerusalem called the "First
Jerusalem Council" in AD 49. This probably marks the serious distinction of Christianity from Judaism, although the two remained closely
entwined for a number of years.

This council in Jerusalem is probably the most important in the
history of the church, not because of the separation of Judaism and
Christianity, but because of the definition of Christianity which came
forth. The real issue before the council was whether the work of
Christ (i.e., the death, burial and resurrection) was sufficient to save
men--i.e., restore them to God. Remember that the basic problem we
have observed in all religions is that they tend away from the true God.
They find other gods and syncretize false worship. We have already

observed how critical the fall was to the history of man. The question the council faced was whether they could accept Jesus' claims as valid and His work as sufficient, or whether they would add some ritual or work. The Jewish leaders of the Church looked at the claims, and proclaimed that the work of the cross was sufficient to reconcile *any* man (whether Jew or Gentile) to God.[8]

There is no record of how many Jews accepted Jesus as the Messiah during this era. Neither do we know when the balance between converted Jews and converted Gentiles swung towards the Gentile side. After the Council in Jerusalem, however, there was an increasingly Gentile flavor to the leadership and expansion of Christianity.

The Nature of Doctrine

As Christianity expanded among the various peoples in the Roman Empire (and even beyond it, although its main strength would lie in the Mediterranean region for several centuries), new converts brought many pagan backgrounds and concepts with them. For Christianity, much like Judaism in Israel, the next two millennia would be a period of attempting to sort out these alien influences and clarifying what Christianity really was.[9]

This could only be done by measuring the issues against the objective standard of Scripture. Invariably there were those who desired to establish another scripture (or gospel) as a higher standard, or set up a higher authority to give the "right interpretation."

Part of the refining process would be building a clear understanding of Who God was and what He had done. As already observed, the process which led to Jesus began with Abraham more than 2000 years earlier. The data about that process was written in a book collated over a 1000 year period. During the first century AD, new data about Jesus was incorporated, and the entire church throughout the empire acceded to the results.[10]

Another part of the process involved sorting out cultural issues as opposed to syncretistic tendencies.[11] Some of those issues are addressed in the New Testament letters to various churches. Further ramifications are addressed in the later writings of the church fathers. Despite their efforts, a number of syncretisms did accumulate over the centuries for various motives.

When issues arose, church leaders held various Councils to evaluate the evidence for different positions. In this manner, Christian doctrine was developed, which has historically been viewed as a set of limits. There is room for different understandings within those limits, but beyond those limits, a belief or doctrine is no longer considered Christian. The church has always used the Bible to determine those limits.[12]

Christianity and the Roman Empire

During the early years, Christianity was considered by the Romans as a part of Judaism, which enjoyed the status of a recognized and thus legal religion. As the two became distinct, the Roman government took a more jaundiced view towards the movement.[13] There were a number of persecutions. The first persecution was under Nero (54-68) when he attempted to blame the Christians for the burning of Rome. The period after Nero is obscure, although it is probable that the persecuting zeal waxed and waned. It is clear that during the reign of Trajan (98-117), Pliny the Younger supervised a persecution in Bithynia (in Asia Minor). It would appear that his efforts were part of a more or less on-going effort rather than a special agenda dictated by Trajan.[14] It was under Trajan that Rome reached its greatest extent territorially.

For the Christians, this general situation continued down through the third century.[15] Under Marcus Aurelius (161-180), Rome began to experience assaults from the east and north. Naturally, the "new" religion, Christianity received the blame for this turn of events. The turn about occurred in 313 when Constantine issued the Edict of Milan which gave toleration to Christianity.[16] The culmination occurred when Theodosius issued an edict in 380 that made Christianity the official religion of Roman Empire.

During the time of persecution, individuals did not convert to Christianity unless they were absolutely convinced of its validity. As Christianity was first legalized (with the Emperor himself a Christian), and then made official, masses joined the movement for social and political reasons. They brought with them the accouterments of their pagan origins.

Ironically, although the leaders were very careful with basic theological issues, this period saw the initial encroachment of syncretistic ideas in other areas. From shortly after 300 come the first reports of prayers for the dead, the signing of the cross, and the use of wax candles.[17] Veneration of angels and saints was evident by the end of the fourth century. Evidently these ideas accreted on the local level and then percolated up through the developing hierarchy. By the time of the Nicean Council in 787, they were beginning to significantly affect theology.[18]

With a relaxation of persecution, the Church began to examine its doctrine.[19] During this period, a number of doctrinal issues came to a head. From the beginning Christianity had averred the worship of the one true God as passed on by the Jews. However, the church also saw that Christ claimed equality and identity with God. For years, the leaders struggled on how to put these two points together. This issue was termed the Arian controversy after the leader of the viewpoint which was deemed invalid.[20] Several other controversies stemmed from this regarding the nature of Christ.[21]

A key figure of the period was Augustine (354-430). Born in North Africa, he journeyed through Italy as a man of the world. He was converted in Milan at the age of 33. Augustine is noted for two significant points. As an older man, he confronted Pelagius, a British Monk on the issue of nature of man.[22] His arguments carried the day against Pelagianism, and were key influences on the reformers several centuries later.[23]

Augustine also was drawn into the question of the role of Christianity in the fall of Rome. Augustine approached the issue by arguing that there were two cities, the earthly (i.e., the state), and the heavenly (i.e., the church). The earthly city is destined for judgment, while the heavenly is destined for the eternal happiness of the saints. This work was instrumental in establishing the extremely strong position of the church in medieval society.[24]

The Medieval Church

The medieval period was predominantly a period of transformation for Christianity. It transitioned from a movement to an organization. Then, as the Roman Empire dissolved, it had to transcend national politics and become an international organization. Later, as Islam was founded and spread, a large part of its traditional territory came under control of a rival religious organization.

The growing power of the papacy illustrated the transformation of the institutional church to an organization. As early as the second century, Christianity began to emphasize a distinction between clergy and laity. By the third century, bishops were becoming more and more prominent as part of the church organization, although the bishop of Rome was still considered by the others (e.g., Cyprian, Bishop of Carthage, d. 258) as the first among equals.

When Constantine moved the secular capital to Byzantium which became Constantinople, the prestige of the Roman bishop was enhanced as a remnant of the old imperial tradition. Increasingly, however, there was antagonism between the bishops of the old and new capital. Some of the issues were theological, such as whether the churches should use images in its worship. Others issues were much more mundane, such as whether clergy should wear beards.[25] These specifics masked political ambitions of the two leaders who actually desired to have authority over the entire church. They produced an increasing sense of division between the two capitals, which led to a final schism in 1054.

The actual issue of division was over the use of unleavened bread in the mass. The eastern church did not. The western church did. In 1053, the patriarch of Constantinople condemned the western church. Pope Leo IX sent an envoy to Constantinople, but the discussions merely worsened the situation. On July 16, 1054, the Roman delegation excommunicated the patriarch and his followers. The patriarch reciprocated and anathematized the Pope and his followers. Until the 1960's, the two churches have gone their separate ways.[26]

After Islam was founded with Mohammed's flight to Medina in 622, it began to spread throughout the Mediterranean world. The process was most effective--accept Islam or die. Although Mohammed mandated that Jews and Christians be allowed to retain their faith, they were taxed, were not permitted to propagate their faith, and subjected to strong social pressure. The net result was that many who had professed a Christian faith turned to Islam.

Islam's most significant effect on Christianity was philosophical. Philosophers Averroes (Spanish Arab, 1126-1198) and Avicenna (Eastern Muslim, 979-1037) strongly influenced the Scholastic movement.[27] Islam also preserved classical Greek thinking, which later helped produce the Renaissance. Thomas Aquinas was profoundly influenced by the works of Aristotle which reached Paris through the Moorish Empire and occupied Spain.

Islam reached its high point in Western Europe when Charles Martel defeated the Moorish invaders from Spain in the battle of Tours in 732. In Eastern Europe, the Byzantine Empire (the eastern remnant of the Roman Empire) held the Muslims back until after the Crusaders conquered Byzantium in 1203. Even then, the city Constantinople was not taken until 1453 (although most of its territory was gone decades earlier).

Within Christianity, two opposing trends were developing. The main leadership was becoming more secular and corrupt as the power of the church increased.[28] This led to a situation where there were actually rival popes (called the "great schism," 1378-1417).

The opposing trend was one of reform. Many within the church took its claims seriously. When they saw the corruption within the system, they attempted to reform it. Invariably, they were persecuted and often martyred. Two early reforming movements were the Albigenses in southern France about 1170, and the Waldensians in central France about the same time. Both groups were persecuted to virtual extinction.

Start of Reformation

Serious reformation attempts began in the fourteenth century. John Wycliffe (1329-1384) pushed for reformation in England, including separation from Roman Catholic rule. He is most noted for his translation of the Bible into English which he completed in 1384, the year of his death.[29] John Huss (1369-1415) read many of Wycliffe's writings in Prague, Bohemia. He was condemned by the Council of Constance and burned at the stake in 1415. His followers, the Brethren of the Common Life influenced Bohemia for a number of years.[30] Jerome Savanarola (1452-1498), a Dominican monk in Florence pushed strongly for reformation from that significant city. Like Huss, he was martyred (he was hanged and then his body was burned).

Martin Luther then might be said to be the first *successful* reformer, although he was able to achieve this goal only by splitting the Church. Luther was a monk in Wittenberg, Germany. In 1511 he traveled to Rome and saw the situation there firsthand. After his return, he became a professor of Bible at the University at Wittenberg. During his studies, he saw Paul's declaration in Romans 1:17 that only by faith in Christ could man be reconciled to God. As he continued his studies in the Biblical languages, he realized that even the venerable Augustine was untrustworthy and only Scripture was an adequate authority.

As Luther evaluated the excesses of Rome in this light, Tetzel began selling indulgences in a nearby town. Tetzel claimed that by buying an indulgence, the purchaser got complete forgiveness of all sin (including sins yet to be committed). On October 31, 1517, Luther nailed to the door of the cathedral in Wittenberg a list of 95 theses or statements regarding abuses that he felt should be debated.[31] Luther's goal was to reform the system. Rome had no intentions of changing, and Luther was excommunicated. As a citizen of the Holy Roman Empire, Luther was challenged by the Diet of Worms in 1521 to recant. Luther refused unless he could be shown by Scripture where he was wrong.

Since he was unable to reform the Church, Luther was forced to develop an organization and liturgy for those who had followed his lead. This quickly became known as the Lutheran Church. In 1555, the Peace of Augsburg guaranteed that territories in the Holy Roman Empire (essentially Germany) which were Lutheran could remain so. This gave the first legal position to the Lutheran Church.

Swiss Reformation

At the same time, Hulreich Zwingli began attacking the system of indulgences in Zurich Switzerland. Already outspoken, he came under Lutheran influence in 1519. In 1523, he published his *Sixty-Seven Articles* in preparation for a public disputation. After the debate, the town council decided that Zwingli had won, and his version of the reformed faith was given legal status. Other nearby cantons followed suit. In 1531, the Roman Catholic cantons in Switzerland waged war against Zurich and Berne. Zwingli was killed in battle, but the reformation lived on and moved on into Geneva.[32]

John Calvin (1509-1564) was converted at the University of Bourges in Paris about 1534. He moved to Basel in Switzerland. There, he studied issues of theology, corresponded with some of the reformers, and in 1536 (at the age of 26), he published his *Institutes of the Christian Religion*. This book, which was later revised and expanded, became the backbone of Reformed theology.[33] Soon afterward, he moved to Geneva where he joined forces with Guillaume Farel who had recently led the acceptance of reformed doctrines.[34]

From Geneva, pastors were sent into France where they acquired a following who became known as the Huguenots. The period was one of turmoil, with several wars and massacres. Peace seemed to come in 1598, when Henry of Navarre, a leader of the Huguenots became King Henry IV. He issued the Edict of Nantes which granted freedom of religion to the Huguenots. This lasted until revoked in 1685 by Louis XIV. After this, the Huguenots fled all over Europe, South Africa and to America.[35]

The reformation spread from Geneva and Wittenberg throughout Europe. While it is obvious the conditions in the church were ripe for reformation, it is also obvious that it was a time where the political realities strongly supported it. Luther was spared because of a rebellion in Spain. Zwingli found favorable soil in the democratic ideas already rife in Zurich, as did Calvin in Geneva. The reformation was not caused by any one man, but rather by a group of men in different places who arrived at the same conclusions in different manners.[36] While they did communicate with one another, they worked independently, drawing similar conclusions from the same standard of authority, the Bible.[37]

Reformation In England

The reformation arrived in England in a very striking manner. While there were many forces working towards it, it was initiated by Henry VIII (reigned 1509-1547) who wanted a divorce. Henry was married to Catherine of Aragon, aunt of the powerful Spanish ruler, Charles V. Deciding that Catherine could not provide him a son (her only child was Mary), Henry asked the Pope for a divorce, which was refused because Charles controlled the Pope. Henry manipulated the English clergy and parliament to separate the English church politically from Rome and to make the king the head of the church. After his divorce, he married Anne Bolyn, who bore him a daughter, Elizabeth. His third wife bore Edward, the son he hoped for. After Henry died, Edward (reigned 1547-53), then Mary (reigned 1553-58), and then Elizabeth (reigned 1558-1603) took the throne in turn following the death of his or her predecessor.

Mary's harsh reaction to the increasing protestant flavor of the country backfired. As a result of her policies, a number of protestant clergy were burned at the stake. This event strengthened the protestant cause in England. Although Elizabeth was Roman Catholic, she could not return to Catholicism because Henry's divorce had never been approved by the Pope. Under the settlement of 1559, she approved a church that had a theology which pleased the protestants, while still retaining much of the ritual of the Catholic Church (the Via Media).[38]

Philip II of Spain had staked a claim to the throne based on his marriage to Mary. Under the instigation of the Pope, Philip gathered together a large armada to sail against England in 1588. The more maneuverable English fleet defeated the armada, and the remnants of the Spanish fleet were ravaged by storms as they circled Ireland while headed for home. As a result, England became a champion for protestantism in Europe, and the stage was set for the Puritan colonization of New England.[39]

A similar political situation occurred in Scotland, where Mary Stuart, a devout Roman Catholic, ruled an independent, increasingly protestant people. To complicate matters, she married the heir to the French throne (he became King Francis II in 1559). John Knox returned from training and study in Frankfort (where he came under Calvin's teachings) at the same time that a number of Scottish nobles covenanted against the Roman Catholic and French influence in Scotland. Under Knox's leadership, Scotland developed a strong Presbyterian Church, which became the state church of Scotland.

Counter-Reformation

Catholic leadership became increasingly concerned over the increasingly successful reformation which was wresting large portions of Christendom from Roman control. They followed four courses of action which collectively became known as the Counter-Reformation. The first was the institution of the Order of the Jesuits in 1534 by Ignatius Loyola.[40] Second was the Council of Trent instituted by Pope Paul III. This council was actually a series of meetings from 1545-63, which addressed the abuses which caused the Reformation. Third was an energetic missions program, which was largely directed by the Jesuits. Fourth was active persecution of Protestants. A prime example of this was the latter part of the Spanish Inquisition.

Roots of Revival

In the early 1720's, a group of young men began to meet together at Christchurch College in Oxford University to study the Greek New

Testament. Called the Holy Club, this group included John and Charles Wesley and George Whitefield. The members of this club were often referred to as "Methodists" by other students for their methodical Bible study and prayer habits.

John Wesley and George Whitefield began preaching in fields and other open air situations in 1739. John Wesley organized his converts into a Methodist society. During his ministry, he is estimated to have ridden over 250,000 miles on horseback through England, Scotland, and Ireland, and preached 42,000 sermons. His brother Charles wrote over 6000 hymns in support of this work.[41]

George Whitefield was considered by many the greater orator. Even Benjamin Franklin spoke highly of his powerful voice and persuasive power.[42] Whitefield, however, was not the organizer that Wesley was. He also retained stronger Calvinist leanings, and as a result, his followers stayed within the established church.

Both Whitefield and Wesley crossed the Atlantic to preach, and both had a profound influence on the Great Awakening. Wesley organized his followers in the newly formed United States, and by 1784 numbered about 14,000 followers there. More importantly, Wesley organized a program of circuit riders who would ride the American frontier preaching and teaching. These itinerant preachers would have a profound effect as Americans moved west.[43]

Western Expansions

As has been seen, by the seventeenth century, the religious picture in Europe was getting very complex. The opening of the western hemisphere was an ideal opportunity for religious groups which had been facing persecution in Europe. The initial colonies in New England were planted by such groups as the Puritans and the Baptists.

The movement to the new world was complex. Generally, the French and Spanish colonies remained Catholic, and the English colonies followed various types of protestantism. Initially, each colony retained its own established denomination, and tended to be intolerant of others. Rhode Island was the most significant exception.

As the colonies began to move inland, toleration increased as the settlers faced the loneliness and hazards of the frontier. This increased toleration was written into the U. S. Constitution as the First Amendment.[44]

One more significant movement must be noted from this period. In 1792, William Carey, a shoemaker in England who became a Baptist minister in 1789, started the modern missions movement. Carey went to India, where he was not only a successful missionary, but also became one of the leading scholars in Sanskrit. Soon, churches from both the United States and Europe were sending missionaries all over the world. In addition to proclaiming the gospel, they have founded schools, colleges, hospitals, orphanages, and other institutions which demonstrate Christian charity.

The Modern Era

The American frontier was a place of religious fervor. This is evident from the number of revivals which swept across it, as also from the number of new religions which emerged there.[45] Jonathan Edwards (1703-1758) was a Congregational pastor in Northampton, Massachusetts. In 1734, a revival started in his church, which spread throughout the colonies. George Whitefield made 7 visits to the colonies during the next 35 years.

The Baptists grew out of this movement as Congregational churches joined with Baptist groups out of England. With the First Great Awakening, the number of Baptists in the south snowballed. Out of the First Great Awakening, the Baptists retained a zeal for evangelism, which continued the growth. Baptists tended to maintain their local independence, but many congregations adhered to several loosely knit affiliations.[46] Today, the Baptists are the largest segment of Protestant Christianity in the United States.[47] The First Great Awakening was followed by a series of revivals over the past two centuries.[48]

While the U.S. was going through a series of revivals which tended to re-emphasize conservative thinking, the churches in Europe were beginning a trend toward liberal theology. While the roots have been traced to Immanuel Kant and as far back as Thomas Aquinas, the "father" of liberal theology is generally considered to be Frederick Schleiermacher (1768-1834). Schleiermacher was a professor at the University of Berlin and he taught that subjective feelings or emotions were the foundation of religious experience. This removed the objective standard of Scripture which Christianity had historically demanded. When religious experience was moved to an emotional base, there were no longer any limits, and modern liberal theology has long since departed from its Biblical foundation.

There have been a number of efforts to re-emphasis that base. In 1910, several conservative scholars wrote a set of books entitled *The Fundamentals*. While this work merely restates the basics of traditional Christianity (the set of limits already mentioned, see above, p. 74), those who do not subscribe to them have denigrated the standards and through ridicule have made "Fundamentalist" synonymous with "narrow-minded" or "bigoted."

Since the Reformation, Roman Catholicism has continued to undergo changes. Two key changes have been doctrinal. In 1854, Pope Pius IX proclaimed the doctrine of Immaculate Conception. This doctrine teaches that Mary was born sinless and lived a sinless life (it thus has no reference to the virgin birth). This has been followed by a 1950 proclamation by Pope Pius XII that shortly after her death, Mary ascended to heaven where she was enthroned as the "Queen of Heaven." Between these two proclamations was 1870 declaration by the Vatican Council that "in matters of faith and morals" the Pope was infallible.

Today, it might be said that Christianity has spread world-wide. Many who claim the title, do not ascribe to its teachings, which, based on our studies of religion as a whole, is not surprising. Those who do look to its founder, Jesus Christ Who, as He ascended to heaven, promised to return in the same manner.

Notes

[1] The term Messiah comes from the Hebrew term for "anointed one." Properly, every priest and king in Israel was anointed. However, in the Old Testament, the term was usually reserved to refer to the king of the nation, especially in the Psalms. From Jewish tradition, a number of these uses are viewed as referring to the ideal king who would lead the nation to a glorious future. A key reference is Daniel 9:25-26, where Messiah is identified closely with the future rebuilding of Jerusalem, and its subsequent destruction. The Greek translation of the Old Testament uses *Christou* for Messiah. The same term is used in the New Testament, where it is translated into English as Christ.

[2] While super-normal signs (commonly called miracles) are an integral part of the Bible, it has frequently been noted that they cluster during three periods--the period of the Exodus, the time of Elijah/Elisha, and the ministry of Jesus.

of Jesus. The signs of the Exodus clearly demonstrated God's power over the
gods of Egypt, and laid a groundwork for the nation and worship of the true
God. The signs of Elijah/Elisha in the middle of the divided kingdom (and the
relatively isolated other instances in the Old Testament) served to refocus
attention back to the God Who claimed their allegiance at a watershed time in
the history of the nation. The signs of the time of Jesus served to validate His
claims to be the Messiah. John states that Jesus did many "other signs" beyond
what were recorded, but the ones that were recorded were done so in order that
the reader might "believe that Jesus is the Messiah, the Son of God (John
20:30-31)." Paul stated that Jesus was "declared with power to be the Son of
God by the resurrection from the dead (Rom 1:4)." Anyone confronting the
nature of Christianity must necessarily come to grips with those claims.
Historically many who have professed to be Christian, have attempted to blow
off these claims. Unfortunately, as C. S. Lewis pointed out, you are then left
with a highly ethical religion built on the teachings of either a liar or a lunatic.
There are a number of excellent works that clarify the issues for someone
attempting to come to grips with those claims, including: C.S. Lewis, *Mere
Christianity*; Paul E. Little, *Know Why You Believe*; and Josh McDowell,
Evidence That Demands A Verdict.

[3] Jesse Lyman Hurlbut (*The Story of the Christian Church*, p. 35), states that
"at the opening of the second century the church was to be found in every land
and almost every city from the Tiber to the Euphrates, from the Black Sea to
Northern Africa, and some think it extended as far west as Spain and Britain.
Its membership included several millions." He does not include evidence that
would take it as far east as Madras, India and possibly even to China. Kenneth
Scott Latourette (*The First Five Centuries*, p. 66) would date the "conversion"
(meaning "the formal acceptance of a faith") of the Roman Empire to 500.

[4] The word apostle means "one sent out." In the ministry of Jesus, a number
of people fit this criteria, although Luke 6:13-16 lists the 12 of the inner circle
as specifically called Apostles. This included Judas, who betrayed Jesus and
then committed suicide. Matthias was chosen by the remaining eleven to take
his place (Acts 1:15-26). Although not among this 12, Paul was considered to
also have been an Apostle. Likewise, James, the brother of Jesus was
considered an apostle (Gal 1:9) Apparently two of the key credentials for
Apostleship were to have seen the risen Jesus, and to have been personally
chosen by Christ. Paul used this argument when challenged about his use of
the title (Phil 3:12). Paul assumed the title and was recognized by others as
an Apostle, although he did not consider himself worthy of that position
because of his earlier record of persecution of the church.

[5] The dates of events in the early church are very problematic. We can date
with fair accuracy key events at the end of Jesus' life and ministry based on the
lunar calendar (cf. Harold Hoehner, *Chronological Aspects of the Life of
Christ*). We can also begin to pinpoint later events as they cross historical

events documented from other sources. However, even the New Testament accounts do not give a good feel for the amount of time occupied by the first few chapters of Acts. Coming from the two ends does not always produce satisfactory results. F.F. Bruce (*The Book of the Acts*, p. 170) places the event of Stephen's stoning prior to AD 36, when Pilate was recalled to Rome, since Pilate would probably have had a mutual understanding with the high priest, and thus turn a blind eye to the stoning. Likewise, he places the conference in Jerusalem shortly before AD 41. This is based on Acts 11:27-29, which reports that shortly after the Jerusalem council, Agabus prophesied a famine. The time frame is the reign of Claudius, which began in 41.

  [6] The first conference was more of a report. The second, several years later, required a decision. Termed the "first Jerusalem council," this second conference demonstrated the pattern that all future church councils took. Leaders met to discuss the implications of an event or movement. Based on the evidence, they set forth the accepted standards. Up to this point, all believers had been Jews, and thus had historically followed the rite of circumcision. Now, uncircumcised men proclaimed their acceptance of Jesus as the Messiah, and the group had to determine what that meant. It should be noted that this occurred some time before the first reference to the movement as "Christian."

  [7] Paul's conversion took place after Stephen's stoning, and before the first Jerusalem conference in 41. There are indications that it might have occurred as early as 34 or even 33, but more likely in 35. This would place the stoning of Stephen relatively close to Pentecost. After his conversion, Paul went off to Arabia for 3 years.

  [8] Obviously, there are some aspects of life that by definition must change if one accepts Jesus as Messiah, or Saviour. That is because these aspects by definition are mutually exclusive. It is like in mathematics, where you cannot have a given number that is positive and negative at the same time. One cannot worship the true God, and some other god at the same time. Whenever one tries to hold up two or more objects at the same time, one of them must *always* occupy a higher position. That higher item then is the true object of worship. Man's tendency is to opt for the most material and sensual, which is why the council warned against idolatry.

  [9] Louis Berkhof (*The History of Christian Doctrines*, pp. 44-51), lists four different sects that split off during this period. These include the Nazarenes, the Ebionites, the Elkesaites, and the Gnostics. The Nazarenes bound themselves to a strict observance of the law, while at the same time holding to Christian doctrine. The Ebionites tended toward Pharisaicism. They denied the divinity of Christ and were strict legalists. The Elkesaites incorporated a form of mysticism of magic and astrology and viewed Christ as an angel. The Gnostics were also mystics who, like the Elkesaites, viewed Christ as a spiritual being who served as an emissary of the supreme God who was other-

wise unapproachable. Both of these were syncretistic, incorporating Hellenistic philosophy.

[10] Moses wrote about 1400 BC. Malachi, the last prophet, was about 400 BC. The problem of inspiration is still one that is not really understood. God was behind it. Men were the instruments. The result is a work which claims a special position and authority (e.g., 2 Tim. 3:16, 2 Pet. 1:21). The various churches throughout the Christendom received copies of the gospels and the letters and viewed them as inspired and canonical. They also received copies of other material including material written by Apostles such as Paul (1 Cor 5:9) which they did not give equal status. The overall conclusion of the church as a whole was verified in the Council of Carthage in 397.

[11] This is a problem even for missionaries today. We grow comfortable with the way we are used to doing things, including worship. Missionaries then tend to bring cultural forms of worship with them. At the same time, newly converted pagans have similar cultural forms in which they feel comfortable. The natural inclination is to transfer those forms into the new spirit of worship. Unfortunately in the give and take, over the centuries a number of pagan concepts have tended to creep in which *can* detract from the true worship.

[12] Louis Berkhof observes that over the centuries, the church as a whole has hammered out doctrine as issues arose. The first issue was the nature of Christianity, which involved a defense against the slander of its early enemies. The main issues argued have been (in historical order) the nature of God (or the Godhead--i.e., the Trinity), the nature of Christ (the first two overlapped considerably), the nature of sin and grace, the nature of the atonement of Christ and salvation, the nature of the church, and finally, last things. The process has always involved a return to the completed revelation of Scripture, and resulted in a fuller understanding of that revelation. It has not resorted to new "revelation."

[13] A number of factors entered into this change in attitude. While avoiding the revolts that caused Jerusalem to be destroyed, the Christians still earned opprobrium along with the Jews for their in-fighting and rioting. As early as AD 50, Claudius noted the rioting in Rome, and lumped the two groups together. On the other hand, the Christians were viewed as suspect because of they turned from the state religions, especially when Caesar was denoted an object of worship. The Christians argued that they had no problem with the state, just the gods behind the state. Rome maintained that the gods were the state, or at least the foundation on which the state was built. In some ways, this was ironic because the gods of this period were largely imported from the conquered lands, e.g., Isis from Egypt, and Mithras from Persia. The difference was that these various cults were syncī .tistic and willing to share the altar with other cults. Christianity would not.

[14] The evidence is a series of letters between the two which have survived. On one hand, Trajan commends Pliny for his efforts, and declares that there

is no set procedure, which suggests an on-going effort. On the other hand, it is argued that if the trials were that frequent, Pliny should have had a better understanding of the procedures (cf. Kenneth Scott Latourette, *The First Five Centuries*, pp. 141-42).

[15] Marcus Aurelius (161-180), Decius (edict of 250), and Diocletian (edict of 303) expended special effort. In between, there seemed to be a lessening of pressure, where Christianity was begrudgingly tolerated, but never legal nor really welcome.

[16] The events of the time reflect an overall changing attitude. Kenneth Scott Latourette (*The First Five Centuries*, pp. 156-9), points out how the fervor of the leaders for the persecutions was already waning by the time that Diocletian abdicated in 305. In the west, Constantius (father of Constantine) who governed the far western portion of the Roman Empire gave the program minimal effort. The eastern ruler, Galerius, issued an edict of toleration on his deathbed in 311. Likewise, Maximinus, ruler of Egypt, Syria, and Asia Minor, granted toleration shortly before he died in 313. Constantine claimed to have seen a shining cross in the sky bearing the motto, "Hoc Signo Vinces" ("By this sign, you will conquer"). He put this cross on the shields of his army, and went forward to meet his rival Maxentius at the Battle of the Milvian Bridge near Rome. Constantine won the battle and his rival was drowned in the river. As a result, Constantine pledged allegiance to Christ, and later issued his Edict of Milan.

[17] The sign of the cross and the use of wax candles are among what are called "sacramentals"—actions or things that produce spiritual effects, i.e., elevate the mind to the contemplation of divine mysteries. Prayers for the dead correlate with the development of the concept of purgatory (formalized by Augustine). The premise is that the state of the dead is not fixed, and prayers from the living can have an effect on their ultimate state. This concept is found in cults in several regions of the ancient world, notably Persia. It probably entered the Roman world through the worship of Mithra.

[18] The Nicean Council of 787 is the last church council recognized by both the Catholic and Orthodox Churches. It ruled on the issue of icons (declaring that they deserved "reverence," but not adoration). Later this was repudiated by the Council of Frankfort in 794 and the English church. Even some later popes did not recognize the validity of this council, although as a whole both the Roman and Orthodox Churches have used it to validate the use of icons.

[19] It must be recalled that in this instance, as with all other doctrinal issues, the problems revolved around man's understanding of the one true God. Positions (usually all sides) were based on pieces of Biblical evidence. The problem lay in how to put the pieces together. Normally a tension was involved. The temptation was (and is) to chose one side or the other. For example, the New Testament refers to Jesus Christ as God and as man. The temptation is to chose one or the other. The church has historically opted to

retain the tension—and then attempted to understand it.

[20] Arius, a leader of the church in Alexandria, proposed that Christ was really a spiritual being created by the one true God before the rest of creation. Another leader in Alexandria, Athanasius, opposed Arius, by emphasizing that the Father and Son (as well as the Holy Spirit) were of the same divine essence (e.g., uncreated and eternal), but possessed distinct subsistences (hypostases). The Council of Nicea, called in 325 to settle the dispute, went with Athanasius as did the Church.

[21] The Apollinarian controversy came to a head when Apollonarius (about 360), bishop of Laodicea, attempted to explain the dual nature of Christ—his humanity and his deity. He argued that man was body, soul, and spirit. The Logos (or divine nature) simply took the place of the human spirit. The church looked at the issue at Alexandria in 362, several times in Rome, and again at Constantinople in 381. Each time it repudiated Apollonarius' view of replacement. Likewise the Nestorian controversy arose over whether the two natures of Christ blended into one God/man nature or remained as two distinct natures. This was not settled until the Council of Chalcedon in 451 which concluded that Christ had two natures and was perfect God and perfect man. Louis Berkhof (*The History of Christian Doctrines*) gives a good summary of the development of doctrine. Reinhold Seeburg (*The History of Doctrines*), William G. T. Shedd (*A History of Christian Doctrine*), and Justo L. Gonzalez (*A History of Christian Thought*) give more extensive studies.

[22] Pelagius argued that man is born neutral. That is, he did not inherit a sin nature from Adam, but could of his own free will chose to sin, or not to sin. He based this argument on the fact that God commands man to do good. From a careful study of Romans, Augustine observed that man inherited a sin nature from Adam, and as a result was prone to sin, regardless of his will. Man was "totally depraved," i.e., could do no spiritual good. The only solution was Christ.

[23] While the Council in Ephesus in 431 condemned Pelagius, not all of the church leaders agreed with Augustine. Many attempted what they viewed a mediating position (semi-pelagianism) which made divine grace and human will equal forces in the renewal of man and limited predestination to God's fore-knowledge of faith and obedience. In this view, man was not "totally depraved," but only weakened by the fall. This became the official position of the catholic church through the centuries. Many of the reformers (especially John Calvin) returned to Augustine.

[24] In addition, Augustine's work established the allegorical method of hermeneutic which had earlier been viewed with extreme mistrust (cf. Milton S. Terry, *Biblical Hermeneutics*, pp. 629-31), although throughout the subsequent centuries a strong strain of a literal hermeneutic survived (cf. Beryl Smalley, *The Study of the Bible in the Middle Ages*, pp. 358-73). Perhaps more importantly, based on this allegorical principle (especially with regard to

the end times), Augustine firmly established the amillennial method of prophetic interpretation which has dominated Christian theology since (cf. Lewis Sperry Chafer, *Systematic Theology*, vol. 4, pp. 264-77).

[25] There were a number of key theological disagreements. First was the Easter controversy. The eastern church, led by Polycarp of Asia (ca. 70-155), argued that Easter should be celebrated on the 14th of Nisan (the Jewish lunar month) regardless of the day of the week. The western church, led by the Roman bishop Anicetus, argued for the Sunday following the 14th of Nisan. The western view won out, but only after the Council of Nicea in 325. Still, because of the lunar calendar, there was the question of correlating Nisan, since it sometimes fell before the spring equinox. Because of differing methods of calculation, the eastern Easter can occur concurrent with or up to five weeks after the western Easter. The eastern church allowed its clergy to marry, while the west didn't. The eastern church allowed its clergy to wear beards, while the west didn't. In 726 Leo III prohibited bowing before pictures or images in church in the east, a practice which was retained in the west. The issue fluctuated in the east, reached a head under Irene who was thwarted by the Nicean Council in 787. In 843, the Eastern Church returned to the use of icons. The final schism came over the use of unleavened bread during the mass.

[26] Leaders of the two churches lifted their excommunications in 1965. In 1975, Pope Paul VI astounded onviewers when he knelt and kissed the foot of Metropolitan Meliton of Chalcedon (the Greek Orthodox Patriarch). The same date, the two churches set up a joint committee for dialogue.

[27] Scholasticism was a movement which lasted from about 1050 to 1350. Beginning in cathedral and monastic schools, it strongly influenced the early development of the modern universities in the thirteenth century. Its focus was to integrate the newly rediscovered Greek philosophy with Biblical revelation. Anselm (1033-1109), Abelard (1079-1142), William of Occam (ca. 1300-1349), Thomas Aquinas (ca. 1225-1274), Albert Magnus (ca. 1206-1280), and Roger Bacon (1214-1294) were key leaders of the movement.   Earle E. Cairns (*Christianity Through The Centuries*, pp. 251-65) provides an excellent summary of the movement and its influence.

[28] R. W. Southern (*Western Society and the Church in the Middle Ages*, pp. 91-169) discusses how the papacy which started with great ideals degenerated over the years. Part of the problem was the increasing syncretism. Part of the problem was the issue of power itself. Part of the problem was that much of the ecclesiastical leadership derived from secular feudal leaders who placed younger sons in the church so that they would not compete with the oldest for hereditary positions. Educated and trained in the courts of Europe, they tended to rise to the top, regardless of their spiritual status. Interestingly, Southern addresses the papacy of this period as a "business."

[29] Protected by powerful friends, and living in relatively isolated England,

Wycliffe died of a stroke before he could be condemned and excommunicated as a heretic. After the Council of Constance (1415, which also condemned John Huss) condemned his teachings, his body was exhumed and burned.
[30] Huss's followers became known as the Moravian church, which persisted through the Reformation and still exists today in the U.S. (*Handbook of Denominations within the United States*, Sixth edition, p. 199-201.) Kenneth Scott Latourette (*The Thousand Years of Uncertainty*, p. 393) points out that Erasmus, a leading humanist during the Renaissance, was educated by the Brethren.
[31] The invention of the printing press in 1456 proved a two-fold factor in promoting the Reformation. Less than two years prior to Luther's posting of the 95 Theses, Erasmus had published a Greek New Testament. It is not clear that Luther had used Erasmus' text prior to posting of the theses, although apparently he had access to a Greek text of some type. Philip Melanchthon came to Wittenberg the following year to teach Greek and Hebrew. Earle E. Cairns (*Christianity Through The Centuries*, p. 314) grounds Luther's declaration of Scripture as the sole authority on Luther's work in the Greek text, but he does not assign a time to this (cf. Bruce Metzger, *The Text of the New Testament*, p. 100). Access to the Greek text was instrumental in the development of Reformation theology, and its spread throughout Europe. When Luther posted his theses, they were quickly printed and distributed throughout Europe bringing the issue to the forefront (J. H. D'Aubigne, *History of the Reformation of the Sixteenth Century*, pp. 100-101).
[32] Because of different backgrounds, as well as historical differences between the Swiss and the Germans (Cf. Jaques Courvoisier, *Zwingli: A Reformed Theologian*, pp. 17-25), Zwingli never joined forces with Luther. Likewise, he repudiated some of his followers who became known as the Anabaptists (forerunners of the Mennonites) because they were more radical. The key issue of division was their insistence on re-baptizing converts (thus, from the Greek, "ana-baptist"--"again baptized").
[33] Calvin, like most of the reformers, had an extremely high view of the nature of God. From their studies of Scripture they saw God as being absolutely sovereign and man, in his fallen state, as totally depraved, i.e., totally unable to do anything to merit favor with God. There was some disagreement on the issue of predestination and grace, especially in Holland. Jacobus Arminius (1560-1609), a Calvinistic theologian, was recruited to refute Dirjck Coornhert who balked at the idea that man was totally depraved. Arminius rebutted Coornhert, although he adapted several points that Coornhert held. Probably a key issue was a greater focus on God's foreknowledge in the issue of predestination. Several followers of Arminius (after his death) drafted five *Remonstrances*, which basically asked for more toleration than had been shown by some very rigid "Calvinists." At the Synod of Dordt in 1618, the *Counter-Remonstrances* were presented and accepted—which have become

known as the "Five Points of Calvinism." The greater stress on the role of
man in salvation advocated by the remonstrances is still evident in a number
of churches today, notably the Methodists, some Baptist groups (e.g., Free-will
Baptists), some Churches of Christ, the Lutherans, Episcopalians, and most
charismatic groups.
    [34] Geneva did not uniformly follow Calvin and Farel. In fact, they were
banished in 1538, but invited back in 1541. Calvin and Farel attempted to use
the state to enforce religious standards. From today's perspective, the methods
they used would be considered excessively harsh, and unwarranted interference
into private lives. At the time, both Roman Catholic and Reformer governments believed they could interfere in their subjects' beliefs and Calvin was
held in high esteem (cf. Hans J. Hillerbrand, *The World of the Reformation*,
pp. 79-80).
    [35] This has been characterized as one of the greatest political blunders in the
history of France. It is estimated that 400,000 fled, many of who were skilled
artisans and professionals of the middle class. The economic blow is deemed
to have contributed directly to France's loss in the upcoming wars with
England (cf. Cairns, *Christianity Through The Centuries*, p. 343).
    [36] From this group of men have arisen most of the major denominations we
see today. Many denominational differences in the U.S. stem from ethnic
background differences. From Luther, we trace the Lutherans. From Zwingli
we trace the Congregationalist and (albeit indirectly) the Mennonites and
Amish. From Calvin, we find the Presbyterian, Dutch Reformed, Christian
Reformed, Christian, Church of Christ, and Disciples of Christ churches. The
Baptists (which are a spectrum of denominations) are from a mixed heritage
derived from Anabaptist, Church of England, Congregational, and Calvinist
strains (cf. Robert G. Torbet *A History of the Baptists*).
    [37] As men turned to Scripture for their standard, the next issue was how to
put the two major sections of the book (the Old and New Testaments) together.
The church had basically followed Augustinian hermeneutics since he had tried
to reconcile the fall of Rome. During the seventeenth century, two distinct
schools of protestant hermeneutics arose. The first was founded in the writings
of Johannes Cocceius (1603-1669) and Hermann Witsius (1636-1708),
following the same principles of Augustine, except it rejected the authority of
the Catholic church. It argued that God had ruled man through two cove-
nants--a covenant of works with Adam; and a covenant of Grace with elect
fallen men in Christ. This covenant of Grace supposedly covers all time from
Adam to the end of the world blurring the distinction between the Old and New
Testaments. The second school was founded in the writings of William Cave
(1637-1713) and Pierre Poiret (1646-1719). It argued that God ruled man
through a series of stewardships (or dispensations)--i.e., the periods before the
Law was given, such as Adam in the Garden, or Noah prior to the flood, were
guided by different standards of faithfulness (hence it is called "Dispen-

sationalism"). The key issue which has separated the two is the relationship
of the nation of Israel and the Church. The Covenant school argues that the
Church has replaced Israel as the focus of the covenant of Grace, therefore
every promise given to Israel applies to the Church (at least in a spiritual or
allegorical sense). The Dispensational school argues that the two entities are
distinct, although both focus on the Messiah (Jesus Christ) and the issue of
promises is not so clear-cut.

[38] After the settlement of 1559, the Puritans gradually achieved a dominance
of the English religious scene which they retained until 1660 and Charles II.
During this period, several key documents were crafted, which have strongly
influenced all subsequent English-speaking Christendom. Under James I (1603-
1625), who succeeded Elizabeth, an authorized English translation of the Bible
was made (the King James or "Authorized" Version). During the reign of
Charles I (1625-1649), the Westminster Assembly drafted the Westminster
Confession of Faith, and the Longer and Shorter Catechisms.

[39] Although the Via Media adopted a Protestant theology, many Protestants
were still not satisfied with the episcopal state church (governed by bishops
with a hierarchy of bishops, priests, and deacons). Some desired a presbyterian (government by a board of presbyters or elders) structure, while others
desired a congregational (government by the congregation) structure (cf.
Cairns, pp. 354-373).

[40] Actually, the Order of the Jesuits was just one of several new orders from
this period, including the Oratory of Divine Love (which produced several
popes called the reforming popes), the Capuchins, the Ursilines, and the
Jesuits. Under an oath of special allegiance to the Pope, purity and chastity,
the Jesuits emphasized education, fighting heresy, and foreign missions. An
early exemplar of the movement was Francis Xavier (1506-1552) who preached
in India, the East Indies, and Japan under Portuguese auspices.

[41] Cairns (pp. 417-18) stresses how Wesley formed his group into a number
of societies within the Episcopal (Anglican) Church. The societies were
subdivided into bands which were subdivided further into classes of 12 under
a lay leader. The Methodists did not separate from the Anglican Church until
after Wesley's death. Wesley broke with Whitefield and other reformers over
the issue of predestination. Wesley stressed man's free will, with salvation
coming through an experience of conversion. He also argued that the Gospel
should have an effect on society. Many sociologists maintain that without the
Whitefield-Wesley revivals, England would have gone through a revolution
similar to that which occurred in France.

[42] Arnold Dallimore (*George Whitefield*, Vol 1, p. 482) quotes Franklin's
Autobiography where he relates how he emptied his pockets into the offering
after he listened to Whitefield's sermon. Franklin never seemed to be as
moved regarding his spiritual state, however.

[43] Clifton E. Olmstead (*History of Religion in the United States*, pp. 252-55),

reports how the circuit system "proved to be an ideal solution to the problem of maintaining a reasonably adequate frontier ministry." In fact, other denominations followed this pattern because of its effectiveness.

[44] It is clear that the founding fathers intended this "separation" clause to refer to the situation out of which the settlers had come, i.e., that one denomination would not be officially sanctioned and supported by the state to the detriment of others (cf. Gregg Singer, *A Theological Interpretation of American History*, pp. 7-50).

[45] Three movements which would fall within the confines of traditional denominations (specifically the Reformed tradition) trace their origins there. All pride themselves on their congregational independence: the Baptist movement (while they trace their roots to Europe, the Baptists are essentially an American phenomenon), the Christian Church/Church of Christ (a unifying movement founded by Alexander Campbell in the early 1800's), and the Bible Church movement (ultimately from both Brethren and Congregational backgrounds—started after World War II by Lewis Sperry Chafer). The Charismatic movement historically has been on the edge of traditional denominations. Theologically it has followed conservative patterns (more Arminian than Calvinistic), but has focused on a spiritual experience. In the past two decades, the Charismatic movement has swept through virtually all denominations, including Roman Catholicism. There have also been a number of movements which have fallen outside the traditional criteria which define Christianity. Most notably they have a revelation which is placed along side the Bible as authority, and they have a different method of salvation. The four most significant are Mormonism (1830), Seventh Day Adventism (1843), Christian Science (1866), and Jehovah's Witnesses (1884).

[46] Robert G. Torbet (*A History of the Baptists*, pp. 512-15) lists 44 Baptist organizations in the United States in 1960. The earliest of today's major Baptist denominations in the U.S. was the Southern Baptist Convention founded in 1845 (barring the National Association of Freewill Baptists, an Arminian group founded in 1727). There are a number of older, but extremely small groups (e.g., the General Six-Principle Baptists which had a total membership of 58 in 2 churches in 1960, but which was founded in 1653).

[47] According to the 1985 *Yearbook of American and Canadian Churches*, 11 of the 50 largest denominations in the U.S. are Baptist, with a total member-ship of almost 26 million. These include 3 of the top 10, and 2 of the 3 largest Protestant denominations. Only Roman Catholicism (with 52 million) claims more members than the Southern Baptist Convention (with 14 million), and only the United Methodist Church and Judaism (as a whole) sit between it and the National Baptist Convention, USA in size.

[48] These revivals might be labeled as follows: The Second Great Awakening (1800-1820), Finney's Revival (1824-1837), the Layman's Prayer Revival (1856-58), the period of the "Great Evangelists" (1880-1935), and some would

add the era of Billy Graham (1950 and following).

PART III

THAT TRAGIC CENTURY

As we study history, we find certain brief periods that are profound in their significance. The sixth century BC was just such a period with respect to history of religion. During the time that the Jewish nation was in exile, the foundation of all of the major religions of the world today (excepting, of course, Judeo-Christianity, already a thousand years old, and Islam which came out of that stream) were laid.

Chapter 6

Avoiding Death By Dying: Hinduism

At about the same time that God moved Abraham west out of Sumer, other forces were moving east, initially through Elam, then on to the plateau that is now Iran.[1] Elam, located on the northeast side of the Tigris-Euphrates valley, served as a natural pathway into the Iranian plateau. Whereas the movement of Abraham was the physical movement of one family, the eastward movement was most likely a migration of ideas, although the Aryan invasion of India was a key factor.

From an early time Elam had shared cultural concepts with the Mesopotamian society.[2] These included mythologies and religious ideas. Elam, on the slopes of the Zagros mountains which divide the Mesopotamian valley from the Iranian plateau, also traded with early tribes on the plateau.[3] This is probably the conduit through which correspondences between Sumerian/Babylonian and Iranian hierarchies of gods can be traced, although current data shows only minimal remnants of the process.[4]

The foundations of Hinduism were laid when the Aryan invaders out of the Iranian plateau moved into the Indus valley. While the Aryans had developed their own religious concepts after the dispersion of Babel, they assimilated aspects of the Mesopotamian culture before they first conquered, then assimilated the Dravidian culture they found in the India. The earliest writings of Hinduism indicate that process. Later writings were layered on that foundation, making Hinduism a good example of a religion that evolved.

The Aryan Foundation of Hinduism

The beginnings of the Aryan strain are lost in the pre-history of Iran. However, there are indications that at one time in that pre-history, the Aryans (or Indo-Iranians) worshipped a single deity, called Varuna.[5] Vedic references to Varuna show him to be a universal monarch who is the guardian of the cosmic law. He is also pictured as creating the universe, and specifically portrayed as forming three worlds: the heavens, the earth, and the air in between (the three realms ruled by the early historical Sumerian triad of gods).

By the Vedic period, Varuna had not only lost prestige, but had been merged or confused with Mithra as part of a triad of gods (Varuna, Mithra, and Aryaman).[6] As later waves of Aryans moved into India, his position was further degraded as this triad was replaced by a second one (Indra [or Vayu, wind], Agni [fire], and Surya [sun]).[7] In the Vedic writings, all that is left are a number of early hymns hinting at Varuna's former status.

The Aryans swept down out of Iran into the Indus valley approximately 1750 BC (within a century or so of when Jacob and his family moved to Egypt).[8] This invasion is described in the Vedic literature giving us a picture of a nomadic, equestrian, light-skinned race conquering large walled cities occupied by dark-skinned city-dwellers. The victory was ascribed to Indra, who was exalted as "the destroyer of cities."

The Aryans did not commit their hymns to written form until long after their amalgamation. By then they had already had a well developed spiritual hierarchy similar to that which we have seen elsewhere. As in other cases, the gods who were exalted exhibited characteristics prized by the people who chose to worship them. This assists in our efforts to distinguish the sources.

The Dravidic Foundation of Hinduism

The most ancient civilization known to have existed in India was located in the Indus valley. From approximately 2500 to 1750 BC, a highly advanced civilization flourished throughout the lower portion of the Indus river and its tributaries.[9] The first excavations of these cities began in the 1930's at Harappa and Mohenjo-daro, but work has been hampered by the high water table in the area, thus little is known about the culture.[10] Most likely, the people who inhabited the valley at that time were the ancestors of the Dravidians, who have subsequently been pushed to the southern part of the Indian sub-continent. Among the most intriguing archaeological finds have been a number of seals which include still undeciphered inscriptions.[11]

In addition to the inscriptions the seals contain images of various animals and apparent deities. One key figure is a being sitting in a Yoga type lotus position with apparent horns and possible attempts at second and third faces protruding from his head. This "horned god" has been linked with the later Indian god Shiva.[12]

Beyond the seals, a number of female figurines have been discovered, providing a link to the worship to a wide-spread "mother goddess" type of cult.[13] Archaeological evidence suggests the worship of the mother-goddess carried over after the Aryan invasion, although it generally died out later.

The seals show a number of animal figures, both mythological and real, many in situations suggesting worship. A large number of figurines of a serpent goddess have been discovered. It has been conjectured that this veneration of animals is a source of the later brahminic concept of re-incarnation which was incorporated during the time of the *Upanishads*.[14]

The Harappan culture came to an end suddenly in the mid-second millennium BC. The prevalent opinion is that the destruction was caused by the Aryan invasion of India. This invasion is mentioned in a series of 1028 hymns or poems called the *Rig Veda* supposedly composed during the period 1500-1000 BC, but which were orally transmitted until about AD 1400.[15] These hymns provided much of the proto-hinduic ritual.

Vedism/Brahmanism

Vedism developed three bodies of literature: the *Vedas*, the *Brahmanas*, and the *Upanishads*. The completion of the *Upanishads* completed the transition from Vedism or Brahmanism to classic Hinduism.

The key body of literature handed down through this period is called the *Vedas*. The total body consists of four sections: The *Rig Veda*, the *Sama Veda*, the *Yajur Veda*, and the *Atharva Veda*.

The oldest section is the *Rig Veda* which consists of 1028 poems. They are hymns addressed to the principal gods of the pantheon.[16] The *Sama Veda* is a selection of excerpts from the *Rig Veda*, apparently designed to assist in the performance of sacrificial rituals. The *Yajur Veda* contains the sacrificial rituals or formulas. This *Veda* lacks the rhythmic nature of the first two *Vedas*. About half of the material is taken from the *Rig Veda*. The *Atharva Veda* is a collection of poetry from the priestly class. It consists of prayers or hymns, some of which have a magical character.

These four *Vedas* became the foundation of religious life in Northern India as the Aryan and Dravidian cultures merged. In some respects, the two cultures never completely merged, for incorporated within these religious concepts came the caste system. Initially, it was built on the basis of occupation and race.

The Aryan invaders had three social classes: the priestly class (the *brahmins*), the ruling or warrior class (the *kshatriyas* or *rajanyas*), and the common people (the *vis* or *vaisya*). At this time, social structure was flexible. The groupings did not becoming rigid castes until after the Vedic literature was completed.

After the Aryans either through brute force or greater numbers overwhelmed the much more advanced civilization, they added a fourth class, the *sudras*.[17]   Initially, it was predominantly Dravidian. According to the "Laws of Manu" (200 BC to AD 200) the *sudras* performed differing forms of manual labor in a sub-hierarchy. The higher levels of this group included handicrafts and artisans, groups we might today call skilled labor.

While there was a large gulf between the *sudras* and the *vaisya*, an even larger gap developed between the *sudras* and an even lower group which was outside of the caste system. This group called the *dasyus* (aliens) is termed today the untouchables. Members of it performed many social tasks which were necessary, but extremely undesirable, most of which involved handling dead animals, e.g., hunters, fishermen, leather-workers, and undertakers.

While the *Vedas* provided the foundations for worship, the Brahmanas explained the process of worship.[18] A collection of writings from the priestly class (*brahmins*) which delineated the Vedic ritual, especially the sacrifices, they are both part of the four *Vedas*, and a supplement to them.[19] In the process, the value ascribed to the ritual changed.   Prior to this time, the ritual was seen as a means of expressing a request to a god which may or may not be honored. Afterwards, the efficacy of the ritual was deemed as dependent upon the skill of the priest in performing it. The knowledge of the ritual became a source of power.[20]

The final segments of the *Brahmanas*, called the *Aranyaka* (the forest books), give meditation guidelines. The *Aranyaka* prescribes meditations which can be used as substitutes for actual sacrifice. They were written as guidelines for those who had reached the ascetic stage of life (see below).[21]

The *Upanishads* (meaning secret teachings) are the final portion in this triad of literature. They explain the *Vedas* and delineate the teachings which became classical Hinduism. Composition probably began about 600 BC, which is the date commonly used to refer to the formation of Hinduism. The number written is unknown. Currently, 108 survive, of which 13 are accepted by all Hindus as revealed writings. The *Upanishads* were completed by 200 BC.

Classical Hinduism

It was during the Vedic period (probably about the time of the composition of the *Upanishads*) that Hinduism developed several patterns which have survived to modern times. The first pattern was based on a concept of four stages of life. Somewhere between 8 and 12, a boy was expected to apply to a teacher and begin the first stage, that of a student. At the conclusion of his studies, (normally after about 12 years) the young man was expected to marry. As a householder, he was to manage the home, have and raise children, and perform the family ritual.[22] He was to earn a living appropriate to his caste, and provide alms for those who had already progressed to the last two stages. At the point where he saw his skin wrinkled and his hair white the man (and maybe his wife with him) began preparing for the withdrawal or hermit stage. In this stage, he at least partially dissociated himself from society and spent more time in the study of the sacred writings, usually in a forest.[23] The final stage was that of an ascetic, where the man devoted himself to meditation hoping to find total detachment from the material world and thus unity with the eternal Brahman (salvation in the Hindu sense).

This period of the *Upanishads* saw the origin of the concept of *karma* and reincarnation. According to this concept (which developed in parallel with the caste system), human beings are born over and over. The status of the new life is dependent upon the accumulated moral quality of the previous lives (*karma*).[24]

Tied in reincarnation was the concept of Brahman and Atman. These concepts attempt to answer the questions, "What is the nature of the universe?" and "Who am I?" Behind the questions was the proliferating hierarchy of gods. It is evident that the Hindu pantheon was in a state of extreme flux and growth.[25]

The philosophers concluded that Brahman was at once the one universal world soul and the creator of the universe.[26] It followed that the entire group of vedic gods were not only subordinate to Brahman, but received whatever power they had from him.[27] If Brahman was the ultimate reality, then what was the self? The *Upanishads* concluded that self was also a mere manifestation of Brahman. Since the physical body dies, the self must then be the non-physical which lies within.[28] This non-physical self (Atman) then is projected to return the Brahman. However, Atman returns to Brahman upon death only if the life was of sufficient merit. Normally, it reappears in another manifestation. The quality of that reappearance is based upon the law of *karma* (i.e., the moral quality of deeds) providing a motivation for moral living in the current life.[29]

The Sutras

Along with the *Upanishads*, the *Sutras* (meaning "threads") were written during this period. The *Sutras* were extensive discussions over a given topic designed to be memorized by brahmin students. While the brahmins memorized the *Sutras* along with the other writings, they never held them in the same regard.[30]

Three key *Sutras* of this period guided both ritual and community living. The *Shrauta Sutras* gave explicit directions for the performing of the vedic rites (or *shrauta*). The *Grihya Sutras* gave explicit directions on the performing of the domestic rites (or *grihya* for the man in the householder stage). The *Dharma Sutras* covered what has been termed "right living." It was the first attempt to delineate a moral code. The *Dharma Sutras* delineated and stressed the importance of ethical behavior.[31]

The development of the concept of Brahman and Atman laid the foundation for Hinduism's noted propensity for absorbing other religious forms. If Brahman was the universal spirit, then it could be argued that all religious forms were merely manifestations of that spirit. This point became the focus of later Hindu philosophy and history.

The Epics

Three other later works strongly marked *popular* Hinduism as the religion evolved. All three are poems incorporating Hindu teaching. While not considered inspired writings in the same sense as the *Vedas*, they are highly esteemed by the Hindu people. Some have said that the common people have a greater affection for these three works than for the *Vedas*. Many later religious developments are traced to these works.

The first is the *Ramayana*. It is an epic poem which tells the story of the exile of Prince Rama and his subsequent search for Sita, his wife. Rama is viewed as one of the incarnations of the god Vishnu. In its present form, it dates from the first century AD.[32]

The second is the *Mahabharata*. This epic contains about one hundred thousand couplets, making it the longest poem in world literature. The story line tells of a war between the descendants of Bharata, an early Aryan king. The descendants are aligned between the hundred Kauravas and the five Pandavas. These two groups of cousins represent the forces of evil and good respectively. Intermixed with the narrative are episodes or asides which incorporate Hindu philosophy, especially the *dharma* of the warrior *(kshatriya)* caste. The *Mahabharata* was probably composed in its present form in the first century AD.[33]

Derived from the *Mahabharata* is the *Bhagavad-gita*, which was probably written about AD 200. The *Bhagavad-gita* tells of Arjuna, one of the Pandava brothers. Arjuna decides not to fight, but is challenged by Krishna. Krishna explains to Arjuna the need to carry out his responsibilities in a noble manner.[34] In the end, Arjuna admits that he had been deluded before and declares his intention to do whatever the god desires and carry out his duties as part of his caste.

These epic poems popularized the teachings of the *Upanishads*, but also modified them. The *Upanishads* were predominantly metaphysical, with a focus on Brahman/Atman. The popular elements which resulted are termed theistic.[35]

Bhakti Traditions

Hindu practice has provided three roads *(marga)* that its adherents could follow. Early Hinduism (out of Brahmanism) focused on either the use of ritual words *(karma marga)* or the learning of mystical knowledge *(jñana marga)*. After the beginning of the Christian era (and apparently after Christianity had been first introduced into India

It included two major movements which exemplified the theistic strains which arose out of the *Upanishads* and Epic periods. The two focus around devotion either to Shiva or to Vishnu.

Shivaism or Shaivism worships the god Shiva. Shiva took the place of Rudra in the Vedic religion, a storm god, who had characteristics of the even earlier Agni. Shiva has several monikers, including "the benign," "the lord of the cattle," "the great god," and "the destroyer." In Hindu thought, however, the destruction of the world precedes its re-creation, therefore is considered beneficial.

By AD 400 a number of groups worshipped Shiva as the supreme god. A strong cult developed in Kashmir between AD 800-1200, but since then it has decreased in strength. Since the seventh century AD, there has been a strong following in the Tamil region of south India.

Shiva has a number of distinct characteristics including four arms. He is often portrayed dancing with his four hands holding a trident, a sword, a bow, and a club. He also normally has three serpents twined around. As "Lord of the Dance," Shiva is portrayed dancing over the spirit of evil, representing the cycle of creation, destruction, and rebirth.

One aspect of Shiva which has attracted followers is his dual nature. He is considered the reconciliation of all opposites, e.g., good and evil, and creation and destruction.

As Shiva became a universal god, new myths incorporated constructive aspects into a dual nature having both masculine and feminine characteristics. As a result, he is often portrayed as Ardhanarisvara, "the Half-Woman Lord." This feminine, world-creating and world controlling aspect is the *shakti*.

Shaktism worships this feminine aspect. It arose from the rural communities in the first or second century AD, where it seems to have derived from the earlier mother-goddess cult. Shakti is normally worshipped under her primary name of Durga.[36]

The second strain is called the Vaisnava tradition. It arose after the fourth century AD along with Shaivism. It expressed devotion to the god Vishnu. Vishnu is one of the earlier Vedic gods. Originally, Vishnu was associated with the sun. Like many of the Hindu gods, Vishnu did not originally hold a high position in the pantheon. However, he appealed to the populace because of his boons to mankind. In later stories he acquired a much higher place, and became part of the chief triad.

became part of the chief triad.

Vishnu is portrayed as the preserver, who embodies mercy and goodness. As the preserver, he has been incarnated ten times. The eighth incarnation was supposed to be in the body of Krishna. As Krishna, Vishnu announced that release from the incarnation cycle could come by devotion to a particular god.

The three gods, Brahma, Vishnu, and Shiva form a triad of three roles of the supreme being: creator, preserver, and destroyer. The development of this concept saw the increase in temple worship, and closely associated with that, image worship.

The Vedantas

Even by the end of the Vedic period, several strains of Hindu philosophy were becoming evident as the leaders sought to understand Brahman and Atman. Hindu tradition lists six schools which were considered orthodox.[37] The largest and most recent school is that of the Vedantas, which essentially has absorbed the others except for the Yoga strain, which has maintained a small but significant following in several forms.[38]

The Vedanta school developed over the last two millennia, but is based on the Vedanta Sutra, which was written early in the Christian era.[39] This obscure document has been the subject of much debate over the centuries.

The oldest discussion available, and perhaps the key commentary was written by Sunkara (788-820) took a monistic view, identifying Atman with Brahman totally. Ramanuja (traditional dates 1017-1137) reacted against this view, and argued that Atman and the world are distinct from Brahman, but not separate. This has come to be considered the mainstream Vaisnava view.

The Puranas

The Puranas were myths, legends, and stories (written predominantly between 300 and 1200) which continued to popularize Hinduism. Buddhism had swept the sub-continent in the third century BC under Ashoka Maurya. Under the influence of the Puranas, Hinduism regained its position of prominence.

This period saw the origin of many of the stories and legends about the various Hindu gods. Since they arose in different areas, the stories are often confusing regarding the details of the pantheon, even though the Veda is the foundation that all supposedly build on.[40]

Muslim Influence

The Muslims began to move into the Indus Valley region in the 8th century, but did not expand further until the 12th century. In 1192, with the Battle of Taraori, the Muslims controlled Northern India as far as Delhi. Over the next twenty years, they completed the conquest.

The Muslims never had firm control, especially with the communication problem of the large sub-continent area. Their domination varied between a few periods of area wide dominion and more frequent periods of widely divided Muslim states.

The Muslim rulers did not have much success in converting the masses, except in the northwest and northeast corners (Sind and Bengal).[41] But likewise, the Hindu masses did not assimilate the new religion. Those who did convert to Islam strongly supported the Sufite (mystic) tradition which has been strongly influenced by eastern mysticism (see chapter 9).

The Sikhs

The Sikhs (meaning "disciples") came out of this period. The founder, Guru (Baba) Nanak (1469-1539) was from one of the strains of the Vaisnava school of Hinduism called Sant[42] in the area called Punjab (northwest India/Pakistan). At this time, there was a great tolerance between Hindu and Islam in this area. Although he was raised a Hindu, Nanak was very familiar with Islam through friends and occupation (working for Muslims).

At the age of 30, Nanak had a mystical experience, after which he decided to follow a new religious path.[43] The foundation of his religion was a rapprochement of Hindu and Muslim teaching. He accepted the Muslim idea of one god, and reinterpreted his Sant background based on Sufite Muslim thinking.

Guru Nanak was followed by nine other Gurus who molded the movement's thinking. Initially, the movement focused on god's love, but after considerable persecution began to focus on the power of its god and became militaristic.

Over the centuries, the Sikhs fought against the Mogul Empire. Finally they achieved an independent state in 1780 in the Punjab region. The main temple (the Golden Temple) is at Amristar. The Punjab was annexed by the British in 1849, after fierce fighting. Through fair administration, the British won the loyalty of the Sikhs, who were disappointed when the Punjab was divided between Pakistan and India in 1947. They are still looking for a separate state.

Modern Hinduism

The collapse of the Mogul Empire in the eighteenth century opened the door to British colonialism. By 1819 (upon completion of the final Maratha war), Great Britain was firmly entrenched in control of the bulk of the sub-continent (lacking Sind and Punjab from the later crown colony). India had already become an objective of the modern Christian missionary movement under the impetus of William Carey in 1792.

The resulting school systems, a developing industrial revolution, and a large urban migration in support of burgeoning trade, had a profound influence on Hinduism. Social changes were profound. A number of new movements appeared within Hinduism, of which only a couple can be covered here as examples.

The Society of Believers in Brahman was founded in 1828 by Ram Mohun Roy. He had studied the Bible under Christian missionaries, but rejected the claims of Jesus Christ's Messiahship. Still, he liked the moral teachings. Remaining a Hindu, he founded a new monotheistic movement which he claimed to derive from the *Upanishads*. His movement had a profound effect in ridding the social structure of India of some of its greater abuses such as widow burning and the great inequities of the caste system.

Helen Petrovna Blavatsky, originally Russian, was strongly influenced by Hindu mysticism. In 1873, she moved to New York, where she founded the Theosophical Society. In 1879, she moved her headquarters to India, where it is considered a reformed sect of Hinduism. Never a significant movement of itself, the Theosophical Society has had a significant role in the New Age Movement (see chapter 10).

Several individual Hindu mystics have had significant influence individually during the past several decades. Perhaps the most mystic of the Vedanta tradition who followed the monistic view (identification of Brahman and Atman) and formed the Students' International Meditation Society (better known as Transcendental Meditation).[44] A second significant figure of the 1960's was Bhaktivedanta Swami Prabhupada, who founded the International Society for Krishna Consciousness in New York City in 1965, better known as the Hare Krishnas.[45] The Hare Krishnas are adherents to the worship of Vishnu as presented in the *Bhagavad-gita* and later commentaries.

Summary

Historically, Hinduism has been limited essentially to the sub-continent of India. In 1947, when Great Britain gave the crown colony its independence, the colony was split along religious lines: Pakistan (former Sind and Bengal regions) was predominantly Muslim, and India was predominantly Hindu. While Hinduism has begun to spread to other areas, its growth has been slow.

At one time in the long distant past was the worship of one creator god. By the time of the earliest Vedic material, the worship of this single god had been transposed into the worship of a triad of gods, with the creator god being pushed to background and in time, the original single god was completely overshadowed. Over the centuries, even this worship was further debased with syncretistic additions and polytheistic developments to the point that estimates of the numbers of Hindu gods range from tens of thousands to hundreds of millions. Still, classical Hinduism is a relatively late religion. Even in its early Vedic forms it appeared about a thousand years after Judaism was founded at Sinai. As later layers were added (the evolution of the religion) the situation became more and more complex and increasingly polytheistic. It is likely that the roots of its pantheistic world view might be found in the extreme polytheism that developed.

Today, Hinduism is a diverse, hard to define religion. Some Hindus are actually atheists (seeing the spiritual aspect of the universe in an impersonal sense), some argue for one god (although they mean a variety of things when they use the term), some argue for many. But many can find a home under the amorphous umbrella called Hinduism.

Notes

[1] A number of scholars have noted Assyrian-Babylonian correspondences in the earliest Hindu writings, especially the *Rig Veda*. These influences are dated long prior to writing down of the Vedic literature between the sixth and fourth centuries BC and thus are part of the earliest Proto-Hindu thought. The language of the *Rig Veda* is "very archaic Sanskrit." On this basis scholars date the initial composition of the work from between 1500-1200 BC (Louis Renou, *Hinduism*, p. 61), to 1000 BC (K.C. Jain, *The Prehistory and Protohistory of India*, p. 204). Jain notes that the names of four of the gods cited in this work are also found in inscriptions dating from at least 1400 BC from central Asia Minor (modern day Turkey, [p. 203]). Unfortunately, data from the second millennium BC is extremely sparse from the Iranian plateau. Still, Albert J. Carnoy, (*Iranian Mythology*, Vol. VI of "The Mythology of All Races," p. 254) sees a strong Sumerian influence in the *Vedas* which he traces through the Iranian period, i.e., prior to the Aryan invasion of India, which took place approximately 1800-1700 BC. The Gutian conquest of both Ur and Elam (about 2240-2115), as well as the subsequent domination of Ur over Elam (during the Ur III period--about 2115-2000) point to a likely period for such influence. As already noted, this was the period that Abraham left Ur for Canaan. From a spiritual warfare perspective, this eastern move seems to be a "mirror-imaging" ploy. As God moved His man west, Satan countered with a move east. But where God tends to work with individuals, Satan works with groups.

[2] *The Cambridge Ancient History (CAH)* (Vol. II, Part 1, p. 256) reflects that the only records we have of Persia during this period come from Elam, especially Susa, the Elamite capital which later served as a capital for the Persian Empire. Further, (p. 271 ff) it notes that the Elamites used Akkadian for our earliest deciphered records, many of which record Akkadian ideas. I.J. Gelb (*A Study of Writing*, p. 213 ff) observes that the Elamites had an indigenous form of writing, Proto-Elamite, which is dated about 500 years *after* the earliest Sumerian, but which is yet undeciphered. A close relationship has been posited between Proto-Elamite and the Indus Valley script dated 300-500 years later, but it too is still undeciphered.

[3] This trade is evident from the use of lapis lazuli in the Ur III culture. The key deposits for this prized mineral (and the closest to Mesopotamia) are found in Afghanistan, directly across present day Iran from the Sumerian-Elam area. Leonard Woolley's account of the excavation of Ur (*Ur 'of the Chaldees'*, pp. 66, 99 and 173) contains several excellent color plates showing the use of lapis in Ur artifacts. While historically gold and silver trade covered similar routes (with significant mining in what is now Turkistan [present day Turkmenskaja and Uzbekskaja former Soviet Republics, and northeastern Iran] and Afghanistan), the source of gold and silver is much more difficult to pin down than

lapis, especially from periods with very limited historical records.

⁴ Albert J. Carnoy, (*Iranian Mythology*, Vol. VI of "The Mythology of All Races," p. 256 and p. 264) places the Iranian cult in an intermediary role between the Babylonian cult and the Proto-Hindu cult. He sees a direct influence on the Iranian cult from Babylonian mythology. As an example, he notes correlations between the Iranian (later Hindu) Indra and the Babylonian-Sumerian Enlil. There also is a correlation between the Elamite goddess Narundi and the Babylonian Ishtar (cf. *CAH*, Vol. II, Part 1, p. 277) who may be reflected in the later Hindu goddess Ushas.

⁵ Gaurinath Sastri (*A History of Vedic Literature*, p. 57) views an antecedent of Varuna as Dyaus, the sky god. He argues that Dyaus is comparable to Zeus in Greek mythology (there appears to be an etymological correlation in the name), however it would appear from the little information available that he could also correlate with An, the sky-god of the Sumerians. Veronica Ions (*Indian Mythology*, p. 16) appears to give the precedence to Varuna, while we would put An before Varuna. Part of the problem may lie in the fact that Varuna is not clearly presented as a god of a given realm of the universe, which would be expected if we were tracing the last memories of the true God.

⁶ Mithra was a god of light (or in India, translated as friendship) while Aryaman was a god of formal hospitality (cf. *The Rig Veda*, translated by Wendy Doniger O'Flaherty). It is likely that this is a process of making gods out of divine attributes, i.e., attributing to a single god a single attribute of the true God. Mithra illustrates the problems we have in putting this material together. He is not mentioned in the earlier Iranian material we have, although he appears to reflect the Aryan strain of the *Rig Veda*. By the time of Zoroaster (6th century BC), he played an significant role in the Persian pantheon as one of the Yazatas or worshipful ones. After Zoroaster, his worship proliferated and spread westward into Rome (AD 100-400), where during the late empire stage it became a major influence before dying out under the influence of Christianity.

⁷ Indra's position as wind or air god again is somewhat reminiscent of Enlil in Sumer. Based on the evidence from Asia Minor, Varuna's displacement had occurred at least by the 14th century BC. The *Vedas* were not written down until at least 2700 years later (about AD 1400). For comparison, the Old Testament was written about 1400 BC (in the case of the Torah) to about 400 BC (in the case of the some of the prophets). With the discovery of the Dead Sea scrolls, we have Old Testament manuscripts dating back at least to 200 BC (cf. Frank Moore Cross, "The Development of the Jewish Script," in *The Bible and the Ancient Near East*, pp. 133-202 and Bruce K. Waltke, "The Textual Criticism of the Old Testament, in *Biblical Criticism*, pp. 47-82), in some cases within a couple of centuries of composition. New Testament manuscripts date from the first century, some from within a century of their composition (cf. Bruce Metzger, *The Text of the New Testament*, pp. 31-35 and Gordon D. Fee,

"The Textual Criticism of the New Testament," in *Biblical Criticism*, p. 130).
[8] Like many prehistorical dates, the date of this conquest has been hotly debated. As K.C. Jain (*The Prehistory and Protohistory of India*, p. 269) points out, the foundation for many of the "traditional" dates, the epic material, is "often conflicting and self-contradictory, and so no satisfactory and acceptable result can be arrived at from these data." The archaeological evidence of the past half century, however, would suggest that this occurred concurrently with the demise of the Harappan civilization in the Indus valley. Jain (pp. 214 ff) argues against this view, primarily on linguistic issues. But his position raises more questions than it answers. Specifically, he is left with an overthrow of the Harappan culture by an unknown force, and a much later Vedic invasion against an unknown civilization.

[9] Archaeological evidence of this culture has been uncovered along the coast of Pakistan and India, from the Iranian border to the northwest to the Gulf of Cambay. Ruins have also been uncovered as far inland as Rupar, about 1000 miles northeast of the westernmost site. While more than 150 sites have been surveyed, the two key archaeological sites are the ruins of the large cities Harappa and Mohenjo-daro. The entire culture has been termed the Harappan culture after the first city. The archaeological work on this culture is still very preliminary, and the dates are tentative, and subject to debate, with some scholars calling for dates both earlier and later.

[10] In this region, the Indus river flows across the vast Punjab plains, dropping but 700 feet in its last 700 miles. Since the time the cities flourished, the ground-level of the flood plain has risen 20-40 feet putting the water table above the levels of most interest to archaeologists.

[11] A number of ties have been made between the Sumerian culture of the lower Mesopotamia valley and the Harappan culture. Harappan seals have been found in the Persian Gulf area. There are similarities in some of the characters. It is likely that the characters were adapted from the Sumerian culture to the Harappan language, probably an early form of Proto-Dravidian, the forerunner of the non-Aryan Indian languages.

[12] Jain, p. 145. John Marshall, a key archaeologist of the Harappan culture notes three correlations: 1) he is three faced, 2) he is lord of the animals (on at least one seal he is surrounded by various animals), 3) Shiva was a *mahayogi* (great yogi).

[13] Jain (p. 144) notes the wide distribution of similar figures westward throughout Mesopotamia, Egypt, Asia Minor, and the Aegean. Alexander Hislop (*The Two Babylons*, p. 20) traces the mother goddess cult back to early Mesopotamia, specifically to Semiramis, the wife of Nimrod (Gen. 10:9-12). While some of his evidence is stretched and some of his analogies are forced, his basic premise that the mother-goddess cult was a contrived imitation of the worship of the true God appears sound.

[14] Ions (p. 11) proposes that the concept arose as the brahmins attempted to

integrate gods from two different traditions, who had differing names and differing representations, but similar attributes or purposes. The idea would be that the priests could then claim that they were worshiping the same god as before—just in a different incarnation or avatar. This is another form of the lie that Satan offered to Eve—"you will surely not die (Gen. 3:4)."

[15] Although no exact date for the initial written form of the *Rig Veda* is evident, it is generally conceded that the Hindus did not begin committing it to writing until well into the second millennium of the Christian era. Even then it was done only in response to Muslim persecutions. Ions (p. 9) observes "Whereas before [prior to the Muslim persecutions] they had valued and relied chiefly on oral tradition—a factor which in itself encouraged the proliferation of mythology—now they set down the scriptures in illustrated manuscripts. The language used was Sanskrit, the classical Aryan language of the Brahmins."

[16] Gaurinath Sastri (*A History of Vedic Literature*, pp. 36-55) observes that the *Rig Veda* mentions a total of 33 gods, with most of the hymns focusing on Agni, Indra, and Soma. He seems to indicate that other gods are implied, but then argues that all are manifestations of the three key gods who rule the three realms, earth, air, and sky.

[17] Norvin Hein ("Hinduism" in *Religions of Asia*, pp. 82-84) points out how the low class workers (i.e., Dravidians) were added to the existing Aryan social structure in order to produce a single social structure. Ironically, this process of merely placing one structure on top of the other produced a situation where many of the social skills came to be concentrated in the lower caste. Thus, while under Hindu theory the top three castes provided the foundation for society, in reality, the non-Aryan *sudras* provided the real economic foundation which has been demonstrated down through the ages.

[18] The *Vedas* (the word means knowledge) contain wisdom considered to have been given to the ancient seers. They are a body of literature encompassing a variety of purposes, and as such stretch beyond the writings given the title, "Veda." There are two main portions, the Mantra and the Brahmana. The Mantra, the earlier portion, includes the four vedas already named. The Brahamanas are prose expansions and explanations of the poetic Mantra. They explain the way of the ritual. As explanations, they are later than the *Vedas*, but necessarily a part of them. The last section, the *Upanishads* explain the why of the ritual. Although last in order, they are said to stand midway between the other two (cf. Sastri, pp. 22-26).

[19] It would appear that many of these began to be written prior to the time of Buddha. As Sastri (pp. 105-6) points out there is no evidence in the Brahmanas of any familiarity with Buddha, while Buddhist texts show familiarity with the brahminic literature. This is not conclusive, however, as will be seen in the next chapter. The Buddhist literature was not written down for several centuries after Buddha. Because of the propensity to transmit key doctrines orally, it is also possible that Buddha could have known of Brahman

ritual before the same ritual was committed to writing.
[20] This is especially true prior to their commitment to written form, which is the key reason they were not written at an earlier date. As Swami Nikhilananda (*The Upanishads*, p. 13) points out, "written words become the common property of all." Since the *Vedas* had to memorized, they could not be learned unless one was able to find a teacher willing to teach them. This provided very strict controls on who was able to exercise religious power. Of course, in times of persecution, this also made it easier to eradicate the teaching—which is the reason that the vedic literature was eventually written down several centuries later.

[21] The Aranyakas were written for those who had sought isolation for meditation. The premise is that the knowing of the ritual is sufficient. Sastri (p. 6) states "it is not always necessary to go through the details of a ritual; it is enough to know it. . . . So, we find Brahmanas often telling us in unambiguous language that one who performs a sacrifice gets the result; the one who knows it also gets the same."

[22] These rituals revolve around the daily observance of the five great sacrifices. These include the recitation of the *Vedas*, offering of waters to ancestors, devotional offerings including a stick of fuel in the sacred fire, offering of food to all beings (god, spirits, ancestors, and humanity in general), and offerings to men (i.e., hospitality).

[23] Since the last two stages may be deferred to a later life, in any given generation only a few men actually leave society. According to Hindu teaching, this renunciation of the world must be performed at some time for all who desire final salvation.

[24] This concept has also been carried over into Buddhism and Jainism (a religion started by a contemporary of Gautama the Buddha). It is clear that the *Upanishads* regard this as a new concept, but it is not clear where the idea originated. There has been evidence of this concept in other cultures, mostly primitive, although some argue that it was present in ancient Egypt. However, in Egypt, what is presented as soul transmigration is a conjectured incarnation (in Hindu concepts, an avatar) of a god (cf. Henri Frankfort, *Ancient Egyptian Religion*, pp. 105-7 and E.A. Wallis Budge, *From Fetish to God in Ancient Egypt*, pp. 75-77). It is clear that tied in with the caste system one result would be to control the society in that it provides a reason that any individual is in a given caste, and a hope for a better future (albeit long term). It would be difficult to project this as either a cause or a source of the teaching, however.

[25] This is evidenced by the fact that the "Hindu Triad" of chief gods remained while the gods changed. Further, after the *Upanishads*, two of the three were gods not evident in the Vedic pantheon (Brahma and Shiva) and the third, Vishnu, had been a minor god in the earlier Vedic pantheon (cf. Ions, p. 40). Further, the number of gods is incalculable. One estimate placed the

practical number at 50,000. In popular accounts, later Hindus espouse thirty-three *crores*, which is ten million. This would place the number of gods and goddesses at 330,000,000 (Banerjea, "The Hindu Concept of God," in *The Religion of the Hindus*, edited by Morgan, p. 51).

[26] This quest has been likened to the Greek philosophical quest, which was occurring at about the same time. One key difference, however, was that the *Upanishads* based their search upon the *Vedas*. The concept of Brahman seems to derive from the description in the *Rig Veda* that the Supreme Being transcended the universe (for example vedas 10.81 and 82 give very exalted views of the creator [Wendy Doniger O'Flaherty, *The Rig Veda*, pp. 34-37]).

[27] This entire issue is very convoluted. While Brahman is viewed at this point as the universal spirit, later Krishna and Vishnu will be elevated to higher positions in different sects. Even so, there are a multitudinous number of other gods, who are on one hand viewed as subordinate, but in another perspective mere manifestations of the overall universal spirit. Renou (p. 36) observes, "The common believer is not conversant with the notion of divine unity." On the popular level, Hinduism has been and remains a polytheistic religion as is evidenced by the popular mythology which is held on a level with the earlier writings by many, and the use of idols in the temples. As Renou (pp. 30-31) states, "For some, perhaps for the majority, the idol is the god himself, and we can classify this as idolatry; for others, symbolical values are true values and the idol is nothing more than what it is in any form of cult in which the sacred is incarnate in some concrete form."

[28] Norvin Hein ("Hinduism," in *Religions of Asia*, p. 107), equates the Atman as 'spirit,' then later as 'soul.' This suggests that the spirit and soul are identical. From a Christian perspective, we would prefer to distinguish the two (e.g., 1 Thes 5:23 and Heb 4:12). The soul is that intangible part of man which contains the mind, the emotion, and the will (which in Freudian psychology is labeled, the ego, super-ego, and id). The spirit is the intangible part of man which contains the capacity to receive and to be motivated by God (cf. Ian Thomas, *The Mystery of Godliness*, pp. 61-74).

[29] Ever since the "Laws of Manu" (written between 200 BC and AD 200) the Hindus have tried to understand how this law works. For example, one school of thought is that *karma* becomes an energy field hanging over the individual head that without warning wreaks retribution, while another school sees it as an internal force affecting the disposition (cf. Hein, p. 89).

[30] The brahmins divided the body of knowledge into two categories, *shruti* and *smrti*. *Shruti*, ("that which has been heard") was deemed inspired, while *smrti* ("that which is remembered") was deemed written by human authors. It was worthwhile, but only explanatory.

[31] Louis Renou translates sample sections of the *Grihya* Sutras and the *Dharma Sutras* in his book *Hinduism*, pp. 105-116. The "Laws of Manu" are a part of the *smrti* which date from shortly after the period of the sutras. They

try to further explain what *dharma* is.

[32] The original form had 5 volumes and was probably composed in the fourth century BC. Later, this was expanded to its present 7 volume form where Rama is viewed as the eighth avatar or incarnation of Vishnu.

[33] Traditionally, the poem is the work of the sage Vyasa, of the early Aryan period. Renou (p. 141) proposes a composition during the second or third century BC, with a redaction during the first century AD. Morgan (*The Religion of the Hindus*, pp. 353-62) gives an extensive summary of the narrative. The Public Broadcasting System has recently made a six-hour miniseries of the work, which also had a theater release in a four hour version.

[34] It is significant that in this work, Krishna is portrayed as conceding validity to other gods (7.21-22). In the process, Krishna claims that when anyone serves another god in faith, Krishna accepts that worship, and whatever the man gets, he gets from Krishna.

[35] The concept of theism in Hinduism is highly confusing to the western student. As Satis Chatterjee ("Hindu Religious Thought," in *The Religion of the Hindus*, p. 207) states, "Hinduism as a religion is centered not so much in the belief in God, as in faith in the reality of spirit and the spiritual order of the world." This spiritual order of the world can be abstract (as presented by the *Upanishads*) or personalized under the control of one or more gods. When personalized, it is termed theistic. This does not mean that the Hindu sees that god as existing exclusive of other gods. Rather, that god could be termed as the primary manifestation of the spirit lying behind the material. Sastri (p. 47) observes that the "Vedic seers tried to find out a single creative cause of the universe which was itself uncreated and imperishable. The result was that they tried to subordinate the gods under one higher being who was competent to control other gods and their activities. Thus, the many gods came to be gradually looked upon as the embodiments or expressions of one universal identity." This view is called "monism," rather than monotheism. Since other manifestations (or incarnations, or avatars) are possible, the Hindus see no problem with worshiping other gods, or even having other gods occupy the same positions in various myths.

[36] This goddess has several names, including Uma, Kali, Devi, Parvati, Candi, Bhairavi, and Camunda, depending upon the myth. Durga is a violent goddess as evidenced by some of her manifestations, such as Camunda, a childless destroyer of life, and Kali, who roams the battlefield delighting in the blood of the slain. Shakti followers either hope that Durga's violence can be directed against forces that threaten them, or pessimistically accept the acts of the goddess as inscrutable. Shaktism or the worship of Durga is of interest as the most developed worship of a female deity in the modern world.

[37] Three schools were deemed heretical. Buddhism and Jainism, both originating in the 6th century BC became separate religions (see chapter 7). At one point, Buddha was a brahmin. Ironically, Buddha was later deemed an

avatar of Krishna. The third school, founded by the obscure Carvaka, was a materialistic group which seemed primarily motivated by anti-clerical and anti-religious ideas. It is seen almost exclusively as an object of polemics, raising some question as to its actual identity.

³⁸ John A. Hutchison (*Paths of Faith*, pp. 150-54) gives a succinct description of each of the schools. The other five schools are:

Nyaya. This is more of a school of logic than religion. This school seeks salvation through knowledge. It was founded by a man named Gautama, who is thought to have lived in the 6th century BC (but, it is stated, was not the Gautama who founded Buddhism).

Vaisheshika. Very similar to the Nyaya school, its basic premise was that the world is made up of small particles (i.e., atoms). It is dated from the 3rd century BC.

Sankhya. A sect without a god, it was essentially a reaction against the monism of the *Upanishads*. It postulated a dualistic spiritual/material universe, in which the individual is not a manifestation of the world soul. It held to an evolving universe. It also claimed that salvation derived from a sufficient realization of this distinction. It is dated back as far as the 7th century BC.

Yoga. Some have argued that Yoga was a physical regime of the Sankhya school. It agrees with the premise that man's basic problem is "bondage" to matter, and salvation lies in realizing the spiritual aspect. It differs primarily in its acceptance of a god, although god is not involved in the realization process. There is an eight step ladder to this realization (involving meditation), and a teacher or guru must guide the initiate up the ladder.

Purva Mimamsa This school rejected several of the main premises of Hinduism, including the world soul (or Brahman). It believed in a real physical universe and individual souls (not mere aspects of the world soul). Religion solely involves performance of the sacrificial rites without any requirement for belief or worship.

³⁹ As in the case of many *Sutras*, the *Vedanta Sutra* is very terse and obscure. Based on the interpretation of it, some have maintained that the writer (Badarayana) was a true monotheist. The *Sutra* can be understood in a variety of ways, however, and has been.

⁴⁰ Norvin Hein (p. 79) likens Hinduism to a river within which run many currents. The *Vedas* would be the banks that "guide" the tradition. One such current from this period was the Tantras, which strongly affected Yoga and several strains of Buddhism, especially in Tibet (see chapter 7).

⁴¹ There is no record that the Muslims of this late period carried out the process of the earlier expansion which required the conquered to either convert or die. Rather, they imposed a poll tax on all non-Muslims, which lasted until Akbar's reign (1556-1605) during the Mogul empire. Frederick Denny (*An Introduction to Islam*, p. 128) states that the Hindus were given a later *dhimmi* (or protected) status because of the *Vedas* and other writings; and "the practical

political necessity of dealing with a vast and varied peoples."
[42] Niels C. Nielsen (*Religions of Asia*, p. 337) traces Nanak's background to the otherwise obscure strain of Hinduism called the Sant tradition. Key to this identification is the Sant position that God was manifest in the world, but was not unified with the world.
[43] According to tradition (*Textual Sources for the Study of Sikhism*, edited and translated by W. H. McLeod, p. 212), Nanak went swimming and left his clothes on the bank. He didn't return for three days, after which he gave no explanation for his absence. Later, he claimed that during this period, he had a vision where he had been caught up to god's presence.
[44] Popularized through his book *Transcendental Meditation* (earlier published as *The Science of Being and Art of Living*). Early followers of Transcendental Meditation (especially during the 1960's) claimed that it was not a religious movement. It is clear from this study that what was meant by this was that it did not have a god in the same sense as Western religion. A survey of some chapter titles from the book verifies that Transcendental Meditation is a form of Hindu thought, e.g., "Attunement with the cosmic life force," and "Karma and the Being."
[45] This movement attracted a lot of attention in the 1960's when the adherents wore the traditional saffron robes of a Hindu mendicant. Since then, the group has opted to wear western clothing, which has given them an appearance of having gone underground. Ken Boa gives an excellent summary of the movement in his book, *Cults, World Religions, and You* (pp. 178-87).

Chapter 7

Under The Bodhi Tree: Buddhism

Siddhartha Gautama who later became known as "the Buddha" was a contemporary of Daniel. He was born approximately 563 BC,[1] when Daniel and many of his countrymen were already in exile in Babylon. The northern 10 tribes had been carried off into exile to Assyria in 721 BC. Daniel and his contemporaries in the first wave of the southern exile were carried to Babylon about 605 BC.

Gautama lived in what is now northeast India and southern Nepal, in the foothills of the Himalayan mountains along the tributaries of the Ganges river.[2] At that time, the Ganges valley was a fertile valley with an agrarian culture. The religion of that area was a form of Brahmanism, a primitive forerunner of what is today called Hinduism.[3] Atop the social structure were the brahmins, who managed the religious aspects of the society, orally passing religious traditions and performing sacrifices. However, the period was one of social turmoil as a result of increasing prosperity and trade.

Another factor that may have contributed to the religious turmoil was the influence of the exiled Jewish peoples. Although God sent the northern nation into exile for its apostasy, not every individual had apostasied. Further, the apostasy problem was largely an issue of syncretism. The nation and its leaders absorbed inappropriate practices and teachings from those around them and distorted the truth. These exiles were transported to Nineveh and other parts of the extensive Assyrian empire. The extent of their influence from there is lost in unrecorded history. However, the Bene Israel people of Western India trace their origins to the same "10 lost tribes of Israel," who left Israel more than a century and a half before Gautama. Given the commerce of the period, it would not be surprising that during this period of turmoil that some exiled Israelite families might have chosen to move further east carrying various "Jewish" ideas (or perhaps more properly, reminders of the true God) with them.[4]

Gautama the Man

Gautama was born into the ruling family of his region, heir of the local raja (or prince).[5] Legend relates that local seers proclaimed to the prince, Suddhodhana, that his son Gautama would end up in one of two careers: a world class emperor ruling over vast realms, or a enlightened religious leader.[6] Being from the soldier class himself, Suddhodhana resolved that it should be the former. He educated his son in all the studies of their culture as well as in the martial arts. The reports (or legends) are that Gautama was an apt student who quickly acquired the skills of a future ruler, although he reportedly spent much time sitting alone reflecting on life.

In order to guide his son, the raja attempted to isolate him by keeping him occupied with various amusements, especially making sure that the young man never saw a sick person, an aged person, a dead person, or a wandering monk. As soon as he had matured (age sixteen) he was married to a beautiful wife, Yasodhara. While somewhat isolated in the palace, he and his friends were kept occupied with various social functions. He was given every earthly pleasure in order to ensure that he would be satisfied and not take up a begging bowl and become a wandering monk himself.

For several years, the raja's stratagem seemed to work. Gautama remained in the palace, and enjoyed a life of luxury. At the age of 29, he requested permission to travel through and visit the realm that he anticipated ruling one day. Despite the efforts of the raja to sanitize the route, in the process Gautama got his first glimpses of old age, disease, death, and wandering monks. This led him to question his life. Shortly thereafter, his wife gave birth to his first child, a son. He named his son, Rahula, "fetter." That day, Gautama resolved to escape the various bonds which linked him to a life he perceived as meaningless.

In many respects, the raja's efforts had backfired for Gautama had not become inured to the tragedies of life most people take in stride. After consideration of what he had seen, Gautama abandoned his wife, infant son, prospective throne, and 13 years of hedonism, and set out to be an ascetic.

For the next six years, Gautama wore the already traditional yellow robe of a mendicant, and wandered the Ganges valley seeking answers to the issues of life. During this period, he sought out at least two religious teachers, practiced meditation after the Brahminic traditions, and attempted a wide variety of ascetic practices.[7] He even became a teacher (or guru) in his own right. But none of his efforts brought him any closer to the answers he sought, nor did they give him peace of mind.

At the end of this period, Gautama reached the extremes of asceticism. Reportedly he had fasted until his backbone could be seen through his gaunt stomach. Realizing that his efforts provided no solution, Gautama abandoned his extreme fast, gathered his strength and retreated to the roots of a Bodhi tree[8] For a week, he sat there in meditation while the *nagas* (serpent kings) first challenged, then approved him.[9] The tradition is that during the full moon of either April or May of his 35th year (528 BC), Gautama was "enlightened," and became "a" or "the" Buddha.[10]

The Enlightenment

Gautama's enlightenment reflected his own experience and earlier schooling. He realized from his earlier years that hedonism did not satisfy. He realized from his time of wandering that asceticism did not satisfy. His conclusion was what is called the "middle way"--the way between those two extremes. Since life is a mass of suffering, and suffering derives from desires rooted in the self, the idea was to deny the self--not satisfy it as in hedonism, nor to flagellate it as in asceticism, but just accept the self, and thus extinguish desire.

This premise is based in the Hindu world premise that man dies and is reborn with his rebirth "body" determined by his behavior in the previous life. Both religions assert the physical world is illusion or *maya*, and that true reality is what they deem Brahman or the universal soul, as opposed to the perceived reality, Atman, the individual soul. This individual soul goes through a process of rebirth or transmigration until the point of enlightenment, or re-unification with the universal soul (a state also called nirvana). Gautama accepted this premise without question. But then his quandary was how to stop this process of rebirth. The goal of both religions is the *dhamma* (or *dharma* in Sanskrit) which is an approach to the spiritual life, or a "maintaining" of the right path, designed to ultimately bring about that enlightenment.[11]

Based on his conclusions regarding the renunciation of self, Gautama developed an eightfold path of self-discipline designed to produce the enlightenment which produced nirvana.[12]   After his enlightenment, Gautama began to teach his conclusions or *dhamma* to mankind. He began with the five ascetics who had left him when he abandoned his fast. They adopted his teachings, and became the first leaders of the movement.

Gautama's Teachings

Apparently, dissatisfaction with the religious status quo was widespread throughout the area. As Gautama's teachings spread, so did the number of converts. He wandered throughout the Ganges valley, teaching and collecting followers for the next 45 years. The accounts report that Gautama the Buddha won his reputation as an implacable teacher who accepted life as it came.[13]

Many of the assumptions of Buddhism derive directly from the Brahminic teachings of the period, teachings which give Buddhism and Hinduism (as the contemporary formalization of Brahminic thoughts) a common view of the origin and goal of life.[14]   While Gautama did more than just restate and organize what he had heard, the basic premise he worked with has been called ethical conditionalism--rebirth in a later life either at a higher state as a result of good deeds in this one, or at a lower state as a result of evil deeds in this life.[15]   Based on this concept, Gautama formalized means by which an individual could increase his chances of a higher rebirth, and ultimately an "emancipation" by stopping the cycle of rebirths.

There are also many dissimilarities between the resulting Hindu and Buddhist thought. One key point is the concept of self. Brahminic teaching had devolved from a monotheistic base to a pan-theistic world view. I.e., beginning with the one true God, it had degenerated to the point that it identified all creation with God. Various attributes of God and later various forces and beings were personalized, being viewed as gods themselves. As a result, brahminic teaching reached a point of identifying the individual soul (the Atman) with the universal soul (the Brahman), making the individual part of the overall.

Gautama rejected this concept in that he rejected the concept of individual soul as a self. Rather, he assumed a phenomenalistic perspective--phenomena alone compose both beings and things. This is apparently derived from the idea that since an individual's memory consists of different sensual inputs, the self is the conglomerate of those inputs, i.e., a collection of perceptions. Since perceptions (and understandings) change, Gautama argued that the individual changed also, or to be more correct, there was no continuous individual but a chain of related individuals, This chain, he maintained, continued on past death through a series of existences.

However, he did accept the brahminic teaching regarding spiritual hierarchies, and incorporated these hierarchies into his ethical conditionalism. These hierarchies incorporated six major sections of beings. Above man was the realm of the gods (incorporating 22 levels above the earth). Below man were four sub-human realms: that of the demons (in the atmosphere near the earth), that of hungry ghosts (on the earth), that of animals, and that of those who dwell in hell below the earth. Man's level was one of mixed pleasure and pain. The levels below man were denoted levels of increasing pain, and the levels above man those of increasing pleasure. Based on the quality of deeds (*kamma* or *karma*) man could be reborn in a higher realm (after a life of merit), a lower realm (after a life of demerit), or as a human being (usually in a lower or higher caste than the previous life, again, depending on merit). According to Gautama *kamma* could only be earned during one's life as a human. Life in one of the other realms gradually depleted the store of merit or demerit acquired during a previous realm, requiring another cycle through the human realm (although a given cycle might require millions of years). All of these realms were viewed as transitory, with the ultimate goal to achieve nirvana, i.e., removal from the continuing series of cycles.

Whatever the sources, Gautama's teaching touched a responsive chord as he wandered the Ganges valley and the Himalayan foothills. Compared to the pessimistic rituals controlled by the brahmins, Guatama's teachings were a religion of hope--not in the sense of redemption and freedom, but a way for the individual to use ethical conditionalism (or the law of *kamma*) to work himself up through the social hierarchy (another carry-over from pre-Hindu Brahmanism) and eventually gain liberation. Compared to the teachings of his contemporary Jina (founder of Jainism), it was a religion of the people, not of an ascetic monastic class. But perhaps it was the personal charisma and discipline of Gautama which was the deciding factor.

Gautama's Ministry

During the next 45 years, Gautama followed the wet and dry seasons as customary for wandering monks during the period. He began ordaining monks, the first group of which were the five ascetics he taught shortly after his enlightenment. Many became monks only after they observed and talked to Gautama, and noted his charisma and balanced view (the middle way) as opposed to the hedonistic and ascetic extremes of the contemporary secular and religious elements of Indian society.

Key to the growth of the movement was his ability to convert, or at least win the personal respect of various religious and political leaders. While refusing to give special social recognition to these leaders, in many ways Gautama made a special effort to win their support religiously. During the first few years of his teaching, he gained a high degree of respect throughout the four kingdoms then situated in the Ganges valley. One reason was the restraint which Gautama placed on his followers as opposed to other alms-seekers. Another reason was the way Gautama carefully reviewed the rules and changed them if there was a negative public reaction. A third reason must have been his intellectual ability, by which he was able to debate with other religious leaders, and pick apart their teachings. As a result, by the time of his death, Gautama the Buddha and his followers were already recognized as a significant religious development in the region.

That is not to say that this group was totally unified. Within eight years after his enlightenment, Gautama was facing significant contentions even among his closest followers, which already threatened schisms. The first significant division was over discipline and cleanliness--a monk had violated one of the rules of cleanliness, and the local chapter divided on how to discipline him, and whether to suspend him or not. While Gautama by personal intervention was able to prevent violence, the argument continued.

Later, as Gautama aged, there were further contentions among the power-hungry who desired him to designate a successor. One such pretender was Devadatta, his cousin and brother-in-law. Repudiated by Gautama, he even attempted to have the leader assassinated. The accounts attribute three such attempts, all of which failed.

As Gautama aged, his personal influence waned, and he complained that the younger monks (in a land where the average life span was less than 25 years, at least three generations removed from their venerable founder) lacked the discipline and zeal the earlier converts had possessed. Still, the fact that the movement retained a large measure of unity indicates his personal charismatic power. Even so, he turned increasingly to rules to regulate what had in earlier days been communicated by example and zeal.

For some, who recalled the earlier glory years, the rules were not enough and led by the same Devadatta, they attempted to enforce even stricter rules. When Gautama refused, Devadatta succeeded in forming his own order, even though he never replaced Gautama. This was the first real schism in Buddhism.[16] As Gautama aged, he appointed "the Teaching" (*dhamma*) as his successor. Each monk was to live as an island with the teaching his guide and leader. What happened throughout the centuries was that successful monks would develop personal followings of students who grasped their teachings, and incorporate them into a widening spectrum of canons.

In his 80th year, Gautama was given a meal after which he became sick from dysentery. Realizing that he was near death, he give his followers directions on the disposition of his body and his last minute instructions. In 483 BC, he died. Gautama's body was cremated. The remains were divided into eight parts which were given to eight different groups for interment. Each of the eight groups erected a monument or *stupa* over their relics. At least 3 of these relic-urns have been rediscovered and are on display.[17]

Early Buddhism

During the following rainy season, approximately 500 of Gautama's followers gathered in Rajagaha to repeat and correct the *dhamma*--- various rules of the order and discourses of Gautama. The resulting canon was memorized and passed on through recitation. The canon was memorized in the local dialect called Pali. Today, the written version of the Pali canon is the primary source of all Buddhist teaching. Each of the various sects have picked up various commentaries or amplifications called *sutras* along the way. The question of which are valid and which are not divides the groups.

Since the death of Gautama, his teachings have spread throughout the world. In the process, there have been a number of divisions and changes, so that Buddhism cannot be regarded as a monolithic religious group any more than any other religion. In 383 BC, another council was held. This second council discussed the inclusion of new rules of discipline. While the proposed changes were decided against, the roots of the primary schism which divides Buddhism today were sown. The group which carried sway began to call itself the Theravadins, i.e., those who support the doctrines of the elders. Those who proposed the changes, claiming to be in a majority, called themselves those belonging to the great community, which became the Mahayana (or "great vehicle" school). By two hundred years after Gautama's death, 18-20 distinct orders or sects had arisen, although many of these later merged or died out.

All of the various schools have attempted to follow the teachings of Buddha as preserved through the various traditions. The basis of these traditions have been four principles (often labeled the "four noble truths") which contain the essence of Buddha's understanding. Succinctly they are: 1) life as we know it on earth is inherently tragic, full of suffering, pain, and sorrow; 2) the cause of all of the suffering, pain, and sorrow is human desire or cravings for the transient things of the earth; 3) (therefore) suffering, pain, and sorrow cease when we give up our desires or cravings; and 4) the way to give up desires or cravings is to follow the eightfold way (the middle way).[18]   The primary differences between the different schools have devolved from point four--how the eightfold way is carried out.

Theravada Buddhism

Early expansion was enhanced by two factors. The first was the continued support of various political leaders in the area who supported the movement financially and built various monasteries. The second factor was the invasion of northwest India by Alexander the Great. Alexander's troops forced him to give up his campaign in 327 BC after he had crossed the Indus river. His withdrawal left a power vacuum in the area which was filled by Chandragupta Maurya (322-297 BC), king of Magadha (during the time of Gautama, a large wealthy region bordering the Ganges on the south). He and his successors conquered to the west and south, incorporating much of the sub-continent into the largest Indian government until the coming of the British. His grandson, Ashoka Maurya (274-232 BC) is considered the greatest king of Indian history, although he ruled a realm he obtained predominantly through inheritance rather than by conquest. He did leave many edicts inscribed in stone enlightening later historians.[19]

Ashoka also became an ardent Buddhist and was a significant factor in its expansion. At about 240 BC, he gathered a great council of Buddhist monks at Pataliputra (today known as Patna) who codified the orally transmitted tenets which led to the Theravada school. The point of contention was the role of the lay person and the community of monks. The group which became the Theravada school stood for a sharp distinction between the two groups, with the monks holding a much higher position social position as well as earning much more merit. It was also much less inclined towards the mystical elements of the Indian culture which had accumulated over the centuries, and which were very evident in the Brahminic teachings. According to Theravadic tradition, this council dismissed some sixty thousand monks. Many were actually brahmins who had used the loosely held standards as a means to advance their own ideas. Others were undoubtedly members of the what became the rival Mahayana school of thought. Ashoka also built numerous monasteries and *stupas* (memorial mounds incorporating relics of some great Buddhist leader, either Gautama or any other revered monk). Tradition sets the number at about eighty-four thousand. He also sent numerous Buddhist missionaries throughout Asia, most notably to Ceylon, or what is now Sri Lanka.

Ceylon became a key Buddhist center. In 25 BC, the fourth conference after the death of Gautama was held in Matale, Ceylon.[20] Here, the oral traditions were written down in the Pali language, providing the first written canon for the Buddhist religion.

Mahayana Buddhism

Shortly after the death of Ashoka, the Maurya dynasty and empire disintegrated, and India was redivided into smaller kingdoms. Many of these new rulers retained memory of the earlier Greek influence, although they continued their patronage of the Buddhist religion in their realms. The coalescing Hinduism provided a second powerful influence.[21]

As a result, Buddhist thinking in India was challenged and modified. One of the key changes was that the person of Gautama as the Buddha was elevated to a position similar to a Hindu god.[22] The movement also became more ritualistic, incorporating temples, art, and other formal institutions.

From about 100 BC to about AD 400 (which overlapped the time that the Pali canon was committed to writing), various new writings (in Sanskrit) called *sutras* (or "discourses") appeared. These purported to be teachings of Gautama which had been lost for a time and then rediscovered. These were adopted by Mahayana school, but not the Theravada school, and contributed to the schism between the two. King Kanishka (AD 77-103) held a council in Jullundur in northwest India which has been viewed as the real start of the Mahayana school. Buddhists from India, Tibet, and China were in attendance. Those from Ceylon and other parts of Southeast Asia did not attend. Various Sanskrit sutras were authorized as commentaries, and were engraved on copper plates, which have survived only in later Chinese translations.

Expansion Throughout Asia

Theravada Buddhism in Burma is dated to the 5th century AD, although there is evidence that earlier Buddhist influences from King Ashoka's missionaries was already in place. Over the centuries it struggled and mixed with local religious ideas and Hindu thought carried by Indian traders. Thailand and Cambodia developed similar mixtures, especially as various tribes migrated south from the China region during the first millennium AD. As a result, while the Theravada school has continued as the dominant form in Burma, Cambodia, Ceylon, Laos, Thailand, and other parts of South and Southeast Asia, it is a hybrid form. This is especially true in Cambodia and Thailand where early Buddhism ebbed under the Hinduism of the medieval Khmer empire centered at Anghor Wat. After the 11th century Buddhism again displaced Hinduism there, but not without being affected itself.

While the Theravada school was moving southeast, the Mahayana school began to move northeast. But again the expansion was not without effect upon the resulting Buddhist thinking. One of the most significant developments of Mahayana Buddhism during this period was the concept of the three forms of Buddha. This theory posited that the Buddha had an all-embracing, universal form, a transcendent form where he could appear as one of many heavenly figures (cf. the Buddha of the boundless light or Amida Buddhism, see below) and a transformation form which he assumed when he existed on earth.

A second very significant incorporation into Mahayana thinking was the assumption that every person had the potential to be a buddha. Beyond this, some potential buddhas on the verge of buddhahood supposedly refuse to enter Nirvana, vowing to withhold their own enlightenment until all others have reached this stages (often termed "are saved"). These individuals are termed *bodhisattvas*. There have been a number of these according to Mahayana teaching.[23] Their key virtue is compassion for humanity.

Other Schools

In addition to the *bodhisattvas*, others have completed the journey to buddhahood, and are indeed now in Nirvana. Interestingly, there are two varieties: those who began their journey as a human, and those who began elsewhere in the universe.[24]

One such bodhisattva of the latter group was Amitabha Buddha (A-mi-to-fo in Chinese and Amida in Japanese). According to the sutras (the earliest of which dates from about AD 400), when Amitabha heard the preaching of a buddha, he resolved to achieve enough merit to create a paradise for gods and men which was free of pain. When he was able to enter nirvana, he chose instead to preside over this paradise in the western region. Known as the pure land, this paradise was achievable by good deeds and meditating on (or faith in) Amitabha.[25]

Another school arose later in the first millennium by the incorporation of Tantras, mystical writings, into Buddhist thought.[26] This school is founded on the basis of using magical rites and mystical meditation to produce the insight which comes through self-discipline in the Theravada school, or through philosophical insight in the Mahayana school. Originating in India, these concepts were carried into Tibet by Padmasambhava in the 8th century.

Ironically, while Tantric Buddhism rooted strongly in Tibet, it contributed significantly to the decline and virtual disappearance of Buddhism from its native India. As Buddhism became more mystical, its Indian devotees gradually moved back into Hinduism. To many Indians, Buddha became viewed merely an incarnation (or avatar) of Vishnu.

Chinese Buddhism

Buddhism began moving to China during the first century BC as Indian monks and traders moved throughout the region. It was not until the following century that it received official acceptance. In AD 61 Emperor Ming-ti (of the Han dynasty) sent to India for Buddhist books and teachers. Initially, the Buddhist teachings were too mystical for the practical Chinese whose thinking had been molded by five centuries of Confucianist and Taoist thought.

An Indian Buddhist named Bodhidharma (in Chinese, Tamo; and in Japanese, Daruma) founded a Dhyana school of Buddhism in China--a school based on extensive meditation to produce enlightenment. This school, after extensive modification by Taoist and Confucian thought, was incorporated into the Chinese religious picture as the Ch'an school, which in Japanese became Zen Buddhism. Pure Land Buddhism was the second predominant form which survived. Again, as in many other lands, the Chinese incorporated Buddhism as just one aspect of their religious lives. For them, Taoism and Confucianism balanced the spiritual portion of their society.

Korean Buddhism

From China, Buddhism spread southwest to Tibet and northeast to Korea. Mahayana Buddhism arrived in Korea about AD 372. At this time, Korea was divided into three strong Kingdoms: Koguryo, Paekche, and Shilla. Each of the three was predominantly Confucianist, having received Confucianism from China during the third century BC. Koguryo, the northernmost kingdom (roughly the area of North Korea today), was the first to receive Buddhist missionaries, followed by Paekche in the southwestern part of the peninsula in AD 384, and finally Shilla (the southeastern portion of the peninsula) about 527.

Once Buddhism had been introduced into all three kingdoms, it spread rapidly, and unification of the peninsula became a goal. This goal was realized by Shillan leaders in AD 668 under threat from T'ang dynasty in China. Buddhism turned out to be more influential in Korea than it had been in the China from whence it came. While the primary early influence was the Tantric school, numerous others were represented. A later strong influence was Zen Buddhism. A Shillan priest, named Wonhyo (617-686) unified the various schools of Buddhist thought which had been carried into Korea into a uniquely Korean form. One of the distinctions was the assertion that the spirit of Buddha is embodied in the universe.

During the next 13 centuries, Buddhism struggled in Korea. Confucianism and Taoism were very strong early opponents who reached their peak in the 15th century. The Koreans also have been historically attracted to various folk religions or forms of spiritism. Protestant Christianity, introduced in 1884, has more recently been the strongest competitor to Korean Buddhism.[27]

Japanese Buddhism

Buddhism was transported on to Japan about AD 552. The primary form of Buddhism introduced to Japan was the Chinese Dhyana school which later became known as Zen Buddhism. For the first 1000 years, Buddhism was predominantly an upper class religion tied in the higher Chinese culture (and writing). Still, as was the case in China and Korea, the Buddhist beliefs amalgamated with local religious beliefs, in this case, Shintoism, a form of spiritism.

As was the case in many eastern regions, the native Shintoism and imported Buddhism were able to not only co-exist, but to mutually reinforce one another.[28] Many Shinto shrines became connected with Buddhist temples.

Tibetan Buddhism

Although there were a few early adherents, Buddhism did not really become established in Tibet until the reign of King Songstan-Gampo (AD 632-649). At the time, the Tibetans followed a form of shamanism called Bon, which presented a world system consisting of a heaven, an earth, and an underworld, all of which were filled with spirits and demons. Tibetan Buddhism was embroiled in a struggle with Bon, as well as a struggle between the Indian Tantric and the Chinese Zen schools. Tantric Buddhism won out over Zen by the early 9th century, but Buddhism was not accepted in general until the middle of the 11th century.

Tibetan Buddhism has incorporated Tantric thought along with the native Bon religious concepts. As a result, there is a great concern with sacred formulas, the use of sacred words, and various devices such as the prayer wheel. Also incorporated is the Bon theory of a divine kingship which has manifested itself in the reincarnating lamas ("superior ones").

Over the centuries, a number of Buddhist sects arose in Tibet. Three predominate today, all basically Tantric. The first and largest order claims to have retain the teachings of Padmasambhava, the founding Indian monk. It is called the "Old Order."

Other orders arose over the centuries ostensibly as reformation efforts. One significant one was founded by an Tibetan named Marpa (1012-97) but is also based on Indian writers. The adherents are called the "Red Hats" in contrast with other groups whose followers wear yellow or black hats.

The strongest order today is the Gelugpa or "the Virtuous." It founded by an Indian named Atisha in 1042 as a reforming effort, and was reformed again by Tsong-kha-pa (1357-1419). It is centered in a large monastery in Lhasa and is led by the Dalai Lama and is the group most familiar to westerners.[29] Westerners call them the "Yellow hats."

Tibet has historically struggled to maintain its identity from China. During the medieval periods, Tibet was often subservient to the Mongols. Over the centuries, the Dalai Lama became the secular leader of Tibet as well as the leader of his sect. After the Manchu (Chi'ng dynasty) conquered China in 1644, Tibet established close relationships which lasted until the 20th century. When China revolted against the Manchus in 1911, Tibet joined in and achieved independence under the Dalai Lama in 1913. This lasted until 1950, when the Communist Chinese took advantage of the attention given to the Korean conflict to occupy Tibet. The Dalai Lama was allowed to keep his religious seat until the unsuccessful revolt of 1959, after which he fled to India.

Summary

The history of the Buddhist religion is complex, and much of it is lost to the modern historian. While we have not seen an overt proliferation of gods, still, we have seen a developmental process similar to other religions. Because of its nature, Buddhism, like Hinduism, tends to absorb ideas and opposing systems. As a result, there are a number of sects with many different beliefs, even within

individual countries. For example, Japanese authorities list 6 major
sects in Japan (the Pure Land and Zen sects, along with 4 other major
Japanese groups) and an unknown number of smaller groups. The
same is true in virtually every Buddhist country. This ability to assimilate also helps explain why Buddhist countries have proven so
difficult to penetrate with Christianity.

Notes

[1] The preferred date for Gautama's birth is 563 BC. Richard A. Gard
(*Buddhism*, p. 59) accepts 563, but prefers 566. H.W. Schumann, (*The
Historical Buddha*, pp. 10-13) notes that based on the data we currently have,
the date must lie between 568 and 544, depending on varying assumptions.
Both also note that Buddhists in Southeast Asia (the Theravada school) prefer
either 623 or 624, which derive from 11th century chronologies, but which do
not correlate with other data.

[2] While geographically isolated, it is evident that some travel and trade
occurred between the two realms. It is clear that trade flourished between the
Persian Gulf region and the Indus valley, on the western side of the sub-
continent, as early as 2400 BC (K.C. Jain, *Prehistory and Protohistory of
India*, p. 122 and 144-3). The settlements in the Ganges were probably part
of the outflow of that civilization. The Indus valley also traded extensively
within the sub-continent itself. While the Indus valley civilization died out
more than a millennium before the time of Gautama, at least indirect trade
must have continued throughout the sub-continent.

[3] See chapter 6 for this background. Buddhism is in reality, one of several
reform movements which occurred in Indian religion at this time.   One
contemporary teacher was Vardhamana or Jina ("The Conqueror").   His
followers were called Jains, "Followers of the Conqueror."   Vardhamana
taught release of the soul from the material world by extreme asceticism,
nonviolence (including avoiding taking of life in any form), and strict
vegetarianism. Today, Jainism has about one and a half million followers.
Historically it was proportionately more significant.

[4] There are a number of Jewish communities throughout Asia which trace
their origins to well before Christ. A number of these claim to be part of the
deported Northern Kingdom which was carried off in 721 BC. The evidence
that trade and travel between the regions goes well back into antiquity would
strongly support this possibility. Certainly Alexander, when he marched to the
Indus River by 325 BC did not feel that he was entering brand new territories,
despite the fact that no empire had stretched that far prior to his time. Tudor
Parfitt studied many of these groups in his *The Thirteenth Gate: Travels*

Among the Lost Tribes of Israel. He notes one group which claims to have descended from Jews who had fled from Nebuchadnezzar—which would put them in India during the life of Gautama (p. 60).

⁵ Apparently, the government of the realm of Sakiya was an oligarchical republic. The warrior class (*khattiyas*) was responsible for various governmental functions. They selected among themselves the local raja who presided over the state council and ran the government when the council was not in session. Thus, the term raja could be translated, prince, ruler, president, or governor (cf. Schumann, p. 3).

⁶ Buddhists acknowledge that little is known of the early life of the founder of their religion. Gautama wrote down nothing. Few, if any, of his teachings were written down until about 250 years after his death. Most were not recorded until about 400 year years after his death. This oral tradition (which became the "Pali Canon") concentrated on Gautama's teachings rather than his biography. It also was an unchecked interpretation based on his followers beliefs that Gautama was an extraordinary being. W. Woodville Rockhill (*The Life of the Buddha and the Early History of His Order*, p. vii) observes "two periods of the life of Gautama are narrated by all Buddhist authors in about the same terms (probably because they all drew from the same source for their information), the history of his life down to his visit to Kapilavastu in the early part of his ministry, and that of the last year of his life." Gard (*Buddhism*, p. 68), states that "the early veneration of the Buddha as Teacher, Victor, Great Man, and Lord or Blessed One in India and elsewhere gradually developed into a Buddha-cult which absorbed non-Buddhist ideas. . . ."

⁷ Tradition states that Gautama lived in dirty places, including cemeteries, refused to wash, wore no clothing, endured the summer sun and winter cold unprotected, and starved himself (supposedly to the point of eating but a single pea [or grain of rice] a day).

⁸ The term Bodhi (or Bo) tree actually means "tree of enlightenment." Traditionally, the type of tree was a variety of fig called pipal (*Ficus religiosa*) which is similar to the banyan (*Ficus bengalensis*), but lacks the support roots among the branches. Both are closely related to the common weeping or Benjamin fig (*Ficus benjamina*) used as a large house plant in the U.S.

⁹ Rockhill (p. 35) translates:

After having remained under the Bo tree as long as pleased him, the Buddha went to where lived the naga [serpent] king Mutchilinda (*Btang-bzung*); and he, wishing to protect him from the sun and rain, wrapped his body seven times around the Blessed One, and spread out his hood over his head, and there the Lord remained seven days in thought.

The Biblical account records the role of the serpent in human history as that of the deceiver. Of course it was the serpent in the Garden of Eden who deceived Eve. The serpent is also characterized in the book of Revelation as the dragon, the Devil, and Satan "who deceived the whole world (Rev. 12:9)." This correlation is strongly suggestive of the origin of Gautama's "enlightenment."

[10] Buddha is a title meaning "enlightened one." One of the items of controversy between the various schools of Buddhism is who might become a buddha. At the time of his assumption of this title, the concept was well known, and more than one skeptic asked if Gautama had become *a* buddha. Later this became a point in the division of the major schools of thought. The Mahayana school limits those who achieve this position to Gautama in this age, while the Theravada school maintains a much more open view. Likewise, the Mahayana school limits the achievement of nirvana to a disciplined few, while the Theravada school includes eventually all living beings, including some by *unmerited benefaction* (cf. Sir Norman Anderson, *The World's Religions*, p. 182).

[11] Sir Norman Anderson, (*The World's Religions*, p. 156) characterizes the Upanishad reformation of Indian Brahmanism as a renaissance of Hinduism. As noted in the previous chapter, it was in reality the birth of Hinduism from the Vedic eclectic animism. He does note that Hinduism was one of three major revolts against the brahminic priestly religion which took place in India contemporaneously. The other two became the Jainistic strain of Hinduism, and Buddhism. Louis Renou (*Hinduism*, p. 19) observes, "if we are to look for a global characteristic of Hinduism, we could consider it the very type of a religion of renunciation." The concept of renunciation is a rejection (or renunciating) of the reality of the world, rather than asceticism, which rejects the things of a real world.

[12] Succinctly, the steps in this path are:

1. *Right understanding*–the individual should accept Buddha's philosophy and reject other, countering philosophies.
2. *Right desires*–the individual should reject such desires as lusts, and resolve to desire only the highest goals.
3. *Right speech*–the individual should be truthful and gentle in his speech.
4. *Right conduct*–the individual's actions should reflect his goals. This includes abstention from killing any living being, from stealing, and from unlawful sexual intercourse.
5. *Right mode of livelihood*–the individual should avoid any work which produces luxury or harms any living thing. He should strive to use his talents and be useful to his fellow man.
6. *Right effort*–the individual should strive to avoid evil, to overcome evil, to inculcate good habits within himself, and to maintain those good habits already present. The ultimate goal is universal love.
7. *Right awareness*–the individual should be aware of the transitory nature of the body, of the feelings of others, the mind, and focus on

completely mastering his own mind.

8. *Right concentration*–the individual should learn to concentrate on a single object, thus demonstrating the mastery of the mind.

The goal of nirvana is based on the dual premise that all life is a mass of suffering, and the "individual" is on a continual path of transmigration from one suffering existence to another. Nirvana is the end of suffering, because it is a place where there are no desires. Thus, when one is able to master desire, one is enlightened, and achieves nirvana.

[13] There are several "biographies" of Gautama the Buddha available. All are derived from the legends written down approximately 4 centuries after his death (the Pali canon). One of the best is *The Historical Buddha*, by H. W. Schumann who supplements the scant personal data available by an extensive knowledge of Indian history and archaeology.

[14] Some of these assumptions are found in the early writings of the Brahmanas (which in an oral form may date as early as the 10th century BC). Many are evident in the *Upanishads* (dating from the same period as Gautama, the 6th century BC).

[15] Historically, we do not know the origin of the concept of "reincarnation" or "rebirth." It does not appear in the earliest proto-Hindu writings, and appears to have been incorporated in the 7th or 6th century BC at the earliest. Spiritually, it is derived from the lie of the serpent in the garden (Genesis 3:4) when he told Eve that after eating the fruit, they would not die. As such, it is a counterfeit of true rebirth which occurs only through the spiritual regeneration of the Holy Spirit as one approaches God through the redeeming work of His Messiah, Jesus Christ. The premise of "ethical conditionalism" is problematic. According to Buddhist teaching, the concept is a natural law— i.e., one automatically is reborn based on the goodness or evilness of one's deeds. However, there is no judge to evaluate the deed, or to weigh the motives–it is the "law of *kamma*." This is critical, because Buddha realized that many actions which are meant for good produce bad results. Therefore, he argued, it is the motive that determines the value for future rebirths. However, there is no clear definition of "good" or "evil" to measure the deeds (or motives) against, nor is there an authoritative source for whatever standards there are. Gautama declared that the motives of greed, hate, and delusion were negative factors (and thus by antithesis, the opposites positive factors). But he merely avers himself as the highest authority--and Buddhists adhere to his teachings.

[16] Devadatta pressed for five points: (1) that future monks would live only in the forest, (2) that they would no longer accept invitations to dine at a patron's house (i.e., eat only from the alms bowl), (3) that they dress only in robes made from rags they gathered themselves (i.e., no longer allow gifts from patrons), (4) that they should no longer live under a roof even during a monsoon, and (5) that they be strict vegetarians (Gautama decreed that

whatever fell into the alms bowl was okay to eat, whether meat or vegetable, unless the monk knew that the meat was slaughtered specifically for him). Gautama supported *encouraging* the first 3, but not the last 2. Ironically, after the schism, Devadatta moved his order to a monastery built by a patron king near the city of Gaya, where the order remained at least a 1000 years.

[17] One was buried in what is now Piprava (formerly Kapilavatthu II) and is now in the Indian National Museum in Calcutta. A second was found in Vesali in 1958 and currently belongs to the Bihar State Department of Archaeology and Museum in Patna. The third was discovered in 1981 in China, having been brought to China in 601 and put into a cave near Beijing. In 1987 it was placed on display in the Beijing Guangji temple.

[18] As can be seen, these four "truths" consist of an observation of the nature of life, an assumption (from Vedic thought) regarding the cause of that nature, a hypothetical solution to eradicate the assumed cause, and a proposed method of accomplishing that hypothetical solution. Judeo-Christian teaching indicates that while there is much sorrow in life, the cause of that sorrow is the fall of man, which is a premise validated by the historical events of the Exodus and the resurrection (cf. Romans 8:18-23). It maintains that the solution is the Messiah who is to redeem the world, again validated by the Exodus and the resurrection. The difference between Judaic and Christian teaching is whether that Messiah has already come, and whether Jesus was that Messiah (see chapters 4 and 5 above).

[19] One of the ironies of Indian history is the fact that while India had long possessed various forms of writing which date back to the Harappan culture (see chapter 6), they were predominantly used for issues considered less important, e.g., contracts and edicts, i.e., things considered not worth memorizing. This is why the teachings of Buddha were not really committed to writing until 400 years after his death (the Pali canon).

[20] This Council of Matale is recognized as valid only by the Theravada school, while the next council, held in northwest India in the first century AD under King Kanishka is recognized only by the Mahayana school. The Pali canon included three bodies of material call the "three baskets." They are the "basket of discipline" (which covers monastic life), the "basket of discourses" (which are the teachings of Gautama), and the "basket of ultimate things" (which are Theravadic philosophy).

[21] The two schools appear to differ over which has really been "contaminated" with Brahminic thought. Mahayana writers argue that the latest writings of the Pali canon (the "basket of ultimate things") are Brahminic, and that the Theravadic school is incomplete. Theravadic writers argue that the sutras of the Mahayana school are Brahminic, and that the Mahayana school is corrupt.

[22] The nature of the Buddha is another distinctive which separates the various schools. Some schools elevate Gautama's position to that of a god, while others view him as an inspired individual who revealed a philosophic truth.

This is especially true of the Theravada school, although to the western observer, the distinction is difficult to maintain. When one walks into a Buddhist temple, whether in Thailand or in Japan or wherever, one will see Buddhists performing acts of worship (burning incense and offering fruit and flowers) before a statue of Buddha, and praying. Some will admit they worship Buddha. Others will maintain, however, that they do not pray to him (although it may be unclear who they do pray to) nor do they worship him, (again, it is very unclear whom they do worship). Richard A. Gard (*Buddhism*, p. 62) states that Gautama "regarded himself primarily as a Tathagata [one who has 'arrived': experienced and transcended the imperfections of life]." Gautama appears to have perceived himself primarily as a holy man who had achieved a level that none of his contemporaries had, but it certainly was a level to which his followers would also be able to achieve. For example, on his death bed, he declared "in whatever doctrine or discipline the Noble Eightfold Way is found in its entirety, there will also be found liberated persons of true saintliness" (Marie Byles, *Footprints of Gautama the Buddha*, p. 204). It is interesting that role of miracles was greatly downplayed. While it is claimed that Gautama had the power to perform miracles, very few were observed by his followers (as opposed to contemporary religious leaders in the area who used miracles [especially levitation] to attract followers [cf. Byles, p. 101]). In this light, it is interesting to compare Jesus who did use miracles or super-normal events to validate his claims, but refused to use them to attract followers (see chapter 5 above).

[23] The Theravada school limits the title *bodhisattva* to the numerous pre-existences of Gautama and the buddhas of other ages. According to this school, there will only be one buddha each of the four ages which fill a lesser cycle of the universe (432 million years). There are 1000 of these in the life span of a universe, which is made up of one billion world systems (an earth, with heavens above and hells below). There are apparently an infinite number of life spans.

[24] The two groups are termed *manushi* buddhas (human based) and *dhyani* buddhas (other than human based). This base depends upon which of the six hierarchies of beings the individual was in at the start of the present age. The origin of the six hierarchies of beings is unclear in Buddhist thinking. Apparently, they just are. This does not explain, however, how the pleasure of the 22 levels of gods dissipates, nor why the 4 sub-human realms are regions of pain—nor why any one being is in any given realm. If the Biblical spiritual hierarchy is valid with its regions of unfallen and fallen angels, and a physical world enslaved by man's fall, one quickly sees a background to Buddhist thinking, and a valid explanation for these various levels (see chapter 2 above).

[25] The origin of this "Pure Land" school is lost. It is thought to have begun in India in the early centuries of the Christian era. Early Chinese proponents include Hui-yuan (333-416) and T'an-luan (476-542). The Pure Land school

arrived in Japan in the 12th century, where it is still the second largest sect.
The dating and the concepts involved, including the paradise in the western
regions, and the concept of faith in Amitabha who will guide to this paradise,
and his origin beyond the human race strongly suggest a Christian influence
(although obviously debased). One Indian tradition is that the apostle Thomas
evangelized India during the first century. Interestingly, some of the concepts
which show up in the supposed records of this trip (*The Acts of Thomas*, dated
at least to the 4th century) include asceticism and avoiding occupation with the
things of this world.

   [26] Tantras are Sanskrit writings covering occult rituals and control of the
physical and mental processes of the body. They arose in India in the 6th
century, where they had a profound influence on the renascent Hinduism,
especially the new Yoga school, although they also showed up in many
Buddhist writings. The goal of Tantrism was a mystical union with the
ultimate reality through meditation. The foundation of Tantric thought in
Buddhism was the unification of the male/female aspects of universal duality
by the symbolic union of a buddha (or bodhisattva) with a feminine counter-
part. The devotee achieved spiritual bliss through meditation on the symbol.
In some schools, this symbolism gave way to literal ritual sexual union,
violating the ascetic and celibate ideals of Buddhism, which led to condemna-
tion of the school.

   [27] Recent polls indicate that Buddhism may have actually fallen behind
Christianity in percentage of adherents, although Korean scholars warn that the
figures can be very misleading because of Korean social conventions which
cause many Koreans to publicly disavow what they perceive might be less
socially accepted religious beliefs.

   [28] Tour guides at various Japanese shrines have stated that 98% of the
people in Japan claim to be Buddhist, while 98% of the people in Japan claim
to be Shinto. While this is an probably an exaggeration, the actual numbers
do show significant overlap. As of 1970, the various Shinto sects claimed
67.8% of the Japanese population while the various Buddhist sects claimed
78.4% [*Japanese Religion: A Survey*, published by the Japanese Agency for
Cultural Affairs]. The difference lies in the focus each religion has accepted
in the Japanese culture. Shintoism is termed the religion of life. It is a family
(extended family including the ancestors) and community adhesive. It is the
religion for the communities to celebrate births, marriages, and community
events. Buddhism is termed the religion of death. It is the religion where one
ponders eternal issues and celebrates death.

   [29] Lama is a title of honor given to leading monks. Dalai Lama derives from
a second honorific given by the Mongol leader Altan Khan in 1578 after the
leading lama journeyed to Mongolia to revive the local Buddhism. The word
means "the sea" indicating one whose wisdom is measureless and profound.
Technically, this group is the result of a merger of the followers of Atisha and

a sect founded by a Tibetan scholar named Tshon-h'a-pa (1358-1419).

Chapter 8

Mystics Galore: Other Eastern Religions

Beyond the Hindu-Buddhist stream, there are a number of religions which fall into the broad category of Eastern Religions. Only four will be covered here, although they have not had the world-wide impact of the modern religions already covered. Historically, however, they have held a degree of significance and major impact both on their native cultures and other religions, and thus play a significant indirect role in the world scene. This is especially true of the Chinese/Japanese religions which strongly influenced the Buddhist stream in those countries. The four religions which will be covered are Zoroastrianism in ancient Persia, Confucianism and Taoism in China, and Shintoism in Japan.

Zoroastrianism

Zoroaster (also known as Zarathustra)[1] as a historical figure was a contemporary of both Daniel and Gautama the Buddha.[2] While Daniel lived in Babylon (part of modern Iraq) and Susa (southwestern portion of modern Iran), Zoroaster lived in the northeast, in an area called Khorezm along the Oxus river (in modern Uzbek former S.S.R.).[3]

Prior to the time of Zoroaster, the Iranians had continued in a polytheistic religion similar to that labeled the "Aryan Foundation for Hinduism" in chapter 6, although most of the details have been lost to history. The information available describes a hierarchy of nature gods,[4] with a number of changes from the strain which moved into India.

Varuna, the early single deity, had already moved into obscurity and had been replaced by the enigmatic figure, Vayu. Vayu is often termed god of the wind although his position might be better termed god of the air, reminding us of the situation in Sumerian.[5] Corresponding to the

early view of three realms in Indian religion, Vayu became the proto-
type for Indra. Little is known about him, except that according to
Persian mythology both Ahura Mazda (the wise lord) and Angra
Mainyu (the evil spirit) offer sacrifice to him. He is the one who
decided that Ahura Mazda (the good god of Zoroastrianism) would
have the better of his adversary.[6]

Zoroaster was a religious reformer, who claimed eight visions of
god. These visions were of Ahura Mazda (later called Ohrmazd), or
the wise lord. Zoroaster's first vision came after years of seeking
solitude and meditation. He described the figure as a radiant being.
In his vision, the visitor provided Zoroaster "an out of the body
experience" in which he was presented to Ahura Mazda and five other
radiant beings. His recollections of these experiences are called the
Gathas, part of the Avesta.

Zoroastrian Hierarchies. From these visions, Zoroaster claimed that
Ahura Mazda was the creator of the physical world and perfect
goodness. He was the ruler and creator of six lesser beings known as
the Amesha Spentas.[7] They were known collectively as the seven attributes. Below this group of seven was another large group of benefi-
cent beings created by the seven. Termed the Yazatas (the adorable or
worshipful ones) they were the various pagan gods of the earlier
Iranian pantheon. While viewed collectively as third in the hierarchy,
individually, they took on (or retained) greater importance in various
areas. One of the more important figures was Mithra, who later
headed his own cult (see p. 146 below).[8]

Ahura Mazda was seen as totally good and just. As totally good, he
could not be considered the creator of evil or even associated with evil.
Rather, another god, equal in power to Ahura Mazda, is viewed the
source of all evil. Angra Mainyu (evil spirit) is the head of an evil
hierarchy which stands in opposition to Ahura Mazda's good hierarchy.

Angra Mainyu's goal is to destroy Ahura Mazda's good creation.
He has a hierarchy that stands counter to Ahura Mazda's.[9] Where
Ahura Mazda creates life, Angra Mainyu creates death. Where Ahura
Mazda produces beauty, Angra Mainyu produces ugliness. Where
Ahura Mazda produces health, Angra Mainyu produces sickness.
Where Ahura Mazda has a hierarchy of gods, Angra Mainyu has a
hierarchy of demons. This hierarchy is the source of all evil, and is a
self existent hierarchy. Thus, evil is something that is beyond the

control of god, although Ahura Mazda is expected to ultimately triumph over his foe.[10]

The Spread of Zoroastrianism. In 539 BC, Cyrus the Great, head of the Medo-Persian empire, conquered Babylon.[11] In his new position, Cyrus ended the exile of the Jewish people and reestablished the Jewish nation as had been foretold by the Jewish prophets Isaiah and Jeremiah. While the religious beliefs of Cyrus are obscure,[12] there is nothing to suggest that he was a follower of Zoroaster. Rather, the evidence available indicates that he followed the traditional Persian pagan worship.[13]

In 522 BC, Darius I Hystapes (Darius the Great) assumed the throne. Although of the royal family, Darius was from a relatively remote branch. As a personal retainer of Cambyses, the son of Cyrus, he made a play for the throne after Cambyses died and was able to retain it. Tradition has it that Darius was taught by Zoroaster as a young boy, after his father, Hystapes, converted to Zoroaster's teachings. Records show that Darius was the first of the Persian rulers to *proclaim* allegiance to Ahura Mazda.

Under Darius and his son Xerxes, Zoroastrianism gradually assumed a strong position in the Persian Empire. It retained this position during the Achaemenid dynasty.

The Decline of Zoroastrianism. Zoroastrianism began to decline initially after Alexander conquered the Achaemenids and ended the Persian Empire. Alexander sacked Persepolis, the capital, and killed many priests. The Macedonian conquest also brought Hellenizing trends, which drew away many followers.

Further pressures came with the introduction of Christianity in the first century AD. The Christians viewed the Zoroastrians as fire-worshipers, based on the central position sacred fire held in their ritual.[14]

Zoroastrianism enjoyed a revival during the Sasanian period (a new Persian dynasty that arose from the Parthian Empire in 224). This was the time of the writing down of the Avesta, the Zoroastrian holy book.

Zoroastrianism began to decline seriously after the Muslims conquered the Sasanian Empire in the 7th century. The Muslims allowed the Zoroastrians the privileges they accorded "people of the book" elsewhere,[15] but still many converted. In addition to the economic and social pressures, many Zoroastrians struggled with the validity of their religion at this point.

One of Zoroaster's contentions had been that there would be a savior a thousand years after Zoroaster, fulfilling the fourth age of history. The Persians expected this about AD 400 (1000 years after the traditional 600 BC time frame). While the year 400 passed without any sign of this savior, the Persians did have the Sasanian Empire. Two centuries later, the Sasanian Empire collapsed under pressure from the Muslims, who proclaimed a new prophet.

The writers of the period attempted to explain the problem in two ways. Some accounted for the delay in the savior by adding three additional time periods.[16] Others looked back at the Avesta and decided that the Muslim invasion was actually the fourth age with its declining social and religious structure. Unfortunately, the cosmic signs foretold to announce it were lacking.[17] Subsequently, Zoroastrianism declined drastically.

Beginning in the 8th century, a group of Zoroastrians moved to Bombay, India to escape persecution, where they have prospered, but not grown significantly. A small group (called the Gabars)[18] also remained in Iran.

Mithraism

Mithra (a god of light) was one of the cosmic rulers (level three) in the Iranian hierarchy. His role was to preserve order or truth. As such, he was an important deity in the pre-Zoroastrian pantheon. Although Zoroaster did not mention him in the Gathas, he has continued to play a significant role in the Zoroastrian hierarchy.

After the Persian conquest of Babylonia, the cult of Mithra incorporated astrology and became a mystery religion. The normal picture of Mithra shows him slaying a bull, which is part of the old Persian creation accounts.[19] Perhaps as a reaction to Zoroastrianism, Mithraism had a late resurgence which actually carried it to Rome. There, it flourished as a serious competitor to Christianity from about AD 100 to 300. It died out about the time that Christianity became the official religion of the empire.

Confucianism

Confucius (from the Chinese Kung Fu-tzu, meaning Kung, the master) was also a contemporary of Daniel. He lived about 551-479 BC in China, where he was a philosopher and teacher in a period of deteriorating social conditions. Little is known about the actual man.[20]

The Environment. This period in Chinese history was primarily feudal, with the Chou dynasty drawing to a close and giving way to smaller states.[21] Increasing social problems produced a group of philosophers whose concern was how to solve the problems of the day. The records we have show that Confucius was one of several who tackled the problem.

The religion of the period was polytheistic, incorporating the spirits of the ancestors as well as various nature gods. A very close relationship was perceived between the spiritual hierarchy and the temporal aristocracy.[22] Behind the scenes of the aristocracy, the spirits of the ancestors and other spiritual beings executed the actual rule of the country. This spiritual hierarchy was headed by the first king, while the temporal rule was headed by the current king.

Guidance for the temporal rulers was procured from the spiritual rulers by means of divination and ritual associated with the ancestral cult. Naturally, this cult centered around the temple where the king worshipped his ancestors, although each subordinate lord would have his own temple for his personal ancestors.[23] Tied in closely with this ancestor worship was an earth altar where the spirits of the soil and grain were worshipped. Again, this was viewed as a material representation of a behind the scenes spiritual power.[24]

This juxtaposition of spiritual and temporal rule helped produce a relatively stable social situation. Over the centuries, the relatively strong central feudal authority lost its vigor, fragmenting the region into a variety of feuding states. As these destabilizing factors entered, it was natural to reflect back to earlier, more enjoyable times. This was, in essence, what Confucius did. He argued that the country needed to return to the way of the ancients.

By the time of Confucius, China was broken into a number of different states of varying size under nominal control of a central authority.[25] The larger states maintained their own power orbits of different small states. There were regular wars as they fought amidst themselves attempting to manipulate and increase the power orbits. Lu, the home state of Confucius, was one of the smaller states which experienced regular turmoil.

The Man. Confucius, himself, had been born of a poor family, and apparently had been orphaned early. As a young man he managed to work as a minor official in the government of Lu. A motivated individual, he was able to secure a good education (at a time when education was usually reserved for the rich or noble). During this period of turmoil, he traveled to other nearby states, and also used his education to form his own school.

According to the traditions, he opened his school to any one who had the intelligence and character to learn. Likewise, his fees were reasonable, within reach of even the poorest. Confucius trained a cadre who would have been unable to receive an education otherwise. He provided a solid education to a group of very able disciples.[26] As they worked into positions of influence, he acquired an extremely loyal following which enhanced his reputation.

This reputation opened up influential posts to Confucius, but he was promoted to higher positions as he demonstrated his abilities as a competent manager. While Confucius did not fall prey to the politics and intrigues which were rampant in the state government, he was also unable to institute the reforms that he had desired.

At the age of 55, he retired and journeyed throughout China, promoting his ideas. Twelve years later he returned to Lu, where he spent the rest of his life writing down his ideas and teaching. Confucius died in 479 BC, apparently a failure since he had been unable to institute his teachings in any of the governments of the region.

Confucius's Teachings. Confucianism has often been portrayed as a non religious philosophical or ethical system. It is true, that Confucius lived in an age of skepticism that deemed the traditional ancestor worship as not efficacious. Confucius himself often seems no better than an agnostic. But it is also true that the traditional behind the scenes spiritual hierarchy provided the *raison d'etre* for his system.

This is evident in the works which Confucius is reported to have compiled or written.[27] The key work was the *I Ching*, or "Book of Changes." *I Ching* is a source of divination by which the adherent could inquire for guidance from the spiritual hierarchy. It is built on a series of sixty-four hexagrams (six line patterns). Each line is either broken or unbroken (Yin or Yang). Based on a ritualistic casting of the sticks, the seeker develops a pattern which he then locates in the book and reads the associated commentary. The process is supposed to give guidance as the spirits direct the pattern of the falling sticks.[28]

In accordance with the needs of his time, Confucius focused on an ethical system designed to administer society. As a result, his concern was on issues of this world. He justified this system on what he termed "the Way of Heaven." This concept of heaven (Tien) derives from the entire spiritual hierarchy we have already noted. Thus when Confucius talked about heaven, he was not talking about a single supreme Being (or God), but a system operating behind the scenes of the material world hierarchy.

After Confucius. When Confucius died, he was a respected scholar and teacher, but his thinking had not had an immediate effect. As his students passed on his ideas, new schools arose, and several schools of thought interacted. A series of philosophers such as Mo-tzu, Yang Chu, Lao-tzu, Chuang-tzu, and Mencius (or Meng Ko) built on his ideas and expanded them.

During the Han dynasty (206 BC-AD 220) Confucianism achieved the goal that the master had sought. As the new dynasty took over (after the brief failures of the Chin dynasty), it needed trained administrators. It found exactly what it needed in the Confucianists. With their emphasis on education, justice, loyalty, and good behavior, they provided a unifying factor that enabled China to remain a single entity to modern times.[29]

Even before its success, however, Confucianism had begun to change. Confucianism appealed to the educated elite. The masses were not attracted by its emphasis on state-craft and service to the ruling hierarchies (both temporal and spiritual).

Shortly after Confucius' death, a teacher named Mo Tzu (479-438 BC) began teaching a system of love and righteousness based on the behind the scenes spiritual hierarchy. Lao Tzu (see section below under Taoism) likewise taught religious concepts which appealed to the masses. Other teachers advocated various systems, many of which were based on divination and various forms of magic.

Over the centuries, Confucianism absorbed a number of these ideas and became for all practical purposes a religious system. Three key changes can be traced. First, Confucianists incorporated Taoist influences (notably the writings of Chuang-tzu, ca. 300 BC). Second, as the Han dynasty incorporated Confucianism, it reiterated the spiritual hierarchy, emphasizing the state rule aspect. This produced an increased emphasis on gods who were concerned with national issues such as harvest yields. Finally, while Confucius gradually acquired increasing status,[30] Confucianism was not generally considered a religion until the seventh century AD. Under the T'ang dynasty (618-907) temples began to be established and sacrifices offered to Confucius.

While some resisted this trend, it was as a religion of the scholarly and administrative class that Confucianism came into modern times. With the decline of China under western pressures, Confucianism declined. As the Communists took over, they repressed it as they did all other religions.[31] Outside of mainland China, however, some have still followed the old studies, especially in Taiwan.

Taoism

Another contemporary of Daniel, Buddha, and Confucius was the enigmatic figure of Lao Tzu (traditional dates 604-517 BC).[32] Lao Tzu (meaning the old master) was supposedly an archivist in the court of the Chou emperor when he was visited by Confucius.

Taoism arose out of the same needs that produced Confucianism. The two schools, however, developed along completely different lines. Confucianism worked to reform social structure and government. Taoism sought to provide spiritual guidance in a sense of right living.

According to the records, Lao Tzu gathered some traditional teaching regarding the Tao (or the way). These, along with his own teachings were incorporated in a book called *Tao Te Ching*.[33] While relatively unknown in the West, it as been asserted that this book is second in world popularity only to the Bible.[34] In addition to *Tao Te Ching*, Taoism depended heavily on the book *I Ching* (see above, p. 149).

The Beliefs of Taoism. The term "Tao" could be translated "the way." There are a number of ramifications of this term, including order, doctrine or guidance. Thus, Taoism is a way of living life. As such, it is a philosophy.

It is much more, however, since it builds on the same spiritual hierarchical background as Confucianism. It is a way of promoting unity between the two realms. From the beginning, then, Taoism has had spiritual ramifications, and so has always been a religion.

The basic premise of Taoism is that the universe is arranged in a dualistic manner, called Yin and Yang.[35] This dualism is a dynamic one. The dynamic process (called heavenly Tao, or just Tao) was evident in the seasons, and the alternation of light and darkness. Light gives way to dark. Cold gives way to heat.

Thus, intrinsic in this concept is a principle of change. Taoists argue that stability derives from a proper balance of the two aspects. This includes the balance between the Tao of the Earth and the Tao of the Heaven (which are themselves opposites). Since Tao alone has no opposite, Tao is the absolute. Everything else is an aspect of that absolute, and is changing.[36]

Since everything is an aspect of Tao, it all must derive from it. As the source of life, Tao is called the ancestor or the mother. In this sense, the Tao is then visualized as a womb from which the visible world has come.[37] Since the entire principle is one of change, all life then must return to the womb from which it came, so life in many ways is determined.[38] As such, there is no immortality (either physical or of the soul). The goal of life is to live as best possible in accordance with the Tao.

This is the principle on which *I Ching* ("Book of Changes) operates, according to Taoism. Since life is determined by the forces of Yin and Yang (the balancing of the temporal and spiritual hierarchies), then the yarrow sticks can be used to determine the present situation, *and the change that is already determined in it.* The source of this information, originally seemed to be a sensitivity of the yarrow sticks to the dynamic state of the Yin and Yang. Later it was viewed as the spiritual hierarchy which was aware of issues that humans are normally not. In either case, the follower can then better chose the way of the Tao.

Chuang Chou (about 399-295 BC) followed Lao Tzu. His work, *Chuang Tzu*, incorporated mysticism into Taoist thought. The mystic was able to put himself beyond the Yin and Yang cycle (spiritual immortality) by becoming identified with the Tao in a mystical sense. This is done through an ascetic discipline.

The Religion. After these writers, a popular form of Taoism sprang up in the second century AD. It was a syncretistic religion which incorporated magical beliefs, traditional Chinese religious elements, and concepts from Buddhism. The incorporation of the traditional elements reinstated the hidden spiritual hierarchy. Under the Han dynasty, Lao Tzu was deified and added to it.

With the incorporation of these other concepts, a number of Taoist sects began to offer a promise of *physical* immortality. One group, called the alchemists, sought to find the elixir which produced immortality through various mixtures involving cinnabar (mercury ore) and gold (a Yin and Yang of metals). Another method used meditation.

With the promise of physical immortality, Taoism became a religion of the Chinese common people as opposed to the elitist position of Confucianism. It really took hold after Buddhism arrived and the people chose the Chinese religion over the foreign import. Early on, there was some difficulty in distinguishing the two as many Buddhist concepts were adapted to Taoism.

Over the past fifteen centuries, the Chinese have supported Confucianism, Taoism and Buddhism. In the process, Taoism has become very complex and almost contradictory. It has remained the national religion of the Chinese people up until the twentieth century. Under the Communist rule, it cannot be practiced openly in mainland China, although there is evidence that it still claims many adherents. It is still very popular in Taiwan also.

Shintoism

Shintoism is a folk religion of Japan. It is a "amalgam of attitudes, ideas, and ways of doing things that through two milleniums (sic) and more have become an integral part of the *way* of the Japanese people."[39] It is essentially a naturalistic mysticism and was probably part of the pre-historic Japanese culture (i.e., prior to the introduction of rice farming about 300 BC).

Originally, Shintoism involved worship of spirits in various natural phenomena such as the sun, mountains, trees, rivers, rocks, animals, and ancestors. This would correlate it to the early Chinese religion which was a background to Confucius. There seems to be direct correlation between the Shinto shrine with the earth altar used by the early Chinese.[40]

The overall concepts centered around maintaining a harmonious cooperation of the various spiritual forces, a concept which is more understood intuitively than intellectually. Under Shintoism, this harmony is the goal of life rather than a seeking for a transcendental world.

Key to the Japanese culture were specific forces which were viewed as guardians of the various clans or specific places. These forces drew that family or social organization together. One of these forces was the emperor as the foundation of the state. Consequently, the emperor is deified, although there are few shrines which relate to specific emperors. All of these forces make Shintoism "a racial religion."[41]

As was the case in many eastern regions, the native Shintoism and imported Buddhism were able to not only co-exist, but to mutually reinforce one another.[42] Many Shinto shrines became connected with Buddhist temples. This has influenced at least the popular conception of Buddhism in Japan.

The difference between the two lies in the focus each religion has accepted in the Japanese culture. Shintoism is termed the religion of life. It is an adhesive uniting the family (extended family including the ancestors) and the community. It is the religion for the community to celebrate births, marriages, and community events. Buddhism is termed the religion of death. It is the religion where the individual ponders eternal issues and celebrates death.

After the upheaval of World War II and the occupation, Shintoism was removed from its position as a state religion and all shrines taken away from the state. With increasing urbanization people are moving away from their homes. No longer a part of a socio-economic network, they no longer feel as bound to the traditional ways.[43] In the process, Shintoism has gradually been losing its hold on the Japanese people.

Notes

[1] Zoroaster was the Greek form of the Persian Zarathushtra. Zarathustra is the form of the name used by the German philosopher Nietzsche in his work *Also Sprach Zarathustra* (*Thus Spoke Zarathustra*). Nietzsche used Zarathustra to propagate his "God is Dead" idea (cf. "Zarathustra's Prologue," [The Modern Library Edition, p. 3], where Zarathustra says to himself, "Could it be possible! This old saint in the forest hath not yet heard of it, that *God is*

dead!" Immediately afterward, he speaks to the people, "*I teach you the Superman*. Man is something that is to be surpassed. What have ye done to surpass man?"). Nietzsche did not reflect Zoroaster's views, but fictionalized this obscure religious leader to reflect his own philosophies.

[2] The date of Zoroaster is currently highly debated. Two periods have been proposed. The traditional date is based on both Greek and Persian tradition that Zoroaster lived 258 years before Alexander, placing his dates about 618-541 BC (which would have him overlap the period of Cyrus the Great). This very specific tradition has never been refuted (cf. "Zoroastrianism," *Encyclopedia Britannica*, 1972 edition). In recent years, an alternative view has been proposed by Mary Boyce (*Zoroastrians*, 1979; cf. John R. Hinnells, *Persian Mythology*, 1985). Boyce proposes that Zoroaster lived between 1700-1500 BC, or about the time of the Aryan invasion of India. She bases her conclusion on similarities of language between the *Avesta* and the *Rig Veda*, (and thus assuming an early date for the *Rig Veda*) along with several references to obscure Greek writers (whose figures are so remote that she then ignores them [e.g., 5000 years prior to the Trojan wars {ca. 1100 BC}]). Boyce completely dismisses the later date as a "western tradition," but she never discusses the issue. The *Avesta* has two parts, the *Gathas*, containing the teachings of Zoroaster, and the remainder which is a compilation of religious works from other sources. Scholarly consensus is that the portion *outside* the *Gathas* (i.e., not written by Zoroaster) is written in much older language. The *Gathas* (the teachings of Zoroaster) are written in Middle Persian which dates from the period between the second century BC to the third century AD. Available copies actually date from the period following (third century AD to the Muslim conquest [651]). Since at one time, the *Avesta* contained a reputed 21 volumes, it is likely that Zoroaster was indeed a 6th century BC reformer, whose works were eventually added to the Persian religious tradition.

[3] The real question regarding the identification of Zoroaster is whether he served in the court of Vishtaspa (Greek Hystapes, the father of Darius I) as related by Persian tradition (cf. A.T. Olmstead, *History of the Persian Empire*, p. 107), or whether Vishtaspa was named after an otherwise unknown king who lived more than a 1000 years earlier (so Boyce, pp. 39-40 and 54-55). While there are difficulties with both views (e.g., differences in the reported ancestry between the two figures), the former view is preferable. In the latter view, Zoroastrianism lasted as a "revealed religion" for more than a 1000 years prior to its popularization. This is especially difficult when first available documents from the Persians reveal that they served other gods than Zoroaster taught (cf. the "Cylinder of Cyrus" and inscriptions from Xerxes in *Ancient Near Eastern Texts*, pp. 315-17). The first references to Ahura Mazda as the god of the Persians are not until the 5th century BC.

[4] Since our information on the pre-Zoroastrian period is derived from Zoroastrian related works, we are handicapped in attempting to reconstruct that

hierarchy. Hinnells notes, "although the gods are often described in mythical imagery, there are remarkably few myths related about them (p. 24)." Perhaps it would be more correct to state that few have survived. Both Hinnells (pp. 24-41) and Albert J. Carnoy (*Iranian Mythology*, in "The Mythology of All Races", pp. 260-319) give a delineation of this mythology, but in both cases, it is already a Zoroastrian revised view.

[5] This reflects the three-fold universe created by Varuna–the heavens, the earth, and the air in between. The initial ruling triad (Varuna, Mitra [or Mithra], and Aryaman) seemed to give each of the gods a separate domain: Varuna, who controlled the rains, had the air; Mitra, who controlled vegetation and fertility, the earth; and Aryaman, the heavens. Actually, even by this time, the situation had become complex with overlapping and changes, and there is a great amount of speculation on the actual roles. Even by the Vedic period, this triad was already being replaced by the triad of Indra, Agni, and Surya.

[6] While this obviously suggests the true God behind the scenes who has been rejected by men as they seek a god more easily understood, the figure is more suggestive of Shiva, the Hindu god who incorporates opposites. The thought is that the Iranians later split that dualistic figure into a good Vayu and an evil Vayu who then received new names to reflect their natures.

[7] The Amesha-Spentas (meaning "Holy immortals) are viewed alternatively as seven attributes of Ahura-Mazda, or "the sons and daughters" of Ahura Mazda (created by an act of the will). It has been claimed that modern adherents to Zoroastrianism do not view these in terms of a pantheon of gods as seen among the Greeks. However, they are still considered spiritual beings who act on a super normal plane to intervene in the affairs of men. While this may correlate to a position equivalent to angels, their actual role would depend upon the powers attributed to them, and the function they serve. Unfallen angels do not desire the worship of men and are quick to reprehend such actions. Fallen angels either accept such worship or direct it to another fallen angel. It is when fallen angels accept such worship that they assume the role of a god. The seven beings are:

Ahura Mazda	(Wise lord)
Vohu Manah	(Good thought)
Asha Vahishta	(Best righteousness)
Spenta Armaiti	(Holy devotion)
Khshathra Vairya	(Desirable dominion)
Haurvatat	(Wholeness)
Ameretat	(Immortality)

Hinnells (pp. 44-49) describes each of these in more detail.

[8] Mithra was viewed as the god who preserved truth by fighting the demons of the lie. Even from early Iranian mythology he was surrounded by other beings who personified various good attributes.

[9] The hierarchy of Angra Mainyu is a mirror image of the hierarchy of Ahura Mazda. Angra Mainyu is considered a non created being, and he is considered the source of the these hostile spirits. The seven hostile spirits are:

Angra Mainyu	(Lord of ignorance)
Ake Manah	(Evil mind)
Azhi Dahaka	(Lie or deceit)
Taromaiti	(False pretense)
Dush-Khshathra	(Cowardice)
Avetat	(Sickness or misery)
Meretheyn	(Destruction)

[10] This type of spiritual structure is termed dualism, because it has parallel hierarchies for good and evil which are equally strong and self contained. It is attractive because it is thought to avoid the problem of "why does God allow suffering?" It still has problems because it does not answer the question of why good and evil exist. According to the Zoroastrian "Myth of Creation," the heads of the two hierarchies lived in two realms separated by a void (Ahura Mazda dwelling in light, and Angra Mainyu in absolute darkness). After Ahura Mazda created the world, Angra Mainyu first became aware of Ahura Mazda, and attacked the wise lord in the only way possible, through his creation. According to Zoroastrianism, Ahura Mazda will someday destroy Angra Mainyu, but how this will be done is not clear. There also is no clear reason given why we should follow the hierarchy termed good and not the other, since the latter qualities would seem to be more advantageous to the self since they are self-serving.

[11] Until 549, the Medo-Persian Empire had been under the rule of the Medes in the persons of Cyaxares (625-585) and Astyages (585-550). Cyrus, a son-in-law of Astyages, rebelled, and with the help of the Babylonians assumed control, although Media was still a prime satrap. Ten years later, Cyrus turned against the Babylonians. This victory is described from two different perspectives. Daniel (Daniel 5) relates the account from inside the walls of Babylon. Herodotus (I:191) describes in detail how Cyrus was able to the city by surprise.

[12] While Isaiah 45 portrays Cyrus as one who is to be sent by God to perform this task, it is clear that it is in God's role as the Sovereign God that Cyrus is sent--not because Cyrus is perceived in any manner as following the true God. The actions described in Isaiah 45 where God states that He will take Cyrus by the right hand demonstrates not only His power over the nations, but the fact that Isaiah declares this at least 150 years in advance demonstrates that He is the God of history. Jeremiah (25:11-12, 29:10) had foretold that the exile would last 70 years. Despite the efforts of Satan and his hierarchy, God demonstrated that He would accomplish His desires.

[13] While Boyce attempts to demonstrate that Cyrus practiced Zoroastrian rituals, the evidence is at best circumstantial. Even more disquieting is the fact

that she attempts to demonstrate how Cambyses, his son, was the first to follow a Zoroastrian ritual, "next-of-kin marriage" (p. 53). This suggests a late date for the ritual, rather than a 1000 year history.

[14] Hinnells (p. 30) notes that Zoroastrians are deeply offended when labeled "fire-worshipers," although fire is considered sacred and is central to their ritual. Still, there is much in the Zoroastrian myth regarding Atar as the personification of fire. Further, he notes that the ritual fire in the temple represents the special place where god's presence is experienced (p. 125). As Kenneth Boa (*Cults, World Religions, and You*, p. 35) notes, while the Zoroastrians deny worshiping fire, "in practice, however, the Parsis [Zoroastrians] treat the fire as much more than a symbol."

[15] As declared by Mohammed, the "people of the book" were Christians, Jews and Sabaeans [a southwest Arabian tribe] (Sura 2:62). The policy for everyone else was to convert or die. Apparently, the sheer numbers dissuaded the conquering Muslims, therefore they allowed the Zoroastrians to retain their religion, carrying out a policy of humiliation at the same time (cf. Boyce, p. 146).

[16] Zoroaster had projected four ages--gold, silver, steel, and iron. The *Bahman Yasht*, a commentary from this period added brass, copper, and lead. This still didn't answer the equally burning question of whether god had abandoned them.

[17] The cosmic signs were particularly significant. A priestly group from early Persian days called the Magi tied their learning with astrology. By the time of the Seleucids (after Alexander) this group seems to have been part of Zoroastrianism, although not much is known about them. They did, however, consistently maintain a distinction between themselves and the group of Babylonians who have been given the same name. Syriac apocryphal tradition draws the Magi who worshipped Jesus at his birth (Matt. 2:1) from the Persian group, but it is impossible to be certain. We recall that Daniel served in Babylon, and after the Persian conquest, in the court of Cyrus the Great. He predicted the time of the Messiah (e.g., Dan 9:24-26). The Magi were watching for a sign, and based on that went to worship as recorded in Matthew. Given these connections, one must wonder how much Judaic thinking influenced Zoroaster?

[18] The Gabars (meaning "non-Muslim") paid the poll tax and were allowed to retain their beliefs--with several restrictions. They were concentrated in Yazd and Kerman (fairly remote cities in mountainous south central Iran), with some in Tehran.

[19] The role of the slaying of the bull is still debated. The suggestion seems to be that by the death of the bull, all other animal life was created, but how this relates to the battle between Ahura Mazda and Angra Mainyu is not clear.

[20] The earliest available biography is from about 100 BC. Since Confucianism was the official doctrine of the Han Dynasty (221 BC to AD 6), this work reflects the high regard in which the man was held. Later writers expanded on

the bits of data that were available. At the opposite extreme might lie the iconoclastic school which concludes that Confucius neither wrote nor edited anything (cf. D Howard Smith, *Confucius*, p.199). Smith attempts to maintain a balanced perspective. He states, "It is possible . . . to become too sceptical. . . . We need to constantly bear in mind that it is not possible to positively to declare that any particular passage . . . is in fact to be attributed to him. It is, however, possible to state quite categorically that after Confucius's death his teachings were taken by some of his close disciples and disseminated to an ever widening circle."

²¹ The Huang Ho (Yellow River) valley of China was probably settled early after the dispersal from Babel, although there is evidence that many elements of "civilization" arrived later (via the route north of the Himalayas [cf. G. Robina Quale, *Eastern Civilizations*, pp. 261-63]). Traditionally, the Chou dynasty united the region about 1122 BC (about a century before King Saul in Israel and 1000 years *after* Abraham) and established a feudal system among the family members of the leaders. This dynasty was beginning to break down by the time of Confucius.

²² The religion of the people seems to have carried over from that of the Shang "dynasty" (1766-1122 BC) which had ruled over the Huang Ho valley until the Chou's invaded from the west. The supreme god in the hierarchy was Shang Ti, who was identified with the founder of the race. The king was the head of the religious hierarchy, and when he died, he joined Shang Ti in heaven where the spiritual dynasty ruled over the land. As other people died, they assumed different service roles in this spiritual hierarchy (apparently directly related to their status on earth).

²³ Beyond this concept of spiritual hierarchy, there are few correlations with any of the religious concepts we have already seen in the Middle East and India. It is evident that the hierarchy which is in place cannot be related easily to any of the other hierarchies.

²⁴ D. Howard Smith (p. 34) places a great emphasis on this earth altar as the source of power for the state. He notes that when a fiefdom was conquered, it was symbolized by the covering of this altar.

²⁵ For example, Confucius in his history of Lu records only two visits from the prince of Lu to the Chou emperor between 722 and 481.

²⁶ Confucius seemed to have a hidden agenda in his school: to produce a political reform that would return China to the golden age of the early Chou dynasty. Incorporated in this (as essential elements of his ethical system) were a national rededication to the worship of the ancestor spirits (the spiritual hierarchy behind the scenes), a reinstitution of right family relationships, a re-emphasis of the cooperative effort and loyalty, and a careful regulation of all human relationships (cf. Smith, pp. 62-63).

²⁷ A collection of works called the "Five Classics" is traditionally attributed to Confucius, although some modern scholars have questioned the dating and

source. As already pointed out, there is good evidence to follow the traditional attribution. The Five Classics were the core of Confucius' educational process. The one book written by Confucius was the *Chun Chiu* or "Spring and Autumn Annals." This is a chronicle of Lu from 721 down to 478 BC. The other four works are older works which Confucius compiled and edited. *I Ching* or "Book of Changes" is attributed originally to King Wen (1150 BC) (cf. John Blofeld, trans., *I Ching*, p. 23). The last three books are *Shu Ching*, "Book of History;" *Shih Ching*, "Book of Poetry;" and *Li Chi*, "Records of Ceremonial."

[28] The inquirer uses a packet of 50 divining sticks, and a set ritual including burning incense to develop patterns from the sticks. By lying out the sticks in a sequence, one ends up with a certain number which represent either a broken or unbroken lines. The process is followed several times to develop six lines. There are 64 possible hexagrams (which allows 4096 possible answers) which are listed in the book, with an obscure text explaining the meaning of each. The explanations are vague allowing the seeker to apply general principles to the given situation. The Yin and Yang are aspects of all the dual principles in the world, e.g., dark and light, earthly and heavenly, female and male, etc. The totality is Tai Chi. The interblending of the two is thought to lie behind all substances and objects in the universe.

[29] While there were several periods of disunity (e.g., AD 220 to 589 and 907-960), the overall pattern was one of political unity. An important aid was the written Chinese language. The pictograms remained a constant, although various dialects developed (Chinese dialects are as distinct as the European Romance "languages"). However, this was a tool of an administrative class that promoted loyalty to the central government.

[30] After Confucius died, he acquired the status of an "ancestor" and thus a degree of worship by his family, even though he was a commoner. The New Text School elevated this status so that by the first century BC, Confucius was the "uncrowned king." Not long after this, the scholar class had a degree of worship for this elevated ancestor. In AD 59, Emperor Han Ming Ti established a cult of Confucius in the schools by decree. Still, it was not until Tang Tai Tsung issued a decree in 630 that temples were built.

[31] Smith (pp. 194-96), draws a interesting parallel between the Confucianism and the "Thoughts of Mao," the official dogma of Communist China. Smith notes that after Communism was firmly in control and the superficial religious aspects of Confucianism eradicated, it began to ease up on its attacks, and actually began to encourage the study of the Confucianist Chinese civilization. He foresees a revival of Confucianist studies, but not as a religion.

[32] Lao Tzu (or Lao Tan) is the traditional author of the book *Tao Te Ching*, the central text of Taoism. As in the case of Confucius, his historicity has been questioned, as well as the validity of the claims of his authorship. The primary attack has been a form of literary criticism that argues that since the

book does not maintain a "single, systematic scheme of thought" (Ninian
Smart, *The Religious Experience of Mankind*, p. 156), therefore the author did
not exist. This argument attempts to impose a 20th century concept on an
earlier age. While there are many holes in our understanding, the earliest
biography dates to 100 BC, and contains many details, such as exact villages,
suggesting at least a degree of historicity.

[33] This title could be translated "Book of the Way and its Power." While
there were books during this age, several times in the history of China, books
were destroyed as new rulers came into power and attempted to wipe out
certain schools of thought (as occurred between the Chou and Han dynasties).
Likewise, Max Kaltenmark (*Lao Tzu and Taoism*, pp. 13-15) observes that the
philosophical schools in China would put together the teachings of the head of
the school in a different manner than we would today. He states, "We must,
then, posit the existence of a philosopher who, if he did not write the book
himself, was the master under whose influence it took shape (p. 15)."

[34] Anne Bancroft (*Religions of the East*, p. 187) asserts that it is second in
number of copies sold only to the Bible. Kaltenmark states that it has been
translated more than any other work of Oriental literature. There are several
English translations, including paperback copies.

[35] Chinese dualism differed significantly from Persian dualism. Persian
dualism posited two distinct spiritual hierarchies, one good and one evil (cf.
footnote 10, p. 156 above). Chinese dualism revolves around observation of
a number of dual principles in the world, e.g., female and male, dark and
light, etc. The source of the concept is lost in the distant pre-history of China,
although it is attributed to Fu Hsi, the first "emperor."

[36] Tao is the inexpressible source of being, but it certainly is not God in the
western sense. It would be easy to visualize Tao as an abstract concept, which
is essentially what the early Confucianists did. The Taoist view was less
abstract, although still quite indefinable.

[37] Since Tao has also been termed "the mother of all things," some have
traced it back to the mother goddess cult which was quite evident earlier
throughout the Middle East (cf. Smart, p. 158). This is probably too simplistic
an explanation, however.

[38] This view is similar to that already noted in Hinduism, except for the
duration. Hinduism depends on the law of karma to return to the monistic
source. Taoism sees death as the follow-on to life (the Yin and Yang principle).

[39] Sokyo Ono, *Shinto: The Kami Way*, p. 3.

[40] Shrines are primarily established as "dwelling places" of the spirits (called
kami). They mark a place where an individual had an encounter with a local
nature spirit and are usually located in conjunction with a rock, tree, waterfall,
or some other natural phenomenon (cf. D. Howard Smith, *Confucius*, p. 34).
As such, there is an affinity with North American Indian religions which

suggests a common foundation predating migratory movement to both regions (cf. Åke Hultkrantz, *Native Religions of North America*, p. 60).

[41] As already noted (chapter 7, footnote 28), most Japanese claim adherence to both groups. While the role of both religions has dropped significantly with the increasing urbanization of Japan, most Japanese still feel equally at home in a Shinto shrine or a Buddhist temple.

[42] Ono, p. 111. He observes how it is interwoven into the culture and customs of the Japanese people.

[43] The pivotal social position of Shintoism has been a key factor which has made Japan so hard to penetrate with Christianity, for, to become a Christian, one must face castigation by his entire community. While there have been three periods of social upheavals where some significant advances were made (the civil wars [1482-1558], the Meiji era [1868-1912], and the occupation period [1945-1952]) since Christianity was introduced in 1549, still, by 1970 all Christian denominations could only claim a total of .7% of the Japanese population. It is one of the ironies of history that the traditional center for Christianity in Japan was Nagasaki, one of two cities destroyed by an atomic bomb in World War II. Still, there is no record of significant opposition to the war there, much as was the case in supposedly Christian Germany.

PART IV

REVELATIONS OF ANGELS AND MEN

Jesus Christ was the water-shed of history. His birth divides time. His resurrection divides all mankind. The key question of the past two millennia has been, "What do you do with Jesus Christ?" The world system has consistently denied the claims that Jesus made, and tries to assign Him a different role than He demands. This is evident within the one major world religion which has arisen since His death. Beginning within the Judeo-Christian tradition, Islam moved itself out of that stream over the issue of who is God's messenger. It has been repeatedly evident with groups that claim to remain within the Judeo-Christian tradition. In both situations men have arisen claiming that an angel from heaven had given them a new gospel.

Chapter 9

The Step-Brother Resurgent: Islam

Islam dates its founding and its calendar from the date Mohammed
fled from the Arabs in Mecca to Medina where he was welcomed as
the promised Messiah the Jewish rabbis proclaimed.[1] Mohammed's
teachings did show a knowledge of Old Testament history, and he
claimed to follow in the same vein as Abraham, Moses, and David.
Soon, it became clear that while he drew on a Jewish background, he
proclaimed an entirely new religion.

Judaism, however, is but one source of Islam. Mohammed also
reacted to the gospel of Jesus Christ, and the polytheistic background
of his region. Actually, the start of Islam preceded the journey to
Medina by several years.

Before Islam

Prior to the institution of Islam, the Arabs of the Arabian peninsula
were predominantly polytheistic.[2] Their worship revolved around a
number of natural objects including stones, trees, and wells. Shrines
to various gods abounded, and each town had its own patron deity.
Some also worshipped what may be called a primitive high god, who
was called Allah.[3] Several districts were also deemed holy centers of
worship, especially Mecca.

From early times, Mecca was a stop along the western caravan route
which stretched from the Indian Ocean to Palestine. Located by several
springs, it was supposedly founded by Ishmael, Abraham's son by his
wife's servant, and step-brother to Isaac, Abraham's heir.[4] By the
sixth century AD, it was a growing trade city with commerce between
Yemen and Palestine.

The center of worship at Mecca was the Kaaba. During the fifth
century, the Kaaba was a small square temple containing a number of
idols and relics. By the time of Mohammed, there were reportedly 360
different images, including an icon of the Virgin Mary. One of the

most important items in the Kaaba was a large stone believed to have
fallen from the moon (and thus sacred to the moon god, Hubal).

The Kaaba was important to Mecca as a magnet for pilgrims. From
before the earliest records, Arabs made pilgrimages to various shrines,
especially to the Kaaba in Mecca.[5] This same Kaaba (although rebuilt)
with the same black stone is the object of the fifth pillar of Islam, the
pilgrimage or Hajj.[6]

In addition to these pagan gods, three major religions were very
familiar in the towns of Arabia by the time of Mohammed. Judaism
had several large communities, especially in Yemen and the city of
Yathrib which later became known as Medina. Zoroastrian traders
from Persia passed through the area regularly, although it is not clear
if any had settled.

There were also a number of Christians spread throughout the area.
As already noted (see chapter 5, footnotes 9 through 12), during this
period Christianity was sorting out several doctrinal issues as it sorted
out apparently contradictory aspects of God, and confronted pagan
ideas brought in by converts. This area of Arabia was caught in the
middle of one such controversy; what was the nature of Jesus Christ?[7]

Mohammed the Man

Mohammed was born in 570. His family was of the Hashim clan of
the Quraysh tribe which held a high position in Mecca from the mid
fifth century on. His father had died shortly prior to his birth. His
mother died about six years later. In accordance with local customs,
Mohammed was given to a foster mother at an early age. Because of
his father's death, his foster father was a poor shepherd in Taif, a small
town in the hills southeast of Mecca.

At the age of five, Mohammed was taken into care by his grandfather, Abd al-Muttalib, who had a position of leadership in the city and
the service of the Kaaba.[8] After his grandfather died a couple of years
later, he was adopted by his uncle, Abu Talib. The death of the
leader, however, left the family without a strong leader, and Mecca
went through a period of unrest. During this period, Mohammed
tended his uncle's sheep and goats and occasionally journeyed with his
uncle's caravans where he learned to trade.

When he was twenty-five, Mohammed was recommended as a skilled
camel driver and caravan manager to a forty-year-old widow, Khadija.

Khadija had been widowed twice, and had inherited a fortune in the process. She liked what she saw in the young man and hired him to manage a caravan to Syria. After a very successful journey, Khadija decided that Mohammed would be a good manager of her estate, and a good husband, so she arranged a marriage with him.

In his new position, Mohammed became a local leader. He developed a good reputation and was well liked. During the rebuilding of the Kaaba in 595, he played a significant role (see footnote 6). With his new position, he also had the time to discuss religious issues. It was a time of flux for Mecca. Several of the Quraysh tribe had repudiated the worship at the Kaaba, and had become Christians. One key convert was Waraqa, a cousin of Mohammed's wife, who translated parts of the Bible into Arabic. Mohammed had many discussions with this learned man.

Mohammed developed a reputation as an introspective person who spent many hours in meditation. As was customary for the Arabs, Mohammed spent the month of Ramadan each year in fasting and meditation. He had discovered a cave on Mount Hira, two miles north of Mecca, where, shortly after his marriage, he began to retreat each year.

Mohammed the Prophet

In 610, during his annual retreat, Mohammed returned home to his wife trembling. He reported seeing a vision of the angel Gabriel.[9] In this vision, the illiterate Mohammed was told to read a scroll. After several protests, Mohammed read the scroll. Upon awakening, he remembered the words,[10] although he was so distraught that he considered suicide. At this point, he heard a voice telling him that the angel was Gabriel and Mohammed was Allah's messenger.

Upon his return home, Mohammed reported fearing for his sanity. Khadija quietly listened to his report and reassured him. Later they visited her cousin, Waraqa, who claimed that Mohammed had seen the same angel who had come to Moses. These two were his first disciples. Mohammed taught "surrender" (islam) to God's will which became the name of his religion. His followers, or those who had surrendered were "Muslims."[11]

For about three years, he quietly told his family and friends about his experience and accumulated maybe forty followers. In 614, he went

public with the message he had received. The inhabitants of Mecca
had no sympathy for this new faith, especially when he preached
against idol worship in front of the Kaaba. Fortunately for Mohammed, the strong tribal system preserved his life since his foes feared
retribution should they kill him. Still, the persecution increased.
Traditionally, the opposition focused on Mohammed's preaching of one
god and his rejection of the use of idols.[12]

A year later, some of his followers moved across the Red Sea to
Abyssinia (although they returned some time later). Mohammed
himself holed up in his uncle's castle east of Mecca, coming out only
during the holy month of Ramadan when a general religious truce
prevailed. By 617, the entire Hashim clan was ostracized within the
Meccan community.

By 619, the pressure was beginning to affect Mohammed. Then
within a few days, both his wife, Khadija, and his protecting uncle,
Abu Talib died. Given the circumstances, Mohammed decided it was
time to leave Mecca. First he went southeast to Taif, the scene of his
early childhood. He was chased out of the city, and returned to Mecca
severely chastened.

When the holy month with its pilgrimages and religious truce arrived
again, he met some pilgrims from Yathrib (the former name for
Medina), an oasis about two hundred miles north of Mecca. They
listened eagerly to his message because they thought he might be the
Messiah the Jewish rabbis in Medina had been proclaiming would
come. Unsure of his reception, they planned to return to Medina, and
to send a delegation the following year with word of whether Medina
would accept him.[13]

Mohammed in Medina

While the delegation from Medina returned a year later and swore
allegiance to him as the appointed Messiah, Medina was not ready to
receive him. Arrangements were made, and during the spring and
summer, his followers began slipping out of Mecca. As word of the
movements got out, the Meccans made plans to kill Mohammed. On
the night of July 16th, Mohammed and his close companion Abu Bakr
snuck out of Mecca and hid a cave in the hills above the city. They
made their way to Medina by a circuitous route, traveling at night. On
September 24th Mohammed arrived in Medina, welcomed as a king.[14]

Soon, Mohammed was acclaimed by many, if not most of the Arabs in Medina. Initially, Mohammed and his followers enjoyed good relationship with the Jews, although it was soon evident that he was not the sought for Messiah.[15] Even so, Mohammed was soon the de facto ruler of Medina. As the relationships with the Jews began to sour, Mohammed directed his followers to pray towards Mecca, not Jerusalem. He also had a revelation which authorized the killing of infidels--those who did not follow Mohammed.

After this revelation, he began sending raiding parties against the caravans traversing between Mecca and Syria.[16] Slowly, Mohammed and his men increased their operations and gathered booty. In January 624, they attacked a larger armed force at Badr, a small town north-west of Mecca. Although outnumbered, the Muslim force was victorious, which they perceived as a direct result of Allah's intervention. It was now obvious that there would be no compromise between Mecca and Medina--between the pagans and the Muslims.

A year later, the Meccans set out in force. They met the Medinans in a second battle on the slopes of Mount Uhud, just north of Medina. Outnumbered four to one, the Muslims were defeated, but the victorious Meccans failed to follow up on this overwhelming victory.[17] As a result, the Medinans resumed their raiding practices. But already, Mohammed was becoming a legendary figure and began to solidify his position with the Medinans and other Arabs.

Two years after the battle of Uhud, the Meccans prepared to attack Medina again. While the Muslims had increased their army to 3000 (as opposed the 750 before), the Meccans had likewise increased their force to 10,000. Mohammed had his men dig a large ditch on the southeastern side of the city. The two armies drew up on opposite sides, and the Meccans taunted the Medinans for their novel stratagem. After a month with just a few skirmishes, the Meccans broke camp and returned home. After the event, Mohammed's revelations again proved how Allah had intervened.

While not decisive in a military sense, the "Battle of the Ditch" swung the pendulum of momentum in Mohammed's favor. He used the occasion to wreak vengeance on the last of the Jews in the Medina area. The Jewish tribe Bani Quariza, living southeast of Medina, had assisted the Meccans (apparently they had planned a rear assault on the Muslims). Angered at their treasonous actions, Mohammed attacked their fortresses, massacred the men after they surrendered, and confiscated their land and possessions. This action changed the entire aspect of the Muslims, presenting them as a fearsome force to be reckoned with. The Medinans who had hesitated before now joined forces, and the Muslims began to expand their conquests.

The Conquest of Mecca

After the "Battle of the Ditch," it was just a matter of time before the Muslims held sway over Mecca, although it was not obvious at the time. A year after the "battle," Mecca sent word to Mohammed that it desired to make peace. Mohammed took this as a sign that the city was almost ready for the taking. He made plans to lead a small force down during the holy month disguised as pilgrims. His plan was that once they were inside, they would surprise the inhabitants and conquer the city. He was thwarted in this attempt when the suspicious Meccans encamped a large army across the approaches to the city.

Mohammed sent his son-in-law, Uthman, to negotiate while he arrayed his forces for a possible battle. Uthman returned with the Meccan ambassador who proposed a "compromise" which really was an insult to Mohammed.[18] Mohammed saw it as a wedge which would eventually give over Mecca, and, over the protests of his outraged advisors, agreed to the terms.

While he waited for Mecca, he continued his conquests of other portions of Arabia and thus gathered strength. Other Arabian tribes began to join his forces, and within two years, he controlled western Arabia from Yemen to the Dead Sea.

In 629, he performed his pilgrimage as per the agreement. He entered the Kaaba per tradition, circled the Kaaba seven times, and embraced and kissed the black stone.

The following year, a minor affair gave him the excuse he wanted to break the agreement. He gathered a large force and advanced on the city, only to take it with but a single small skirmish. Mecca belonged to the Muslims.

As ruler of Arabia, he entered the city on camelback, dressed in the traditional white garments of a pilgrim. He made his pilgrimage to the Kaaba, and had the idols removed. Beyond that, he treated Mecca with the reverence due a holy city, although he kept his political capital at Medina.

After he finished his pilgrimage, he continued his campaign. While he now had control of the key cities, there were a number of tribes which had not surrendered. These surrendered over the next two years as it became clear the Mohammed and the Muslims were firmly in control.

It was not until 631 that he proclaimed Mecca off limits to pagans, and proclaimed the revelation that all Muslims were to conduct the pilgrimage to Mecca at same time of the year as earlier pagan rituals (Sura II:197). Mohammed led the next pilgrimage to Mecca, the first for Muslims only. Shortly after that, Mohammed died, on June 8, 632, almost exactly ten years after he had slipped out of Mecca, a hunted fugitive.[19]

Islam as a Religion

Becoming a Muslim is remarkably easy. All one must do is to publicly declare "There is no god but Allah (or God) and Mohammed is the prophet of Allah."[20] According to Muslim doctrine, one must utter this but once in his lifetime--but then the other doctrines and duties become incumbent upon him. There are five of each.

The five doctrines are: faith in the absolute unity of God (i.e., a form of unitarianism),[21] belief in angels,[22] belief in the prophets and scriptures,[23] belief in the final judgment,[24], and belief in divine decree and predestination.[25]

To the outsider, it appears that Islam has maintained a fairly narrow doctrinal position and a strong degree of unity through the years. Actually, dissent and divisions began immediately after Mohammed's death. Some of the appearance is undoubtedly because of the simplicity of the doctrines. Still, lesser points have been heavily debated, and a number of sects have arisen, although many of them are as politically oriented as religious.[26]

Much of the appearance of unity stems from a greater emphasis on the performing the five duties, also called the five pillars of Islam. These are so important that some call Islam a system of orthopraxy-- "right practice". In many ways, this emphasis on right practice has obscured differences of opinion.

These five duties are: an open profession of faith (see above), prayer five times a day, giving of alms (standardized at two and a half percent of income), fasting (which specifically means Ramadan, and then from dawn to dusk), and the pilgrimage to Mecca. The *jihad* or holy war is often viewed as a sixth pillar.[27]

The basic beliefs and duties are laid down in the Qur'an, the sacred book of the Muslims. In addition to the Qur'an they have the *hadith*, the traditional collection of sayings and actions of Mohammed and his companions. These relate many incidents in the life of Mohammed, but also relate many stories which are now disputed. While the Qur'an has been standardized (see footnote 10), the *hadith* have not. In fact, there are a number of collections. Moreover, many individual *hadith* which were once accepted are now rejected.[28]

Islam After Mohammed

Most histories of Islam are essentially histories of the Arab conquest of the Middle East (which predominantly lies outside the scope of this study).[29] For the Muslim of the seventh century, there was no concept of a secular government, or of a separation between state and church. The conquest began with Mohammed, who conquered the Arabian peninsula. It continued with his successors to the point that a century after Mohammed's death the empire stretched from Spain to Pakistan.

Mohammed did not leave instructions for a successor. It was a given that as a prophet and giver of the Qur'an, he would have no successor. But Mohammed was also the head both of the Islamic state, and the Islamic religious system. Abu Bakr, a close aide of Mohammed was selected as the first Caliph (deputy). Not everyone was happy with this selection. Some felt that Ali, the son-in-law of Mohammed should have been the successor. It was here that the first divisions were experienced (although the military successes united the Arabs remarkably for the first century).

The minority that argued for Ali became known as the Shiites (derived from the Arabic *Shi'at Ali*, "the party for Ali"). As a minority, they focused on religious government, which they felt centered in infallible *imams*, who physically descended from Ali (and thus from Mohammed). When the Umayyads (a group from Mecca who originally opposed Mohammed) took over the Caliphate in 661 and moved the capital to Damascus, the Shiites reacted, were persecuted-- and flourished in number. From this political beginning, the Shiites evolved their own *hadith*, and body of law (or *Sharia*) based on it.[30] The Shiites eventually dominated in what is now Iran, Pakistan, and southern Iraq.

Although Ali acquiesced to the selection of Abu Bakr as Caliph, another segment of the Shiites did not. They were called the Kharijites. Their initial premise was that the Caliphate should be decided by a free election. The Kharijites also placed an equal stress on faith and practice.[31] The majority party became known as the Sunnis. They have maintained the mainstream of Muslim thought over the centuries. Sunni doctrine solidified in the 9th century, predominantly in opposition to concepts that other groups brought in from the outside. The basic premises of the Sunnis are a literal interpretation of the Qur'an (as opposed to rationalistic speculation), and obedience to the prophetic *sunna* (meaning literally custom, it denotes the guidelines transmitted via the *hadith*, rather than the Qur'an). The Sunnis are the dominant party in most of the Islamic world.

As in the case of Judaism (in its formation of the Talmud), most of the discussion and controversy since the time of Mohammed has been on the application of the Qur'an and *hadith*. As such, one of the predominant institutions in Islamic society has been the body of legal scholars. They have assumed a role somewhat between that of a rabbi or pastor and a judge. Currently, there are four *recognized* schools in the Sunni tradition,[32] and three in the Shiite tradition.[33]

Sufism

Even by the 8th century, mystic strains began to enter the Islamic world. As the Islamic conquests brought in outside influences, a number of groups sought to retain orthodox purity. Starting from urging right practices, the Sufite movement increasingly emphasized the use of asceticism to achieve piety.

Strictly speaking, it is not a separate sect, but a movement that transcended the various schools. For this reason, it is not listed in a number of works which cover the Islamic sects. However, there are a number of *hadith* accepted by many Sufi, that are not recognized by the traditional schools. Likewise, most Sufi meet in small groups for training in meditation. In this process, a number of orders have developed as disciples clustered around specific teachers.[34]

Modern Sects

During the past couple of centuries, there have been a number of

reform movements. Perhaps the most significant reform movement
was the puritanical Wahhabi movement founded by Muhammed ibn
Abd al-Wahhab in 1744. During a time that the Ottoman (or Turkish)
Empire (centered in Istanbul) was declining, al-Wahhab began
preaching against Sufism. He won over the strong house of Saud in
Arabia. At this time, the group could not withstand the force of the
Turks. During World War I, the Saud family was able to take power
over most of the Arabian peninsula, including Mecca and Medina.
Immediately, they destroyed a number of shrines in Mecca, and
refurbished the rest.

Over the centuries, other sects have arisen, especially within the
Shiite school with its emphasis on the *imam*. Two must be mentioned
which arose in the 19th century. Both today are considered separate
religions.

Babism. Early in the nineteenth century, a school arose in Iran which
looked for the imminent return of the twelfth *imam* (see footnote 33).
As the followers of this school of Shiite Islam spread throughout Iran,
one adherent, Mulla Husayn, encountered a young man named Siyyid
Mohammed Ali in 1844,[35] and immediately proclaimed him the
promised one they were looking for.

That December, Ali (or the Bab) made a pilgrimage to Mecca where
he proclaimed his message. The Sunni authorities ignored his
declarations, while Shiites arose in opposition. During the next three
years, however, he did acquire a significant following. The Bab was
imprisoned while the authorities attempted to decide how to handle the
situation.

He still proclaimed his message which sought to establish a society
based on Muslim principles, but which incorporated the newly
emerging scholarship and science. While he emphasized the role of the
Qur'an, he rejected many of the teachings which had accumulated
through the years.[36]

He also began to teach that since god was unknowable, he made
himself known in a number of manifestations, including the Jewish
prophets, Jesus, and Mohammed. He angered the Muslims by arguing
that Mohammed's teaching would be supplanted by a later prophet,
foretold in the Muslim teaching of a coming *imam*.[37] While the Bab
assumed this role for himself, he also anticipated another who would
follow him, which he entitled, "he whom God should manifest."

After a trial and caning in 1848, his following increased. Fighting broke out between the Babites and the Shiites. Many of the leaders of the movement were killed as the Shiites purged the country. This purge was directed by the Prime Minister when the old Shah died in 1848 to be replaced by his 16 year old successor. The Bab himself was executed in 1850 by a firing squad.[38]

Baha'i. In 1844, a young man named Mirza Husayn Ali accepted the teachings of the Bab, and began corresponding with him in prison. He took the name, Baha (Splendor or Glory). The Bab expanded that to Baha'ullah (Glory of God). After the death of the Bab, Baha'ullah became a key leader of the still growing movement.

Three years after the Bab's death, the Shah, jealous of his Prime Minister's power, had him executed. The new Prime Minister was a relative of Baha'ullah, and persuaded the Shah that the solution to the Babites was to exile Baha'ullah, rather than execute him. Baha'ullah and most of the Babites moved to Baghdad, which at that time was in the Ottoman Empire. While in prison, before the exile, Baha'ullah assumed the title, "he whom God should manifest," styling himself as the fulfillment of the Bab's prophecy.

Most of the Bab's followers accepted this declaration, but many did not. They followed Mirza Yahya, a younger half brother of Baha'ullah, whom the Bab had appointed as his successor before he died. As a result of the subsequent fighting, the Ottoman government banished Mirza Yahya and his followers to Cyprus and Baha'ullah to Palestine.[39] Baha'ullah died there in 1892.

The Baha'i or the followers of Baha'ullah, got a new start when his son, Abdul Baha, came to the United States in 1912. He established a temple and a U.S. headquarters in Wilmette IL (in the Chicago area). The world headquarters remained in Haifa. The Baha'i faith has grown from this start,[40] and established a small, but cohesive world-wide organization.[41]

Conclusion

On the surface, Islam seems to be an exception to our pattern of development from monotheism to polytheism. Still, we have seen a very familiar patterns of schism and division which reflect countering authorities within the overall group.

From its start of attempting to fulfill Judaism and Christianity without a resurrected Messiah, Islam has become a strong force in the world religious scene. Historically, it has been racked with controversy over the issue of how to adapt to a changing world. This is especially true today, as has been evident in Iran during the past decade.

Notes

[1] Mohammed's move from Mecca to Medina (formerly called Yathrib) is termed the Hijira (more properly, the *Hijra*, which means "emigration"). The Muslim calendar is a lunar calendar of 354 days dated after the official start of this emigration, July 16, 622. Mohammed arrived on September 24.

[2] A significant number of the people in Arabia were Christian, Jewish, or Zoroastrian, all of whom claimed to be monotheistic. In addition, Frederick Mathewson Denny (*An Introduction to Islam*, p.58) cites a number of Arabs before Mohammed who did not claim membership in the any of the religions cited, but who were *hanifs* (i.e., "true believers"), which he terms "generic monotheists." The Pickthall translation of this term is "upright men" (see Qur'an, Sura 3:67), but it refers to men who were not idolaters.

[3] Allah is derived from a contraction of the Arabic *al-ilah* meaning "the god." Denny (p.56) states that Allah "was the high god of the great trading city of Mecca and especially of the Quraysh tribe, into which Muhammad was born." He compares this concept with those we have previously noted in other cultures (see chapter 1 above, especially footnotes 9 and 10). It is indeed possible that Ishmael and his descendants (the probable ancestors of the Arabs, cf. S.D. Goitein, *Jews and Arabs*, pp. 19-32) had carried the worship of the true Creator God with them when they left Abraham. However, it is clear that by the time of Mohammed, whatever remained of the worship of the true God had been distorted and obscured by the introduction of pagan elements (cf. Sliman Ben Ibrahim and Etienne Dinet, *The Life of Mohammad, Prophet of Allah*, p. 47). Mohammed demonstrates this when he claims new revelation rather than any sort of restoration.

[4] The story of Abraham, Sarah, and Hagar is found in Genesis 16. Since Abraham and Sarah were old without children (86 and 76 respectively) Sarah gave Hagar (her Egyptian maid) to Abraham to be a surrogate wife and mother. When Ishmael was born to Abraham and Hagar, Sarah became jealous. The jealousy increased after Isaac was born 13 years later (Genesis 21). At this time, Hagar and Ishmael were sent off into the wilderness of Paran (central Sinai) on their own, where an angel of the Lord showed her a spring. Muslim tradition maintains that this spring was that of Zamzam at

Mecca about 700 miles southeast (Muhammad Husayn Haykal, *The Life of Muhammad*, p. 27-28).

[5] The pilgrimage to the Kaaba required the pilgrim to strip himself naked as a sign of humility, touch the sacred stone with the right hand and kiss it, circle the Kaaba seven times. Today, the circling of the Kaaba is made clothed. The stone is called the Black Stone (it is actually a dark reddish-brown). Tradition is that originally it was milky white, but became black from absorbing the sins of countless pilgrims (although Islam argues that there is no redemption for sin). Today, there are several other rituals performed during the pilgrimage. All but one date from before Mohammed (Robert Payne, *The History of Islam*, p. 5).

[6] Muslim tradition claims that the Kaaba was originally built by Adam, rebuilt by Abraham and Ishmael after the flood had destroyed it. It was rebuilt again approximately AD 595 with the assistance of the young man, Mohammed. Already Mohammed was showing leadership skills, for when the time came to replace the black stone, the four families of Mecca argued about who would have the privilege. Mohammed was picked to arbitrate. He placed the stone on a coat, had representatives from each family take a corner, carried it to the new location, where he lifted it into place. The Kaaba was destroyed again in the 10th century, at which time the black stone was broken into several pieces. These pieces have been replaced, held together by a silver setting. The Muslims claim they do not worship this stone. Still, when they bow in worship (5 times daily), it is to the black stone. Also, during the Hajj, they still touch and kiss the stone hoping for forgiveness of sins.

[7] The councils of Nicea in 325 and Chalcedon in 451 had put together the evidence and concluded that Jesus was one Person who had both fully human and fully Divine natures (cf. Charles C. Ryrie, *Basic Theology*, p. 247). This conclusion had repudiated the opposing positions of several groups in the near east. In Egypt, the Coptic church (along with the Jacobite church in Syria) had adopted a view called the monophysite (or one nature), which argued that there was only one nature which was neither fully human, nor fully divine. This conclusion also repudiated the Nestorian view of several groups in Syria, Persia and Arabia which argued that there were two natures which never mixed. The arguments between these three groups were continuing up through the time of Mohammed. He was confronted by the different viewpoints as he talked with Christians (cf. Haykal, pp. 55-56 and 61). Haykal, however, does not feel that these sectarian arguments were the only reason that Christianity did not take hold in Arabia. He states "polytheism has been the strongest appeal of paganism to weak souls in all times and places (p. 18)." No strong Christian leader had appeared in Arabia, and the Christians that were there retained many of their pagan trappings. This set the stage for Mohammed with his charismatic personality and his strong appeal to worship one god.

[8] Abd al-Muttalib set forth to clean out the Zamzam, the traditional spring

during a drought in 530. In the process, he found treasure left over from the last king in the area. He then became rich and famous as the "guardian of the well." The year 570 is called the year of the elephant because the Abyssinian viceroy of Yemen, with an army mounted on elephants, advanced on Mecca that year to destroy the Kaaba. The reason for this expedition is unclear. Haykal suggests an attempt to establish a rival shrine in Yemen (p. 40). Payne proposes that the viceroy was a Christian and desired to erect a cross over the sanctuary of the moon god (pp. 6-7). Tradition maintains that after the Meccans fled, an epidemic hit the Yemeni army which then retreated.

[9] The biographers report that this vision occurred in a dream (Haykal, p. 75). The angel named himself as Jibra'il, which is given the English translation Gabriel. Gabriel (both Hebrew and Greek) is the name of the angel who appeared to Daniel to explain the prophecies regarding the nation of Israel (Daniel 8:16), and Mary to announce the birth of Jesus as the Messiah of Israel (Luke 1:26). While the Arabic is not an exact cognate of the Hebrew, they both mean "strong one of God." This does not necessarily mean that it was the same angel. Since Mohammed preached a different Jesus (just a human prophet rather than the Messiah) than that presented in the New Testament, his testimony must be rejected (2 Cor 11:4). Paul's warning in the same passage that Satan could disguise himself as an angel of light (2 Cor 11:14), and his servants as servants of righteousness (2 Cor 11:15) is highly enlightening. Given the spiritual hierarchy which rules the world behind the scenes, it would not be surprising that Mohammed could have an actual vision of a real angel who claimed a name familiar to him from his discussions with Jews and Christians. But if Jesus proclaimed that there were be false christs (or messiahs), it then follows that servants of the father of lies would also lie.

[10] These words are recorded in Sura 96 of the Qur'an (or more usually Koran, meaning either reading or recitation). This was the first of four such visions he had in his lifetime, although there were a number of other occasions when he had "revelations." During his lifetime, the followers of Mohammed memorized the revelations. After Mohammed's death a number of those people were killed in battle with the loss of some suras. After that they were committed to writing and were gathered into several collections of differing lengths. During the early 650's (about 20 years after the death of Mohammed) Caliph Uthman organized an authoritative collection and destroyed all others. This version has 114 chapters or Suras arranged in an apparently haphazard order. Muhammad M. Pickthall (*The Meaning of the Glorious Qur'an*, p. xvi) argues that the order is "from inmost things to outward things."

[11] Islam is the denominative noun form of the verb *taslim* denoting surrender. This itself is a derived verbal form of the basic form *salam* which denotes soundness, peace, or security. Muslim is the participial form of the verb.

[12] Sydney Nettleton Fisher (*The Middle East: A History*, p. 35), states "They feared that the adoption and practice of these beliefs would, through the decline

of the pilgrimages, ruin Mecca as a flourishing commercial center." It is perhaps ironic that the exact opposite has happened as Islam has become the world's second largest religious grouping (claiming 860 million adherents by 1988). Well over a million pilgrims crowd Mecca each year as they fulfill their *hajj*.

[13] It was probably during the interim, Mohammed had his second vision. According to the tradition, Mohammed was awakened by Gabriel who took him to Sinai and Bethlehem, where Mohammed offered prayers. He then was taken to Jerusalem where he entered the Holy of Holies of the Temple (the Temple had been destroyed in AD 70) where he found Abraham, Moses and Jesus praying together. From here he was taken to the Seventh Heaven and the presence of the Creator. After being embraced by God who blinded him with his glory, Mohammed was returned to Mecca. Muslim scholars still debate the significance of this vision. Some claim that it was a physical journey. Others (based on the report of his wife that he never left her side that night) claim it another vision (Ibrahim and Dinet, p. 89).

[14] It is ironic that Payne (p. 29) and others describe the prophet's entry to Medina as that of a king, for in many respects Mohammed seems to have founded an empire as much as a religion.

[15] During this phase, many of the rules of the new religion were formulated, including making Friday the Sabbath to be different from the Jews and Christians. At this time, Mohammed directed his followers to pray three times daily towards Jerusalem. However, as Payne (p. 32) observes, "he was a man whose revelations came from a God infinitely remote from Jahweh."

[16] Shortly after the raiding parties began, one of the parties, thinking it followed the written orders of Mohammed, attacked a caravan before the end of the holy month. Mohammed berated the group for attacking in the holy month--then "received a revelation" that such an action was permissible since the greater evil was the disbelief of those attacked (Sura 2:217).

[17] Mohammed was lethargic in his leadership in this battle, and discouraged by recent defections. Payne (p. 39) comments that he did not have "the exhilarating knowledge that God was fighting on his side." In this battle, he committed several tactical mistakes, and lost control of his troops. He himself was severely wounded and reported dead. Based on this report, the Meccans returned home with their booty, convinced that the Muslims were no longer a serious threat. The sections of the Qur'an dated from this period provide great insight into that book and its revelation. Payne states "every page of the Quran during this period is filled with oaths and maledictions against his enemies, not only in Mecca, but among the Jews and "hypocrites" in Yathrib (p. 41)."

[18] According to the terms offered, Mohammed had to abandon his "pilgrimage" that year, but the Meccans would clear the city of all other pilgrims for 3 days every year following so the Muslims could conduct their pilgrimage to the Kaaba. Also, no Meccan young men would be allowed to follow

Mohammed without the authorization of their guardians, and any who did would have to be returned. Any Muslims who decided to leave and go to Mecca would be permitted to do so. This agreement was to last at least 10 years. After agreeing to the terms without a quibble, Mohammed had a revelation on the way back to Medina which proclaimed it a great victory.

[19] Mohammed died of an ordinary fever in the arms of his favorite wife, Aishah (he had 10 wives and 2 concubines after Khadija died). He was buried beneath the floor of her house in Medina. Later a mosque was erected over the site. Although he had several wives, he had no son who survived past infancy, and thus no male heir.

[20] Hassan Ayub (*Islamic Belief*, p. 17) notes that upon the recitation of this statement one is entitled to all the privileges given to Muslims. He also asserts that in the case of a mute, merely the intention to make the statement suffices.

[21] Ostensibly, the monotheism of Islam is in distinction to the pagan polytheism which Mohammed encountered in Mecca and Arabia. It is evident, that it is also in reaction to the Christian concept of the Trinity, which Mohammed had encountered early in his discussions with Christians. For example, Sura 112 specifically argues against John 3:16 when it declares that Allah does not beget. Likewise, in Sura 5:69, Mohammed argues that the Christians and the Jews believe in Allah (i.e., one God), but in 5:75, he argues that Jesus, as Messiah was no more than a mortal messenger, not part of the Godhead as He claimed to be. To do this, he must also deny that Jesus was crucified (Sura 4:157).

[22] Mohammed sets forth a spiritual hierarchy similar to that found in the Old Testament. He argues that there are two categories of angels, fallen and unfallen. Gabriel and Michael are two unfallen angels mentioned. Satan (or Iblis) is the head of the fallen angels. He was cast out of heaven for failing to bow down to Adam. Below the level of angels are another category of spiritual beings called jinn (singular: jinni, often translated into English as genie). While spiritual beings, some of them became Muslims (Sura 72:14).

[23] There are twenty-some prophets mentioned in the Qur'an (Ayub, p. 76). Most are from the Old Testament, including Adam, Enoch, Noah, Abraham, Ishmael, Jacob (who later became Israel), Elijah, Elisha, David, and Solomon. Of the writers of the prophetic books, only Ezekiel, Zechariah, and John are included. Jesus is included as a prophet as is Mohammed. Logically, there is nothing that would argue that Mohammed is the final prophet. The closest the Qur'an comes to this position is to state that Mohammed is the seal of the prophets (Sura 33:4). While S. Abul A'la Maududi, (*Finality of Prophethood*), maintains this is the case, his argument is against other Muslim schools. The Muslims maintain that the Scriptures given to the Jews and the Christians were once valid, but were then corrupted, therefore they do not accept them.

[24] For the Muslim, there is no mediator. This is one of their objections to Christianity--that Christ can be a mediator between God and man. However,

later doctrine (the mainstream), based on the Qur'an (e.g., Sura 2:255, which says no-one can intercede with God *except by His permission* [italics added]) has come to give Mohammed the role of interceder. Even so, in Islam one must face God in the final judgment *totally on one's own merits*. This will occur on what is called the Last Day, when all who have ever lived will be assembled before God. According to Muslim doctrine, each person's deeds are written in a book, which will be examined at that time. It is ironic that some Muslim traditions state that this examination will take place in Jerusalem, on the site of the Dome of the Rock (also the site of the Jewish temple). The hope is that at this time, the individual will qualify for eternal paradise. The alternative is eternal hell. Paradise has been described in very sensual terms aimed at attracting men, although spiritual delights are supposedly more important. Little is said regarding aspects of paradise for women. Muslims also believe that if they are killed in a *jihad* (or holy war), they are guaranteed paradise. Otherwise, the qualifications are unclear.

[25] Islam is often viewed as a very fatalistic religion. In some respects it is. In other respects, however, it does attempt to balance determinism and free will. Muslims are adamant that Allah is omniscient and omnipotent, and that he has the will to do anything. Still most struggle with the fact that man seems to act from his own will. They would see man's freedom limited by Allah, however (cf. Ayub, pp. 65-72).

[26] Ayub (pp. 240-51) lists three major and about fourteen minor sects which have appeared over the centuries. He notes several causes for these issues, primarily political issues and the conversion of many from Jewish, Christian, and Zoroastrian backgrounds. They brought new presuppositions which challenged Qur'anic doctrine. Ayub comments that the major issues began arising during the Abbasid period (the third dynasty of Caliphs [if the early Caliphs at Mecca were the first], centered in Baghdad during the period 754-1258).

[27] Denny (p. 123) argues that for the Muslim, the *jihad* as holy war is only one aspect of *jihad*. He would include a spiritual type of *jihad* aimed at expanding Islam through peaceful means such as preaching and establishing educational institutions.

[28] John A. Williams (*Islam*, pp. 57-58) points out how modern Muslim scholars admit that many individual *hadith* are spurious, and different schools have different bodies of *hadith*.

[29] More information on the expansion of the Islamic empire is available in any Middle-Eastern history book (such as Sydney Nettleton Fisher, *The Middle-East: A History*, although it is now somewhat dated). A well-written history of the expansion of Islam is Robert Payne's, *The History of Islam*, recently reprinted.

[30] A number of influences affected Shiite theology, including Greek philosophy, and teachings from Zoroastrianism, Christianity, and Judaism. As

a result, some of the doctrinal differences are significant. Some Shiites add to the creed, "There is no god but Allah, and Mohammed is his prophet," the phrase "and Ali is his comrade." Other differences include allowing the pilgrimage to Mecca by proxy, or allowing a pilgrimage to the tomb of a Shiite saint to take the place of a pilgrimage to Mecca. Some of the schools also incorporate teachings of transmigration, and other eastern teachings.

[31] Over the centuries, the Kharijites have been noted for their attempts to retain the purity of early Islam. Today, there are still several groups, predominantly in North Africa.

[32] The four surviving schools all date from the 8th and 9th centuries. The Hanafi school (founded by Abu Hanifa in the 760's) is considered the most liberal, and is dominant in India, Central Asia and Turkey, and the Cairo region of Egypt. The Maliki school (founded by Malik ibn Anas about 780) centered in Medina. Today it is dominant in North Africa. The Shafii school (founded by Muhammad ibn Idris al Shafii about 800) broke off from Maliki school by placing a higher emphasis on *hadith* than the traditions of Medina. Today it is primarily located in Malaysia and the regions around the Indian Ocean. The Hanbali school (founded by Ahmad ibn Hanbal in the early 800's) placed an even higher value on Hadith. This school was very conservative and was persecuted by the Baghdad Caliphate for its opposition to governmental liberalism.

[33] The Shiite schools agree with all the Sunni schools on the authority of the Qur'an and the *sunna*, however they differ regarding which *sunna* are valid. The Shiites place a great trust in their *imams* (literally, "leaders"), who they view as divinely guided. While different *imams* have founded different smaller schools, all are physical descendants of Ali and Mohammed's daughter, Fatima. Three Shiite schools predominate. The Zaydis are closest to the Sunnis since they do not regard their *imams* as more than human. The Isma'ilis (or "Seveners") focus on Ishma'il, the seventh in the line, but see an unbroken chain of *imams* to date. They see a mystic second layer of meaning to the Qur'an which is given by the *imam*. Several more notorious groups such as the Assassins and the Druze came from this branch. The Ithna 'Asharis ("Twelvers") disavow Ishma'il in favor of his younger brother Musa. They list twelve *imams* in the chain, the twelfth of which mysteriously vanished in 874, but who will reappear before the judgment day to save the world. They disavow any second level of meaning to the Qur'an, although they place belief in the *imam* as an article of faith (Muslims who fail here are regarded as inferior).

[34] Denny (pp.270-91) lists about a dozen mystics with their orders, most of which are totally obscure to Western history. One which has caught the western popular imagination is the Mawlawis (founded by the mystic Jalal al-Din al-Rumi [or Rumi] in Turkey in the 13th century), popularly called "whirling dervishes" (from the Persian *darwish*, meaning "mendicant") because

of their ecstatic dance. One other early mystic that should be mentioned is Rabi'a (who lived in Basra, Iraq late in the 8th century). Rabi'a was one of the few women who has achieved any form of status in Islam.

[35] Taking the title the "Bab," meaning "gate," Siyyid Ali-Mohammed was born in 1819, a descendent of Mohammed. From a poor family, he received minimal education. Tradition says that he had extraordinary wisdom and a spiritual nature.

[36] William S. Hatcher and J. Douglas Martin (*The Baha'i Faith*, pp. 24-25) see much of the Bab's teaching as a reaction to the "mental world that had changed little from medieval times, except to become more obscurantist, isolated, and fatalistic" which prevailed in 19th century Islam. They argue that the Islamic Republic, which was established by the Ayatollah Khomeini in Iran in 1979, typifies this mind set.

[37] The Bab attempted to incorporate all religion in his teaching. For example, he labeled the anticipated Jewish Messiah, and Jesus's promised "Comforter" (the Holy Spirit) as the same manifestation to blur the distinctions between Judaism and Christianity.

[38] The report is that the first firing squad of 750 Armenian Christian troops fired at the Bab and his companions, and when the smoke had cleared, not a shot had scored--and the Bab was missing--only to be found in his prison cell. A second squad of Muslims was assembled, and the bodies were riddled (William S. Hatcher and J. Douglas Martin, *The Baha'i Faith*, pp. 18-19).

[39] Today the Babist group has all but died out. The Baha'i religion has succeeded it, and kept the Bab and Baha'ullah's teaching alive.

[40] In addition to teaching the oneness of God, the Baha'is teach the unity of mankind, and the unity of all religion. Each religious leader is considered appropriate for his time and culture. The corollary to that is that Baha'ullah is considered the leader appropriate for today. The Baha'i emphasize their other teachings (such as the unity of religion and science, equality of men and women, universal education, and abolishing extremes of poverty and wealth) which makes their movement attractive, especially on the college campus.

[41] As of 1988, the Baha'is claimed more than four and a half million followers, worldwide. Walter Martin (*The Kingdom of the Cults*, p. 253), questions that figure based on the number of centers, and small U.S. membership.

Chapter 10

New Gods or Old?: Modern Religious Movements

Our premise has been that man is a religious creature. Further, we have posited that in his search for religious answers, man is very open to a variety of religious sources which take him away from the true God. We have observed how over the centuries, new religions have arisen. Some came from "revealed" sources, i.e., interaction with members of the spiritual hierarchy. Others developed as men attempted to answer the basic questions of life--with or without a spiritual guide. We have also traced the multiplication of sects within the various religions as individuals reported further "revelation" or posited slightly different answers.[1]

The origins of the most of the major world religions are clouded by the obscurity of pre-history. However, the process continues even today, around the world. H. Byron Earhart reports several hundred *new* religions in Japan alone within the last century and a half.[2] Edmond C. Gruss observed a newspaper report that posited 2500 to 5000 new religions in the United States since World War II.[3] A survey like this cannot even begin to cover that degree of proliferation. Therefore, we will look at a sampling to demonstrate the process.

Since we know that historically most of these new sects or religions die out rather rapidly, we have chosen samples that have shown a greater lasting power. Further, in accordance with our premises, the religions chosen are significant within the confines of the modern Judeo-Christian tradition. The movements which will be covered are: Mormonism, Christian Science, Jehovah's Witnesses, and the New Age Movement. Several other significant movements could be considered including the Unity Church, communism, and secular humanism.

Mormonism

Joseph Smith Jr, the founder of Mormonism, was born in 1805 in Sharon, Vermont. His grandfather was characterized as a universalist. His father was uninterested in organized religion. His mother was from a Presbyterian background. In 1816, after a number of moves dictated by financial need, the family settled in Palmyra, New York.[4]

Palmyra, New York was in the middle of what has been termed "the burned over district."[5] Between 1799 (the Second Great Awakening) and 1824 (under Charles G. Finney), a number of religious revivals swept through the area. These waves of religious fervor were broken by periods of cooling ardor and conflicting ideas as new immigrants entered the area.[6]

Joseph Smith Jr. was 10 when his family settled in this turbulent area. Despite his father's lack of religious concern, Joseph's mother and several of the children joined the Presbyterian church. Later, Joseph recorded that he questioned which church he should join because of the strife he saw in the churches of the period. He stated that as he questioned he had his first vision at the age of 14, where he was told that all creeds were wrong and he was to join none of the churches.[7] It is also implied that he became aware at that point that he was to receive a special revelation in the future.

Mormonism dates its founding to Joseph Smith's second vision on 21 September 1823. In this vision, Joseph Smith claims that an angel named Moroni[8] told Joseph about a collection of gold plates. The next day Joseph Smith visited the site where those plates were supposedly buried--a hill "convenient" to his home.[9] Joseph reportedly found a box with the plates, a breast plate, and the Urim and Thummim (the device used by the Old Testament High Priest to discern God's will). According to Joseph, he was not allowed to take the plates home until 1827, and even then was not to show them to anyone else.

Using the Urim and Thummim, Joseph began translating using a scribe to write as he spoke.[10] Still, the scribes were not allowed to look on the plates.[11] Eleven early followers had a *spiritual vision* of the plates, but signed affidavits as witnesses. As Martin Harris declared, "I saw them with the eye of faith."[12] The resulting book was published and the Church of Jesus Christ of Latter Day Saints was officially established in 1830.

This new church was not welcomed in its founding community and encountered increasing hostility, apparently because of the character of its founder. A year later, Joseph Smith had a revelation that the new church should move to Ohio. They settled in Kirtland (near Cleveland). Amidst the ferment of the western frontier, Joseph Smith and his teachings began to attract followers. They also attracted adversaries and hostilities. More than organizing a church, Joseph began to organize a new social order looking to the point that he would lead his people to the new promised land or Zion.

The only question was, where was this land? Scouts returned from out west with glowing reports about the region of Independence, Missouri, the start of the Santa Fe trail, and a major trade center with the Indians.[13] They formed a small colony in the area. Smith hesitated to move the rest of the group because of the failures his representatives had met in converting the Indians. In May of 1831, he had a revelation that established Zion in Jackson county Missouri, near Independence. Joseph, himself, retreated to a farm south of Kirtland where he studied, rewrote the Bible, and gave forth a number of revelations.[14]

Trouble soon erupted in the Independence region.[15] Early in November 1833, more than 1200 Mormon settlers were driven from their homes.[16] The following year, after a revelation, Joseph led a small army to help the exiles. The arrival of this small army turned the governor of Missouri against the abused Mormons. Now Joseph Smith had another revelation that his men were to return to Kirtland--their journey had been a trial of faith. He prophesied, however, that Zion would be redeemed on Sept. 11, 1836 (an event which never occurred).[17]

Back in Kirtland, he focused on church organization and expansion. He occupied his people in building a temple. He established a bank with the flimsiest of assets.[18] The first reports of polygamy emerged during this timeframe.[19]

After the bank failed, Joseph sent the key leaders associated with it on a missionary journey to England. During the next six months, the church began falling to pieces. By January, 1938, Joseph Smith had to flee west. His followers in Missouri viewed the disastrous situation in Ohio as an answer to the prayers--to bring Joseph Smith out west. He was followed by 600 followers and they established a new city, Far West, on the north side of the Missouri River.

The situation was no better here, and soon there was open fighting between the Mormons and the non-Mormons. The Missouri government entered the fray on the side of the non-Mormons and the non-

Mormons prepared to kill every Mormon they could find.[20] The
Mormons were saved by the restraint of several of the state militia
leaders as the Mormon leaders surrendered.

Joseph Smith and most of the leadership were taken to Liberty to
await trial for treason. Brigham Young, who had joined Smith after
reading the newly published *Book of Mormon* in 1830, assumed a de
facto leadership. In the following February, he led some 10,000
Mormons to Illinois.[21] Joseph Smith joined them there after "escaping"
during a change in venue.[22]

In Illinois, Joseph Smith and associates founded the city of Nauvoo
(supposedly taken from Hebrew meaning "beautiful place"). Nauvoo
quickly grew from nothing to the second largest city in Illinois in 1844.
In addition to the exiles from Missouri, the first of a large stream of
converts from England began arriving in 1840.[23]

But the tensions which led to trouble in Missouri soon arose in
Illinois. Rumors of the practice of polygamy began to circulate, as
well as tales of bizarre rites and sexual orgies. While not based on
fact, the tales soon had their effect, and a wide-spread distrust of the
Mormon community spread through the region. This was reinforced
by the formation of the Nauvoo militia, which by 1842 included 2000
men (even though city militias were common during that era).
Complicating the issue were lawsuits and internal strife.

By 1843, Joseph Smith and the Mormon leadership were actively
looking at a further migration to the west. Again, Joseph hesitated--and
the Mormons remained in Illinois, setting the stage for Joseph's
demise.

The climax was precipitated by Joseph Smith as he attempted to
suppress internal dissension. A number of close associates began to
express dissatisfaction with his tight control of the community. They
instituted lawsuits, and requested indictments against Smith on the
charges of adultery, polygamy, and false oath. They also opened a
newspaper, the *Nauvoo Expositor*. When the paper opened, it attacked
Smith's financial manipulations and his "moral imperfections."[24] Smith
responded by destroying the paper.

This action precipitated a violent reaction in nearby Carthage and
Warsaw. Mobs gathered, as well as the local militia. On the advice
of his brother Hyrum, Joseph turned himself over to the authorities and
was taken to Carthage to await trail.[25] Late in the afternoon of June
27, 1844, the militia stormed the jail, and Hyrum and Joseph Smith

were killed. Regardless of his other shortcomings, Joseph Smith had organized well. With the ruling Quorum of the Twelve Apostles, and other levels under them, the church was well organized for the next step. The only question was, who would take Joseph's place. Joseph had earlier designated his son, but he was only thirteen.[26] Others desired the position. The Twelve appointed Brigham Young, and the majority of the church followed this decision.

Several groups splintered off during this period.[27] The only significant one is the Reorganized Church of Jesus Christ of Latter Day Saints (which claims to be the legitimate LDS church).[28] It followed Joseph Smith's son, rejected polygamy and several other teachings of the soon to be Utah church.

Brigham Young organized the majority for a trek west. After months of preparation, he led the first train west in February 1846. By that fall, Nauvoo was virtually deserted. After earlier scouting expeditions, the Mormons knew exactly where they were headed--the Salt Lake Basin.[29] That did not lessen the trials of the journey.

Actually, the Salt Lake City area was merely the heart of the migration. The Mormons moved throughout the virtually empty basins of the Rockies from Arizona north to Idaho. Over 15,000 migrants left Nauvoo and other areas in the Midwest for "Deseret" (a word from the *Book of Mormon* supposedly meaning "Honeybee"). They were supplemented over the next couple of decades by skilled converts from England and other places in Europe.[30]

As early as 1849, Utah attempted to be admitted to the union as a state. Concern over the tight control the church had over the civil government prevented this, however. It was not until the 4th church president proclaimed a new revelation that supposedly banned polygamy in 1890 that Utah[31] was finally admitted as a state.

Over the years, a number of new revelations have occurred as various social issues arose. For example, in 1978, priesthood rights were granted to blacks for the first time.[32] These new revelations, however, have been on relatively minor issues. The church doctrine continues to follow the polytheistic teachings that Joseph Smith wrote in the 1830's.

Christian Science

The founder of Christian Science, Mary Baker, was born in New Hampshire on July 16, 1821. Her father was a strict Calvinist, whose theological positions troubled her all of her life.[33] She was the youngest of six children, three sons and three daughters.

When she was twelve, she was scheduled for confirmation in the Congregational Church. However, Mary could not accept the idea of unconditional election and eternal punishment since she knew that at least some of her older siblings had not professed faith. In the turmoil, Mary became sick.[34] Although she soon recovered, Mary developed a reputation as a sickly young person.

At the age of 22, Mary Baker married George Washington Glover of Charleston, South Carolina. The couple moved to Charleston where she was exposed to the sufferings of slavery. Six months after their wedding, George contracted yellow fever and died. Mary moved back to her New Hampshire home. Three months later (September 1844), she gave birth to a son whom she named after his father.

As a result of depression and illness, she was unable to care for her child, and the infant was given to a neighbor to nurse. Later, Mary and her family contracted Mahala Sanborn, the daughter of a blacksmith to care for the young child. The nurse became extremely attached to the child.

Mary's mother died in 1849, and her father remarried about a year later. After her mother's death, Mary again entered a period of depression/illness. Near the time of the remarriage, Mahala planned to marry and move away. She desired to take George Jr. with her, and after serious discussion, it was decided that she should do so (apparently because of Mary's ill health).

Three years after her father's remarriage, Mary remarried to a Dr. Daniel Patterson (a dentist, but also trained in homeopathy).[35] One of her goals in this marriage was to regain custody of her son. After the marriage, Dr. Patterson refused to allow that. Her time of marriage with Dr. Patterson was one of ups and downs. She was bed-ridden much of the time, and her husband tried to establish a solid practice. After 12 years of marriage, much of it spent in separation, she divorced him on the grounds of adultery and abandonment.[36]

Before that occurred, however, the couple heard of a Phineas Parkhurst Quimby, a healer from Portland, Maine. Quimby, a doctor "by courtesy only," had studied mesmerism (hypnosis). He had reached the conclusion that much of healing depended on the patient's mindset.[37] Mary went to visit Quimby, and after talking to him decided that she was healed. They communicated for the next four years, until Quimby died in 1866.

The relationship between Quimby's teachings, and Mary's teachings is complicated and highly debated.[38] Christian Scientists totally downplay any relationship at all, and argue that they are entirely two different items. While there is no doubt that Mary Baker Glover founded the religious organization, an honest appraisal of the situation reveals that many of ideas she cohesed and popularized derived from this period and her study with Quimby.[39]

Both followed a principle which might be labeled simplistically as "mind over matter." The primary difference was that Quimby viewed the mind as stronger than matter, while Mary came to the conclusion that matter is unreal and the mind is the only true reality.[40]

Mary Baker Glover later dated her discovery of the principles of Christian Science to the aftermath of a fall on February 3, 1866 (less than a month after Quimby died) in Lynn, Massachusetts, where she hurt her back. She claimed that she was told that she would not survive. The doctor claimed otherwise.[41]

For the rest of her life, Mary Baker worked on refining and publicizing her teachings which at that time she called Mind-Science. Convinced that her "miraculous" healings were scientific, she was determined to find a way to reconcile it with her view of God and the Bible.[42] Her first effort at a book closely resembled material she had written for her associate, Quimby.[43] Over the next several years she revised and edited, and finally renamed her process "Christian Science."[44]

During this period, she began teaching and set her goal at establishing her own church.[45] Since she was unable to find a publisher for her book, a couple of associates pooled the money to pay for the publication of the first edition in 1875. This book, *Science and Health* was continually revised throughout her life.[46] This was also the year that the first Christian Science meeting was held, the first step towards the church she desired. This goal was realized in 1879, when on August 23, the state charter recognizing the incorporation of the Church of Christ, (Scientist) was issued.

In the interim, Mary Baker married her third husband, Asa Gilbert

Eddy, one of her students and followers, in 1877.[47] Eddy died in 1882 of heart disease. Mary Baker Eddy refused to accept this verdict, but argued that he had died of "mesmeric poisoning."[48] While the basic premise of Christian Science is the power to heal, the sad fact is, that there is no demonstrated case where Mary Baker Eddy actually healed an organic disease.[49]

During the next decade, Mary Baker Eddy dedicated herself to advancing her church and her book. The church was originally Congregational in structure. With increasing dissent, she dissolved the church in 1892, and reorganized it--with full control retained in a board of directors that she appointed.[50] In 1895, the "Mother Church" in Boston was dedicated.

She became more and more reclusive after 1889, retiring to Concord, New Hampshire where she concentrated on meditation and writing. She still retained control of her church until she died in 1910. To ensure that there would be no false teaching, she dictated that there would be no teaching at all. Each church would have a First Reader and a Second Reader instead of a preacher. In place of the sermon, the First Reader would read selected passages from *Science and Health*, without any explanatory remark. The Second Reader would read from selected passages from the Bible, again without remark. The passages were originally selected by Mary Baker Eddy. Today they are selected by the board of directors.

Jehovah's Witnesses

The movement called Jehovah's Witnesses must be considered to have two founders. The organization was actually founded by Charles Taze Russell, born in 1852 in Pittsburgh, Pennsylvania. His replacement, Joseph Franklin Rutherford, so changed the organization, that many Jehovah's Witnesses are unaware of the role that Russell played in its history.[51]

Little is known of Russell's youth.[52] Like Mary Baker, he had a problem accepting the judgment of God taught in the Presbyterian and Congregationalist Churches in which he was raised. By the age of seventeen, he had characterized himself as a skeptic. Soon after that point, however, he came into contact with the remnants of the Adventist group which had followed the teachings of William Miller who had predicted the second coming to be in 1844.[53]

Based on his readings, he became strongly interested in Bible study and in 1870 organized a Bible class.[54] Over the next several years he became disillusioned with the Adventist view of a physical return, and began teaching a spiritual return. On this basis, he joined with N. H. Barbour in 1876. This joint venture included publishing a magazine and a book.[55]

By 1879, Russell had split off from Barbour over the issue of the atonement.[56] He started his own publication, *Zion's Watch Tower and the Herald of Christ's Presence*. This publication led to rapid growth for the movement. Within a year, some thirty groups had sprung into existence in seven states. It became organized in 1881 as the Watch Tower Tract Society with Russell as its manager, and was given a legal charter in 1884.[57]

Russell continued to pursue his primary interest of examining Old Testament prophecy. In 1886, he published *The Divine Plan of the Ages*, which was the first of a planned seven volume series. Originally the series was to be entitled *Millennial Dawn*, but later it was changed to *Studies in the Scriptures*. The final volume was actually published by Rutherford after Russell's death. At the same time, he continued to produce the *Watchtower* on a bi-weekly basis. These writings were the only approved method of understanding and interpreting Scripture.[58]

Undaunted by Miller's two-fold failure to date the second coming, Russell jumped in and proclaimed that the second coming would be in 1914.[59] This and subsequent attempts by the movement to nail down the date have failed.

In 1916, Russell died on a train passing through Texas. Russell had left a will giving his desires for succession by a committee of 5 which he named. However, he also had implemented a program for voting at business meetings that allowed each individual one vote for each ten dollars contributed to the movement. In January 1917, Joseph T. Rutherford was elected president in what in retrospect appears a ramrodded vote.[60]

Almost immediately, Rutherford began making changes which affected the structure and beliefs of the movement.[61] The major change, which sullied the reputation of the Jehovah's Witnesses for years, was the decision not to support the entry of the U.S. into World War I. Beyond telling his followers to avoid military service, he identified the U.S. government as part of the present day Babylon which was to pass into oblivion.[62] Rutherford and seven associates were tried on conspiracy charges under the Espionage Act of 1917. All were found guilty and sentenced to prison. Rutherford was sentenced to 20 years in the Federal Penitentiary at Atlanta.

Although the Brooklyn offices were closed, Rutherford continued to run the organization from prison. After the war and the Allied victory, Rutherford requested a retrial. On May 14, 1919, the convictions were set aside, and the organization revived.

This period saw the transition of the movement from a loosely knit group of "Ecclesias" with much local autonomy to a centrally controlled organization. Rutherford held the control.[63] He became a very prolific writer who displaced Russell as the guide of the organization. Rutherford also changed the name of the movement to Jehovah's Witnesses in 1931. He gave the movement the organization it has today. It was under Rutherford that the Jehovah's Witnesses achieved a reputation of an antagonistic group that was embattled against the world.[64]

Rutherford died on January 8, 1942 of cancer. He was succeeded by Nathan H. Knorr, the then vice-president. Knorr continued Rutherford's policies.

While Rutherford had attempted to eradicate all corporate memory of his predecessor, Knorr attempted to solidify Rutherford's status as the key writer and innovator. Under Knorr, all new publications come from the Watchtower headquarters unsigned. Under Knorr's leadership, the movement grew from a little over 100,000 to over one and a half million.

Knorr did institute the New World "translation" of the Bible. This work is a carefully orchestrated editing of the Biblical text so as to incorporate the movement's doctrines are incorporated.[65] Like both of his predecessors, he dated the end of world, placing it with much pomp and anticipation in 1975. Again, the date passed without incident.

Knorr was replaced by Frederick Franz in 1977. This period seemed to be a high point for the movement. It is estimated that more than a quarter of million followers left the movement in the 1970's. Franz died at the end of 1992, and was replaced by Milton G. Henschel.[66]

During recent years, there is evidence that the movement is changing once again. The tone of the literature has been scaled down over the past decade. There are rumors that local groups are holding Bible studies, and some key leaders have been removed because they questioned the Biblical base of some doctrines. What remains to be seen is how much the group with change under the new leadership, as the generation that was to remain through Armageddon passes away.

The New Age Movement

There is still widespread disagreement on how to characterize the New Age Movement. Despite its widespread familiarity and influence, a 1991 poll showed that only about 28,000 Americans claimed to be "New Age."[67] While certain writers have expounded key philosophies supposedly of the group, there is no cohesive external organization.[68] Its adherents deem it best understood as a network of groups or movements.[69]

In reality, what is currently called the New Age is the mere visible manifestation of a spiritual hierarchy, with the higher levels in the not physically visible spiritual realm.[70] As such, we see only pieces of the whole, and often these pieces seem but remotely connected. The primary visible connection lies in certain beliefs and teachings held in common.[71]

The New Age is perceived as a phenomenon of the 1980's. Actually, it is the most recent manifestation of eastern mystical thought, albeit in somewhat new packaging. Originating with the *Upanishads* in the 6th century BC, we have already seen how this mystical thinking predominated in Hinduism. We have also seen its spread into Buddhism and its inculcation as a mystic form of Islam in the Sufite tradition.

This Eastern Mysticism was introduced into Western Culture by a variety of means during the 1800's. Examples include the various religions which derived from Quimby,[72] spiritualism which swept the U.S. during the 1850's, and the Transcendental Movement of 1836-60.[73]

Another source was the efforts of Helena Petrovna Blavatsky. During the 1850's and 60's, she traveled throughout the world (notably India, Tibet, and Egypt) as she studied mystical religion. She ended up in New York in 1873, where she founded the Theosophical Society in 1875.[74] She published her foundational work, *Isis Revealed*, in 1877 which built on a theme of an unknown ancient civilization in India which was the foundation of all wisdom.[75] The headquarters of the society was moved to Adyar, India in 1879. Blavatsky incorporated occultism and spiritism in her works as was especially evident in her second book, *The Secret Doctrine*.[76]

After Blavatsky's death in 1881, the society split several times. In 1907, Annie Besant, a British social reformer, was elected president of the remnant of the international society. In 1909, she "discovered" a young Hindu named J. Krishnamurti, whom she adopted and proclaimed the world teacher and new messiah.[77] In 1929, he renounced this claim and went his own way. Besant ran the society until her death in 1933. She was followed by Alice Bailey who wrote 24 books from 1919-1949 supposedly dictated by the Ascended Master, Djwahl Khul. The term New Age comes from these books.[78]

From its founding the Theosophical Society has remained a somewhat obscure fringe group. The philosophies underlying it, however, have been spreading throughout Western Society, and since the 1950's have surfaced in a number of forms. This surfacing began with the counter-culture "Beatnik's" of the 1950's who were fascinated by the Zen school of Buddhism.

They were replaced by the "hippies" of the 1960's. The philosophies underlying this generation were definitely from the east, including their gurus, and the use of drugs for mystical experience.[79] The 1970's began bringing the New Age concept out. Several sources point to 1975 as the year the movement went public (exactly one century after the founding of the Theosophical Society).[80] But it was a combination of Marilyn Ferguson's *The Aquarian Conspiracy* in 1980 and Shirley MacLaine's *Out On A Limb* in 1983 which made the New Age a known entity.[81]

Beginning with the 1970's, a number of "channeled" works have supplemented Blavatsky and Bailey's writings.[82] Actually, one of the first was Jane Roberts, who began to channel the being Seth in 1963. Since her death in 1984, a large number of other channelers purport to be channeling the same being.

Today, the New Age movement is more diverse than ever. Further, there have been several overt marketing schemes of New Age concepts, including the rainbow (which as the symbol of God's promise to Noah of no more floods is also a Jewish and Christian symbol). The multiple references of the symbols creates complications as it sometimes becomes very difficult to sort out what actually New Age.

Is there a conspiracy as Ferguson and others argue?[83] Based on the evidence of New Age writers such as Ferguson and Saraydarian, we conclude that some type of conspiracy is involved. However, we would observe that the actual conspiracy aspect of the movement is in the spiritual realm, behind the scenes, rather than in the hands of men. Men and women who believe that they are directing a world changing movement by their involvement in some aspect of the New Age are likely to find themselves pawns being moved by the actual world-rulers.

Summary

As we have surveyed the history of these movements, we have spent much of our effort on the founders of the first three. That is because in many respects, these individuals molded and defined the movements (the New Age Movement is much more diverse in its origins). That factor is one reason these movements are often termed "cults."

One scholar of Church history observed that "cults" manifest specific needs in the lives of their founders. Out of these needs, the founders construct a theology which then brings them out of their lethargy.[84] In our survey of several modern religious movements, we see aspects of this observation. More than this, we see a consistent patter of rejection of the True God in the lives of the founders.

In the case of Mormonism, Joseph Smith hungered for prestige and answers to several questions about the history of the Americas. He struggled with the number of denominations on the frontier. He also struggled with the issue that his father would have nothing to do with religion, while his mother was at least moderately religious. He lived in religiously turbulent times. The *Book of Mormon* provided some answers. While that book may have had its source in a novel, it is still possible that Smith encountered a member of the ruling spiritual hierarchy in his quest. As leader of a religious movement who had actual visions his hungers were met in a way that he was never able to receive as a treasure hunter and seer in his youth.[85]

Mary Baker Eddy struggled early with a father who retained a strong sense of justice and legalism in the church.[86] From an early age, she proved extremely sensitive to suffering, whether among the farm animals, or the turbulence of school life. She also struggled with her health. She sought a god who would not be judgmental, and found a god of the mind--suffering was of the material world, and thus not real. While Mary Baker Eddy did not report the visions that Joseph Smith, Buddha, and Mohammed did, this does not rule out an interaction with the spiritual hierarchy, especially after her encounters with Quimby.

The issue of Charles Russell is more difficult. Like Mary Baker

Eddy, he struggled with God's sovereignty, and yet became a strong Zionist based on his study of prophecy and God's control of history. His successor, Joseph Rutherford, seems to have been interested in the power aspects--he built a personal empire. Both built a religion which centered around their position as president, which probably answered their individual needs, or at least their desires.

The New Age movement raises a different question. Russell Chandler observes that "when people lack faith in a transcendent Creator God, they turn to the magic, rituals, and human devices of the Broad Way to find meaning and empowerment."[87] We have observed that historically there has been an effort on the part of the spiritual hierarchy to produce a counterfeit designed to draw men away from worship of the true Creator God. As such, the New Age is a hybrid-- the old lies wrapped in new packaging. In the next chapter we will examine why this package is so attractive to men.

Notes

[1] We have observed how the world and mankind in general are in spiritual rebellion against the Creator God. The factors of human nature which incite men to establish their own religion would come under the category of psychology of religion. That would be an entirely different study.

[2] H. Byron Earhart, *Religions of Japan*, pp. 21-22. Earhart reports several dozen of what he calls the "*larger* New Religions" (italics added), and several hundred total. The largest two, Tenrikyo (came out of Shintoism) and Soka Gakkai (came out of Buddhism), report several million followers each. The Japanese Agency for Cultural Affairs (*Japanese Religion*, pp. 225-6) reports that Tenrikyo has severed any ties with its Shinto past, while Soka Gakkai is still considered a Buddhist sect. Tenrikyo demonstrates the process. It was founded when Mrs. Miki Nakayama was possessed by a "creator deity." She then committed to spread the message of this spirit. This movement claimed almost two million adherents as of 1970.

[3] Edmond C. Gruss, *Cults and the Occult*, p. 5. Gruss cites a *Los Angeles Times*, December 1, 1978 article which places this number "within recent years." It must be observed that the first three movements covered in our sample all arose in the 19th century, and that these are but a few of the movements from that period. In fact, it will be observed that a number of other movements are tied in with the history of these three, including the New Age.

[4] This was the first stable home for the Smith family from the moment that

Joseph Sr. and Lucy Mack had married in 1796. As Leonard J. Arrington and David Bitton (*The Mormon Experience*, p. 9) put it, "a combination of poor judgment, bad luck, and adverse circumstances conspired to keep them continually on the move."

[5] The "Burned Over District" is the portion of western New York which received its name from the number of revivals which swept though it during the late 18th/early 19th century. Kenneth Scott Latourette (*The Great Century: Europe and the United States*, "A History of the Expansion of Christianity," vol. 4, pp. 192-96) notes that there was an emotional element to all revivals. This swept many people along with those experiencing genuine conversion. After a number of passes, many who did not experience genuine conversion became inured to the emotional draw. Cf. Fawn Brodie, *No Man Knows My History*, pp.13-15.

[6] In the zeal of the era, religious questions dominated the local culture, as did a number of questions regarding the origin of the Indians and Indian artifacts.

[7] This vision was not recorded by Joseph Smith until 1838 (approximately 18 years later), although he published his first autobiographical sketch in 1834 (Brodie, p. 24). Some have questioned the reporting delay, suggesting that it is a later invention. Mormon history argues that Joseph Smith reported it to his family (Arrington and Bitton, p. 5). Arrington and Bitton (p. 7) note, "in the strict sense, historical research can never either confirm or disprove alleged supernatural appearances." We have already noted (see chapter 9, footnote 9) how spiritual beings from Satan's hierarchy disguise themselves as angels of light, so we cannot rule out an actual vision. The question then is whether the gospel that Joseph Smith (and Moroni) preached is the same as that presented in the New Testament. A number of discrepancies show that the "gospel" according to Joseph Smith is different (cf. Col 2:18 and Gal 1:8-9), and thus must be rejected. We might note, however, that there is strong evidence that the gist of the historical theme (if not much of the book itself) of the *Book of Mormon* is from another source–a novel written by Solomon Spaulding (or Spalding), a Congregationalist pastor from Pittsburgh. Beyond the similarity of themes, a common use of a strange form of King James English, and use of the same names; the manuscript for Spaulding's novel disappeared from a print shop which Sidney Rigden, an early companion of Joseph Smith, frequented (cf. Wayne L. Cowdrey, Howard A. Davis and Donald R. Scales, *Who Really Wrote The Book of Mormon*). It should be noted that Spaulding wrote two novels. Cowdrey, Davis and Scales argue the *Book of Mormon* copies his *second* novel. The Mormons argue that his *first* novel was nothing like the *Book of Mormon*.

[8] Moroni, an angel, was supposedly the last prophet of a branch of the Jewish nation that migrated to America and then vanished. The fact that Moroni is called both an angel and a former prophet illustrates one of the non-

Christian tenets of Mormonism. According to Mormon doctrine, there is a multiplicity of gods. All men pre-existed in, and came from the same spiritual realm. After death, they become angels or gods (apparently in different spiritual realms from which they came--specifically, either in the celestial, terrestrial, or telestial kingdom [in descending order, none of which is a place of punishment or hell]). The system is very complex, but succinctly, it is a polytheistic belief which maintains that its god was once a man (i.e., Adam) and that men will become gods. Cf. Walter Martin, *The Kingdom of the Cults*, pp. 176-198 for an evaluation of the theological system.

[9] The hill (Cumorah) is where Mormon (the father of Moroni) supposedly buried the gold plates in the 4th century AD. Mormon was allegedly a general of one segment of the Jews who migrated to the west coast of South America. This group was called the Nephites (supposedly from the Northern Kingdom). The other segment was the Lamanites. These two segments were descendants of Lehi, supposedly of the tribe of Manasseh, part of the Northern Kingdom, but who lived in Jerusalem, part of the Southern Kingdom until he left about 600 BC. The hill Cumorah was the location of the last major battle between the two segments in AD 385. This battle virtually annihilated the two tribes. The book is called the *Book of Mormon* after Moroni's father.

[10] The Urim and Thummim were a pair of items kept in the breastplate of the Old Testament High Priest. They were used to discern God's will, probably as either a "Yes-No", or an "Either-Or" form of lot. They were never used to translate. The Jewish nation spoke and used Hebrew for religious purposes from its inception to date (even after the use of Hebrew was lost in the exile--centuries after the supposed time of Lehi's migration to the Americas [cf. the discussion on the Mishnah in chapter 4 above]). According to Joseph Smith, the plates were written in "Reformed Egyptian." This was still some ten years before the *publication* of the first translation of hieroglyphics from the Rosetta stone which was discovered in 1799, but not widely publicized. Champollion completed his initial work in 1821-22 (cf. Brodie, pp. 50-52). Smith purports that Jews from Jerusalem, instead of writing in Hebrew, used a script that no one else is recorded as using. In 1967, papyri which Joseph Smith supposedly translated as the final section of the *Pearl of Great Price* were located in the Metropolitan Museum. When Mormon Egyptologists translated these papyri they discovered that it was not the *Pearl of Great Price*, but part of the standard funerary texts buried with each mummy (cf. Cowdrey, Davis and Scales, pp. 22-24). Every attempt to validate the source of the *Book of Mormon* as historical has ended up a failure-- which has then been downplayed by the church.

[11] After two months of "translation," the first 116 pages disappeared. Supposedly, Smith's scribe Martin Harris took them with him and Lucy Harris stole the manuscript, apparently destroying it. She told Smith, "If this be a divine communication, the same being who revealed it to you can easily

replace it (Brodie, p. 54)."   Smith was in a quandary for he feared that
enemies might publish the stolen pages in an altered form (Brodie, p. 55, cf.
Arrington and Bitton, p. 13).   Loftes Tryk (*The Best Kept Secrets in the Book
of Mormon*, pp. 18-29) argues that in reality Joseph used the "loss" as a means
to change the story and scribes.   We might contrast this situation to that of
Jeremiah, whose scroll of prophecy was burned by the king (Jeremiah 36:20-
32).   The Lord repeated the revelation, adding to his previous judgments.
Note, further, however, the difference here between revelation and translation.
Lucy Harris' admonition still rings true—if it *was* translation and the original
was still there, why could not Smith re-translate?   This is especially true if the
Urim and Thummim did the translation.   Still, Smith was unable to "re-
translate" the lost portion, and the following summer he received a "revelation"
that *he was not to do so*.   Rather, another set of plates, previously undisclosed,
covering the same period were provided "which covered exactly the same
period in Indian history as the lost manuscript. . . . Once he had translated it,
he could go back to the old plates and carry on, presumably from page 117
(Brodie, p. 55)."   The fact that the resulting English *Book of Mormon*,
"translated" from plates hidden since AD 420 (and apparently previously
translated from Hebrew into the mysterious "Reformed Egyptian"), contains
extensive quotations from the 1611 edition of the King James Bible is also
extremely suggestive (Jan Karel Van Baalen, *The Chaos of the Cults*, p. 191).

[12] Brodie, p. 78.   The declarations of two groups are included in every copy
of the *Book of Mormon* as the "Testimony of Three Witnesses," and the
"Testimony of Eight Witnesses."   The first three witnesses *all* later quarreled
with Smith and left his church, although two returned.   Three of the eight also
"apostatized" and left the church, never to return.

[13] One of the basic tenets of Mormonism is that the Indians are the descendants of the lost ten tribes of Israel (cf. chapter 4, footnote 16).   "The Latter-
day Saints had the responsibility, according to this theology, of introducing this
'covenant people' to the *Book of Mormon* and teaching them the ways of their
ancestors, who once followed Jesus" (Arrington and Bitton, p. 145—which, of
course, ignores the point that the supposed migration occurred approximately
600 years prior to Jesus).   According to Mormon doctrine, when Jesus spoke
of other sheep, he referred to the Indians, and after his resurrection, he
appeared to the Nephites in America, where he taught them the same Christianity he left behind in Palestine (cf. James E. Talmage, *A Study of the Articles
of Faith*, pp.. 141 and 172).   The descendants of the Nephites reverted to a
pagan religion.   Soon after the founding of the church, Joseph sent out a
number of representatives to various tribes, where they met with little success.

[14] Another basic tenet of Mormonism is that the Bible is accurate, *in so far
as it is translated correctly*.   One of Joseph Smith's goals was then to
"retranslate" the Bible, correctly, although there is no indication of what he
was using as an original.   The revision added a prophecy in Genesis 50

To Serve Other Gods

foretelling Joseph Smith, and a prophecy in Isaiah 29 foretelling the *Book of Mormon* (among other changes). After Smith's death, this "revision" was published by the Reorganized Church. The Utah church does not use it, asserting that Smith never completed his final revision (cf. Brodie, p. 117). In addition to the *Book of Mormon*, two other books were published by Joseph Smith during this period--*Pearl of Great Price*, and *Doctrine and Covenants*. These three books constitute the real authority of Mormonism, not scripture. In fact, Mormon doctrine derives primarily from the last two.

[15] A number of factors were at work, including the slavery issue (most of the Mormon converts were Northerners and anti-slavery, while many of the old settlers were pro-slavery), the normal frontier mindset, and the communal nature of the settlement (Brodie calls it "communistic," [p. 140], but Karl Marx was but 15 years old at the time).

[16] Temporarily, they settled in Clay county, across the Missouri river. Walter Martin (*The Kingdom of the Cults*, p. 153) cites Sydney Rigdon's "Salt Sermon" as an instigating factor, which "virtually challeng[ed] the whole state to do pitched battle with the 'saints.'" At this time, Rigdon was a close associate of Joseph Smith and one of the leaders of the Missouri group. Later he was expelled from the church.

[17] Joseph stylized himself as a prophet of God, yet his record as a prophet was abysmal. The Biblical mandate for prophets was one hundred per cent accuracy (Deut 18:20). The penalty for failure was death. Brodie (p. 417) notes that Smith "was nimble in extricating himself from failure." Despite his record and the questionable source of his authority (cf. footnote 13), Smith maintained to his death that the *Book of Mormon* was "the most correct of any book on earth, and the keystone of our religion (Brodie, p. 276)."

[18] This period was one of extreme speculation, which turned into the panic of 1837 when President Jackson forbade U.S. agents to accept anything but gold or silver in payment for land. Watching land prices escalate, and remembering his promises to the Missouri group, Joseph Smith decided to form his own bank in the fall of 1836. It was denied a charter, but Smith decided to open it anyway. Caught up in the crash after Jackson's decree in July 1836, the bank became one of many that crashed. At this time, it was calculated that the Mormon leaders owed non-Mormons over $150,000 (close to $1.5 million in 1991 dollars). Ironically, the nation-wide crash saved Smith's reputation, casting the bank failure into the light of a petty indiscretion, rather than fraud (Brodie, pp. 194-207).

[19] The charge of polygamy has continued to haunt the Mormons to this day. Early in the history of the church, Joseph Smith is reported to have had at least two affairs (Brodie, pp. 119 and 181). After these, he introduced the idea of a restoration of polygamous marriage with a revelation (cf. Arrington and Bitton, p. 197). The fact that this "revelation" was quietly kept within the inner circle for several years demonstrates how the leadership perceived the

revelation would be received. It did not become widely known until the 1840's. *Doctrines and Covenants* [section 132] states that it was recorded in 1843 (this new revelation supposedly overrides an earlier one in the *Book of Mormon* which forbade polygamy [Jacob 2:24-27]). It did not actually get promulgated until after Smith's death in 1844, although rumors of its existence began as early as 1835 (Brodie, pp. 186, 297-308, and 334-47). Mormon historians have attempted to downplay the issue, emphasizing the Mormon practice of "sealing for eternity" which could be construed as a "spiritual marriage." Arrington and Bitton (pp. 185-205) argue that it was only a minority (they calculate 1% of all Mormons up to the late 1970's) who participated in the practice. Further, they claim most participated only out of obligation to the church (including the men). While they declare that it enabled many women on the frontier to avoid spinsterhood, they aver that it created more problems than it was worth. When Utah attempted to be admitted to the union (in 1890), church president Wilford Woodruff proclaimed later revelation which stated that the Mormons were willing to obey the law of the land (but which did not actually reject the previous revelation). Still the issue of polygamy arises regularly. On June 26, 1986 (almost 100 years after the practice was "banned"), the *Dallas Morning News* carried a major article regarding a case in Colorado City AZ which had split the town. Even more recently, a Utah lawyer, Elizabeth Joseph, wrote an article proclaiming her participation in a polygamous marriage (with 8 other wives)--and extolling the social benefits of the system (*Dallas Morning News*, May 24, 1991).

[20] Mormon histories of this period (up until the migration to Utah) present the Mormons as a peaceful people who were violently attacked without provocation. Even Brodie (pp. 208-255), who takes a jaundiced view of Joseph Smith has this perspective. In reality there was give and take on both sides. Arrington and Bitton [p. 57] observe, "the fatalities, with few exceptions, occurred when Mormon defensive units were functioning as troops in the field"). Still, it appears that the non-Mormons both here and later in Illinois over-reacted. But, it must also be observed that these frontier men perceived a direct threat to their well-being. The nature of the threat they perceived has not been fully explored. Arrington and Bitton (p. 46) state "there was the repugnance felt for a religion that challenged many accepted values. . . . most felt that its beliefs were superstitious, disgusting, repellent. What was apparently most galling was a mixture in Mormonism of what seemed to outsiders as a primitivistic reversion to 'unenlightened,' even 'un-American,' beliefs."

[21] The estimates range from a low of 8000, to between 12,000 and 15,000.

[22] Reportedly, Smith was able to bribe the sheriff who then sold them horses. Their guard "conveniently" got drunk and went to sleep. Smith and those with him fled on the horses.

[23] Arrington and Bitton (p. 68) report that several factors, including, "the

206   To Serve Other Gods

depression of 1837, social oppression, Chartist schemes, and disillusionment with the Church of England" made the English open to conversion. Portrayal of America as a New Eden persuaded many to migrate west.

[24] William Law managed a curiously subdued newspaper, given the times and the purpose for which the *Expositor* existed. Still, the first issue contained affidavits that the long rumored "revelation" authorizing polygamy did exist—within the higher levels of leadership. It was a bomb-shell in the community. As Brodie (p. 375) puts it, "Those who were practicing polygamy feared a massacre by the anti-Mormons; those who had been kept in ignorance were overwhelmed by the realization that all the surreptitious gossip might after all be true."

[25] Joseph had a premonition that this would be the end. He is reported to have told his family, "If Hyrum and I are ever taken again, we shall be massacred, or I am not a prophet of God (Brodie, p. 383)." Actually, Joseph did not need the mantle of prophethood to anticipate that event. His statement must also have been colored by a certain degree of depression as he could see his empire unraveling. Brodie makes an interesting observation, which would certainly be apropos regarding Smith's claim to be a prophet. "Joseph lacked one useful capacity of the natural leader; he was unable to gauge the repercussions of his policies upon the opposition (p. 156)."

[26] This designation of successorship is denied by the Utah church (cf. Brodie, p. 381).

[27] There are still several listed in the *Handbook of Denominations in the United States* . None have a membership of more than two or three thousand. All have denounced polygamy, but still adhere to the *Book of Mormon*. Other teachings vary. Sidney Rigdon headed a small group called the Church of Jesus Christ. It moved east to Pennsylvania. James J. Strang took another group to Wisconsin, where he was murdered in 1856. A third group is centered in Independence, Missouri, where it is holding the land (lots) for the anticipated building of the temple that Joseph Smith had foreseen. It is called the Church of Christ (Temple Lot).

[28] The Reorganized Church claims that it is the direct continuation of the Latter Day Saint Church. This has been upheld by two court decisions [1880 and 1894] which have ruled it the legal continuation of the original church. This position has been further vindicated by the 1983 discovery of a document in Joseph Smith's handwriting naming his son as his successor. The Reorganized Church did not cohese until 1852, and did not select Joseph Smith III as its president until 1860. Although still characterized as "Mormon" in doctrine it swung back strongly towards orthodox Christianity. One of the most significant points of deviation from orthodoxy is that it has an open canon of Scripture—leaving room for further revelation.

[29] At that time there was one white settler in the basin, a trapper named

Miles Goodyear. The Mormons bought him out.

[30] Census reports showed that Utah territory (just part of the settled area which included Nevada, Utah, and parts of Idaho, Wyoming, Oregon, California, and Arizona), had a population of 11,380 in 1850, and 143,963 in 1880. The actual migration stretched out over a several year period with the first 1700 arriving the summer of 1847. The number who perished en route is unknown.

[31] The Mormons desired to name their state "Deseret." When it entered the union as a territory, it was given the name "Utah" after the Ute Indians in order to give it a more neutral appearance.

[32] Under early Mormon teaching, the blacks were viewed as under the curse of God, and thus not eligible for the priesthood. This position came under attack during the civil rights movement. In 1978, a new revelation opened the priesthood to blacks.

[33] The primary struggle that Mary Baker Eddy had was with the concept of judgment. She refused to accept a God who would condemn anyone to Hell (cf. *Retrospection and Introspection*, p. 13). Likewise, she could never accept the concept of the fall of man (as recorded in Genesis). In fact, she stated that if the fall had occurred, it destroyed the entire foundation of Christian Science (*Miscellaneous Writings*, p. 14).

[34] Her biographers report that when she was examined by the pastor before the congregation, she answered regarding her salvation, "I can only say in the words of the psalmist, 'Search me, O God, and know my heart; try me, and know my thoughts; and see if there be any wicked way in me, and lead me in the way everlasting'" (Sibyl Wilbur, *The Life of Mary Baker Eddy*, p. 31). She never professed faith in Jesus Christ, and didn't join the Congregational Church until she was 17.

[35] Homeopathy is a form of medical practice which is based on the "law of similars." This principle posits that a cure can be effected by giving a drug that in a healthy person would produce the same symptoms being experienced by the patient.

[36] Mary spent her time in bed reading and learning. She read the Bible, many of her husband's books on homeopathy, and talked frequently with neighbors who discussed religious issues. A key area of thought was the healings recorded of the early church. During this period, Mary had close relationships with a number of Spiritualists (such as Mrs. Kidder in Groton), which her biographers have felt compelled to downplay.

[37] Quimby had never studied actual medicine, but had worked with several mesmerists during the period, including Charles Poyen, a French hypnotist, and John Dods, who had published a book called *The Philosophy of Electrical Psychology*. Working with Dods, he concluded, "it was not the medicine that was doing the curing but the patient's confidence in the doctor or medium (Wilbur, p. 85)."

³⁸ Walter Martin (*The Kingdom of the Cults*, pp. 112-17) unequivocally states that her book *Science and Health* "is filled with numerous plagiarisms from the manuscripts of P.P. Quimby and from the writings of Francis Lieber, distinguished German-American publisher and authority on the philosophy of Hegel." He shows a number of examples on these pages. As an ironic aside, Martin also ascribes the manuscripts of Quimby as the actual source for another gnostic sect, the Unity church. In this case, Quimby's writings were used by Charles and Myrtle Fillmore in their magazine *Thought* and other Unity publications.

³⁹ Salem Kirban, *Christian Science*, p. 23. Kirban cites a number of manuscripts written by Quimby and Mary Baker Glover which clearly show that at the time she recognized Quimby as a primary source of her learning. (Cf. Stephen Gottschalk, *The Emergence of Christian Science in American Religious Life*, p. 68). Wilbur, a Christian Science follower, argues that there is no relationship between Quimbyism (which she terms "Mesmerism gone astray" [p. 90]) and Christian Science. Yet on the same page, she tells of the first visit to Quimby: "Gazing fixedly into her eyes, he told her, as he had told others, that she was held in bondage by the opinions of her family and physicians, that her animal spirit was reflecting its grief upon her body and calling it spinal disease. He then wet his hands in a basin of water and violently rubbed her head, declaring that in this manner he imparted healthy electricity. Gradually he wrought the spell of hypnotism, and under that suggestion she let go the burden of pain just as she would have done had morphine been administered. The relief was no doubt tremendous. Her gratitude certainly was unbounded. She was set free from the excruciating pain of years. Quimby himself was amazed at her sudden healing; no less was he amazed at the interpretation she immediately placed upon it, that it had been accomplished by *Quimby's mediatorship between herself and God.*" (Italics added. This is the actual distinction between the two. Quimby viewed the healing a physical process, Mary viewed it a spiritual one.)

⁴⁰ Gottschalk quotes H.L. Mencken who stated, "Christian Science is the theory that since the sky-rockets seen following a wallop on the eye are an illusion, the eye is one illusion and the wallop is another (p. 66)."

⁴¹ Cf. Kirban (p. 20), who quotes an affidavit sworn by Dr. Cushing in 1907. Kirban also cites other documents from Mary where she claimed to have originated the principles in either 1853 or 1864.

⁴² Cf. (*Science and Health*, p. 109) where she states

Christian Science reveals incontrovertibly that Mind is All-in-all, that the only realities are the divine Mind and idea. . . .

For three years after my discovery, I sought the solution of this problem of Mind-healing, searched the Scriptures . . . . I knew the Principle of all harmonious Mind-action to be God, and that cures were produced in primitive Christian healing by holy, uplifting faith; but I must know the Science of this healing, and I won my way to absolute conclusions through divine revelation, reason and demonstration. The revelation of Truth in the understanding came to me gradually and apparently through divine power. When a new spiritual idea is borne to earth, the prophetic Scripture of Isaiah is renewedly fulfilled: 'Unto us a child is born,' . . .

[43] Wilbur (p. 159) states: "She began to systematize her ideas and to write out a new manuscript, not entirely different from those she had prepared for Quimby. She still believed Quimby had shared the truth of divine healing with her, . . ."

[44] Actually, it is neither "Christian" nor "Science" in the normal definitions of these terms. Eddy stated in *Retrospection and Introspection* (p. 39), "I named it Christian, because it is compassionate, helpful, and spiritual." In *Miscellaneous Writings* (p. 22), she stated "Science is neither a law of matter nor of man. It is the unerring manifesto of Mind, the law of God, its divine Principle."

[45] Wilbur records Mary telling a companion in the early 1870's "I shall have a church of my own some day (p. 211)."

[46] In 1906, the decision was made to stop numbering the editions after 416 (William Dana Orcutt, *Mary Baker Eddy and Her Books*, p. 101). Ostensibly *Science and Health* was to promote Bible study. Since it was to be the determination of how to interpret Scripture, its real goal was to supplant the authority of the Bible. By 1893 she was seeking to publish this "Bible study aid" in "Bible paper" which Oxford press limited solely to Bibles and Prayer Books (Orcutt, p. 64) so that it would be "more similar in physical appearance" to the Bible.

[47] She was 56, but on the marriage license wrote in 40. Cf. Martin, pp. 111-121 regarding Mary Baker Eddy's personal integrity.

[48] Kirban, p. 31. She actually issued a statement containing this view to the *Boston Post*, June 5, 1882. Obviously, Mary Baker still had certain ideas regarding the mesmerism that she had learned from Quimby.

[49] Martin quotes Alfred Farlow, Chairman of the Publications Committee of the Christian Science Church and President of the Mother Church in Boston as stating that "he did not know of *any* healing *ever* having been made by Mrs. Eddy of *any* organic disease in her lifetime (p. 141)." Even the authorized biography by Wilbur which puts events in the best possible light reports at best circumstantial evidence.

[50] Today the board consists of five permanent members and is self perpetuating. All other churches are considered branch churches of the "Mother Church," although they have their own directors and by-laws (which must adhere to the provisions of the "Mother Church").

[51] Russell's organization was called the Watchtower Bible and Tract Society. When Rutherford took over, he changed the name (as well as many of the

tenets) of the group. Gordon E. Duggar (*Jehovah's Witnesses*, p. xix) states from personal experience, "It is most doubtful that even Jehovah's Witnesses themselves know the history of their organization. Their early publications are not available to them from The Watchtower Society, and their history is published in changing biased stories."

[52] Apparently Russell did not write a journal as did Joseph Smith, nor did he authorize an official biography as did Mary Baker Eddy. Herbert Hewitt Stroup (*The Jehovah's Witnesses*, p. vi) notes the difficulty he experienced in researching the movement: "Since the movement is in many ways a 'secret' one, the members were loathe to give me openly any information." Since the movement does not write of itself, the best information comes from former members who have left the organization, however, as indicated by Duggar, many of them suffer from ignorance regarding their own organization.

[53] William Miller was a zealous Bible student who felt that he could determine the date of the Second Coming by the numbers given in Daniel 8. He concluded that it would be on March 21, 1843. When the event did not occur, he recalculated that it would be the following year, which proved to be another failure. Miller admitted he was wrong, and told his followers to return to their regular churches. Some didn't go, including Ellen G. White a follower who then claimed several visions. The crux of these visions changed the nature of the Second Coming. The year 1844 was now the time that Christ entered the "Holy of Holies" to investigate the lives of His people to determine who is eligible to receive the benefits of the atonement. Her group united with two other Adventist groups to form the Seventh Day Adventists. According to Stroup (p. 15), Russell used the Great Pyramid of Egypt to assist in his determination of the Second Coming.

[54] Russell's qualifications were meager. He assumed the title of "Pastor" (although later the movement disclaimed any clergy and lambasted groups who possessed a clergy) without any credentials. He claimed advanced training in theology and Biblical languages. In a lawsuit in 1913, he had to admit that he had neither--after he had perjured himself (not only on this issue but on the issue of ordination). In addition to these misrepresentations, Russell also ran into problems regarding "Miracle Wheat" which the movement sold for a $1 a pound (government investigation subsequently revealed its quality to be less than average), sending "imaginary" sermons to newspapers for publication (the imaginary part was in regard to where [and if] it was delivered), and a divorce suit from his wife who found him conceited, egotistic, and out of line with other women (cf. Martin, pp. 35-42, and Anthony A. Hoekema,*The Jehovah's Witnesses* p. 13).

[55] N. H. Barbour headed a small splinter Adventist group in Rochester NY. He also taught a spiritual second coming and published *The Herald of the Morning*. Russell joined in the publication of this periodical and the book *Three Worlds or Plan of Redemption*. Included in the book was the teaching

that Christ had returned in 1874 (invisibly).

⁵⁶ The exact nature of this argument is somewhat uncertain. Anthony A. Hoekema (*The Jehovah's Witnesses*, p. 11), states that Barbour "began to deny that the death of Christ was the ransom price for Adam and his race." Martin (p. 87) notes that in later writings, both Russell's and the organization's positions were unbiblical since they view the work of Christ as incomplete "until the survivors of Armageddon return to God through free will and become subject to the Theocratic rule of Jehovah."

⁵⁷ The date of this charter, December 13, 1884 marks the official beginning of the movement which has come to be known as the Jehovah's Witnesses. Many date the founding of the movement to the organization of the first Bible study group in 1870. Even the scraps of evidence available suggest that this group was at best a forerunner. Horowitz (p. 51) argues that because of the changes brought in by Rutherford, "it is not correct to say that Pastor Russell was the founder of 'Jehovah's Witnesses.'"

⁵⁸ As in the case of the other movements covered in this chapter, the ostensible authority for the Jehovah's Witness Movement is the Bible--but only as interpreted by the movement. In the case of the Jehovah's Witnesses, this is a nebulous authority. During the life of Russell, the authority centered in him and his *Studies in Scriptures*. Martin (p. 41) states, "Think of it-- according to the 'Pastor' it is impossible to understand God's plan of salvation independent of Russellite theology, and to relegate one's study to the Bible alone void of Russell's interpretations is to walk in darkness at the end of two years." After Russell, this authority shifted to Rutherford, who gradually displaced Russell, then totally undermined him. Russell's works are no longer available from the society, and Jehovah's Witnesses are not allowed to read his works. In fact, according to former Jehovah's Witnesses, many do not know that Russell ever had anything to do with the group. Since Rutherford, the authoritative documents are unsigned.

⁵⁹ Apparently, he had earlier marked 1874 as the year of the return (Duggar, p. 35), but nothing happened. In 1878, he decided that the year was to be 1914. When nothing occurred in 1914, he moved it to 1915, which also proved a bust (Duggar, pp. 37-38). After these failures, it was decided that in reality, 1914 marked the end of the age of the gentiles, and Jesus now assumed the role of the Millennial King in heaven. His successors attempted to determine the date of Armageddon. Rutherford proclaimed 1925, and his successor, Knorr opted for 1975. Both, of course, passed without incident. Hoekema's comment on the situation is extremely apropos: "In trying to show how this final fulfillment occurred, however, the Watchtower authors become quite badly confused (p. 94)."

⁶⁰ Rutherford was the chief legal counsel for the movement at the time. Although not mentioned in Russell's will as one of the proposed five directors, Rutherford's name was the first suggested for the presidency, and the

nominations were closed immediately after his nomination (Stroup, pp. 13-14). William J. Schnell (*Thirty Years A Watch-tower Slave*, p. 34) maintains that the subsequent anti-war editorial policy of the *Watchtower* was deliberately construed to take the spotlight off the manipulation Rutherford used to gain the presidency. David Horowitz (*Pastor Charles Taze Russell*, pp. 36-37) records how Russell was a strong Zionist as a result of his prophetic interests, and how Rutherford changed the entire tone of the movement, including making the Jehovah's Witnesses the "new people of the covenant, the second choice of Jehovah."

[61] Many of the followers of Russell did not appreciate the results. Some broke off and formed their own movements. Stroup (pp. 14-15) includes the Standfast Movement, the Paul Johnson Movement, the Elijah Voice Movement, the Eagle Society, and the Pastoral Bible Institute of Brooklyn. Martin adds the Dawn Bible Students Association (p. 34).

[62] Duggar (p. 15) observes that while Russell discouraged military service, he told his followers to go ahead and join the army if they had to, but to seek non-combatant positions. Rutherford's troubles were not only with the U.S. government. The Canadian government banned all Watchtower publications because of their seditious and anti-war positions.

[63] William Schnell describes this transition in his book *Thirty Years a Watch-tower Slave*. Apparently, individual earlier groups had the potential of being orthodox Christian in most facets (p. 14). Under Rutherford, this freedom was curtailed as he began to dictate a standard non-orthodox belief pattern which all Jehovah's Witnesses now must follow (cf. pp. 26-28).

[64] Duggar argues that Russell has already laid the foundation for that attitude when he states "the theme of us vs. them, anti-everybody, was developed even more (p. 15)." Incidents like the previously discussed anti-war stance in 1917 suggest the Rutherford played a much larger role in the development of this attitude. However, since much of the history of the group is necessarily derived from the limited "official" material, part of this impression may be a result of Rutherford's suppression of his predecessor's works (cf. Duggar, pp. 25-26).

[65] Both Duggar, (pp. 25-37), and Martin, (pp. 63-85) discuss in detail how this "translation" differs not only from other translations, but misrepresents the original languages. Duggar (p. 63-67) notes that none of the "translation" committee had adequate credentials for the task. Of the five, only one had any language training and he was unable to translate even a basic verse from Hebrew in a Scottish court trial.

[66] Duggar (p. 76) cites the Watchman Fellowship report of 287,838 abdications and an estimated U.S. loss of 3% in 1977. Losses over a several year period in the mid-seventies have apparently been made up in the late 1980's and the movement is currently reporting growth. This is based on statistics of the Jehovah's Witnesses Yearbooks, which do not give actual

membership numbers, but record distribution accounts, from which approximate membership can be derived. Watchman Fellowship also notes that after the death of Franz, the organization is nearing a leadership crisis since Milton Henschel is probably the last of the "anointed remnant" to take this leadership position. This group, the generation of 1914, is viewed as the only ones truly "born again, and is the group that supposedly will not pass away prior to Armageddon (*The Watchman Expositor*, 10:2, 1993, p. 3).

[67] This poll was published April 10, 1991 in *The Dallas Morning News*. Commissioned by the Graduate School of the City University of New York it was based on a survey of 113,000 people.

[68] The two key recent works are Shirley MacLaine's *Out on a Limb*, which popularized the basic concepts, and Marilyn Ferguson's *The Aquarian Conspiracy*, which explicates its goals and ideas.

[69] Cf. Elliot Miller, (*A Crash Course on the New Age Movement*, p. 14), who observes that the term some New Agers use is metanetwork, or a network of networks.

[70] While we have adapted this as a premise of the counterfeit religions, this concept is exactly what New Age writers claim. For example, H. Saraydarian (*The Hierarchy and the Plan*) discusses a transcendent hierarchy which is governing earth from a spiritual realm. This hierarchy is made of humans "who have triumphed over matter," (whom he calls "Masters of the Wisdom") assisted by a being called Sanat Kumara and what he calls "Solar Angels." Sanat Kumara is termed "the Lord of the World" who is "the sole repository of the Will" and is "the divine prisoner of this planet (pp. 17-18)." Frithjof Schuon in his *The Transcendent Unity of Religions* universalizes the concept and maintains that there is a distinction between what he calls the exoteric and the esoteric aspects of religion. The exoteric aspects are those of the visible realm. The distinctions between different religions lie there. The esoteric aspects in the invisible [spiritual] realm. It is in the esoteric arena that Schuon sees the unity of religions. This transcendent unity becomes a foundation for New Age concepts.

[71] The two key concepts are the concept of monistic pantheism and reincarnation. Monistic pantheism is the view that all is one (monism) and that god is everything and everything is god (pantheism) (cf. Marilyn Ferguson, *The Aquarian Conspiracy*, pp. 372-86 and Fritjof Capra, *The Tao of Physics*, pp. 10-12)). Lowell D. Streiker (*New Age Comes to Main Street*, pp. 29-30) objects to the use of these "buzz words" (actually, they are technical terms, not buzz words), and prefers "panentheism" (which he then redefines for his own use). Based of his redefinition of "panentheism" as "the divine is present in everything," Streiker then muddles all forms of mysticism, no matter what the belief of the mystic.

[72] Quimby, himself, does not seem to have followed eastern religious beliefs. He derived his ideas from Franz Anton Mesmer (1734-1815). However, his

214 To Serve Other Gods

teachings accorded well with eastern religions, philosophically. Each of the movements which derived from his work incorporated eastern religious concepts. We have already discussed the relationship of Mary Baker Eddy to Quimby. Unity was founded by Charles and Myrtle Fillmore in 1895. Myrtle Fillmore, raised a Methodist, came to Christian Science out of Transcendental-ism in 1887, then converted her husband. Charles had already studied the writings of Spiritualists and Theosophy. They began to publish their own magazine, but had a falling out with Mary Baker Eddy over copyright violations. During the early 1890's Hindu and Yoga thought including reincarnation and vegetarianism, were incorporated into their teachings. The Unity Church International was officially founded in 1924.

[73] This movement was guided by authors Henry David Thoreau, Ralph Waldo Emerson, and Walt Whitman and is highlighted in every American Literature book. They were deeply influenced by eastern mystic writings, especially the *Bhagavad Gita* and the *Upanishads*.

[74] Theosophy is the concept that man can come to a knowledge of the metaphysical through intuition or revelation from seers. The concept derives primarily from Upanishadic thinking, which as we have already seen, arose during the time of Daniel and the exile of the Jewish nation. Blavatsky was not the first to incorporate these concepts in Western Culture. Meister Eckhart (13th century) and Jakob Böme (16th century), both German mystics, are often considered theosophical thinkers. Rudolf Steiner (*Theosophy*, English translation 1922) was a German contemporary of Blavatsky, who seemed to arrive at his conclusions independently. Jan Karel Van Baalen (*The Chaos of Cults*, p. 62) quotes Blavatsky as characterizing her theosophy as "the same Spiritualism [that she had practiced before] but under another name."

[75] Michael Gomes (*The Dawning of the Theosophical Movement*, p. 7) notes that the Theosophical Society now identifies that civilization as the Harappan culture of the Indus Valley (see chapter 6). This then supposes that all true wisdom was discovered by the Dravidic culture, and then somehow passed on secretly through Indian culture. As already noted in Chapter 6, it is indeed likely that certain concepts carried over into Hinduism from this Dravidic culture, including the mother-goddess cult, certain Yoga concepts, and possibly the concept of reincarnation (although it is more likely that this latter concept was introduced during the time of the *Upanishads*, several centuries later). However, Theosophy builds on the premise that one of the masters living in Tibet (named Djwhal Khul) dictated the teachings to Blavatsky and later to Alice A. Bailey. Thus, Theosophical teachings were supposedly new "revelations" beginning in 1875 (Saraydarian, pp. 29-31).

[76] Reflecting its Indian origins, Theosophy is a pantheistic religion with gnostic overtones. It incorporates seven planes of progression through which the souls of men must travel as they work to Devachan (equivalent to nirvana).

[77] The Theosophical concept of messiah differs radically from that of Judeo-

Christian teaching. According to Blavatsky and Besant, there is a group of men who have progressed through the seven planes, but instead of proceeding on to Devachan (or nirvana), remain to supervise human progression/evolution. They are called masters or mahatmas (among many other names), and dwell throughout the world passing on the esoteric teachings to whoever is willing to be taught. One group, centered in Tibet, was supposedly the source of Blavatsky's teachings. When a Theosophist advances far enough, he or she may be possessed and used by these masters. Above these masters is another, "one supreme teacher." When this master possesses a person, then the Theosophists claim that a christ is among them.

[78] The concept of a new age derives from astrology which measures the trip of the sun through the Zodiac. The age is defined by the constellation of the Zodiac in which the vernal equinox occurs. Each age is approximately 2000-2100 years. Currently, we are in the age of Pisces, or the fish. According to these teachings (cf. Eva Dowling, "Introduction," to *The Aquarian Gospel of Jesus the Christ*, pp 9-10), the Taurian age (age of the bull) began with Adam, followed by the Arian age (age of the ram) which began about the time of Abraham. The next age, the age of Aquarius, is supposed to be an age of spiritual harmony, peace, and prosperity. The exact beginning of this new age is problematical but supposedly it will be within 25 years of the turn of the millennium (between 1975 and 2025).

[79] Two important centers which arose during this period were Esalen in California, and Findhorn in Scotland. These are but two of several communities which developed out of 1960's style communes. They provided what became New Age teaching, and reinforcement to New Age followers through newsletters and networking (cf. Ferguson, pp. 136-41 and 332-37).

[80] This date appears in a number of places, but publicly there is little significant that happened then. Saraydarian (p. 28) states that 1975 was to be a year that the Hierarchy met (coincidentally, his book was published in 1975). Methods of inculcating New Age concepts include movie, TV, games, music, stress and motivational seminars, and educational programs. Ferguson states "Beginning in 1975, California groups began organizing road shows-- conferences and seminars all over the country (p. 141)."

[81] The *New Age Journal* and Mark Satin's *New Age Politics* (1978) preceded these works, but were not as effective in attracting attention.

[82] Channeling is the same process that formerly was known as "trance mediumship, one of the most ancient practices known to humankind" (Brooks Alexander, *Spirit Channeling*, p. 12). Alexander quotes one "channeler" as saying, "channeling is a form of voluntary possession (p. 6)." Jane Roberts was significant since she was the first published by a "respectable" publisher (Prentice-Hall). It is now so accepted and popular that there is even a directory telling who is who in the field (*Channelers: A New Age Directory* by Robin Westin). Westin notes several "channelers" in American history,

including Edgar Cayce (1877-1945).

[83] Several Christian writers (notably Constance Cumbey, Texe Marrs, and Dave Hunt) have picked up on Ferguson's declaration of an "Aquarian Conspiracy" and attacked everything that smacks of New Age. In the process, they have drawn criticism upon themselves for their inclusiveness. For example, Chandler maintains that Dave Hunt denies "that psychology can be 'Christian'" (p. 231). Chandler notes that Alice Bailey does outline a plan (which has been echoed by more recent writers such as Saraydarian). However, he questions whether this is a "present, organized conspiracy" as we think of it.

[84] John Hannah made this observation in his teaching of the cults section of Church History at Dallas Theological Seminary. His definition of a cult includes five facets. It is recent in history (probably 200 years or less); it denies essential tenets of orthodox Protestant theology; its founder is conceived as a prophet and demands obedience; it places some other authority as equal to or higher than the Bible; and it is "inclusive"—only they have the truth, all others are lost. Others give slightly different definitions. Walter Martin surveys the psychology of cultism in his *Kingdom of the Cults* (pp. 24-33). His survey focuses on the membership, while Hannah's focuses on the founder.

[85] Brodie discards any hint of the supernormal in her biography. She also discards the idea of the Spaulding connection, but views the *Book of Mormon* as a novel that Smith wrote by himself (p. 36). She states, "perhaps in the beginning Smith never intended his stories to be taken so seriously, but once the masquerade had begun, there was no point at which he could call a halt (p. 41)."

[86] Wilbur's comment here is enlightening: "Her mother she thought a saint, her father an embodied intellect and will (p. 22)."

[87] Chandler, p. 312. He contrasts the broad way of mankind, which consists of four lanes, doubt, denial, disobedience, and death, with the narrow way of trust in Jesus Christ.

Chapter 11

The Right Road Or A Rabbit Trail?

The "Way" or some synonym has cropped up regularly in our examination of the different religions, demonstrating belief that the adherents
had found the right road to lead through this life and into the next.
Buddhism focuses on the eightfold *path*. Hinduism has its three *roads*.
Taoism has been translated "the *way*." Early Christians were termed
followers of "the *way*." Muslims use the term the straight *path* in
reference to the lifestyle of one surrendered to Allah. The Old
Testament uses "way" to refer to lifestyle.

How does one sort out all of these claims? We have seen a number
of similarities in the origins of all the religions we have examined. We
have also seen strong contrasts. When we evaluate, we really only
have three choices: 1) all religions developed as manifestations of the
same psychological needs and consequently are of equal value; 2) all
religions merely fulfill superstitious needs and thus are equally of no
value, especially to enlightened modern man; 3) one religious tradition
is right and the rest are wrong (in which case we must carefully chose
the right one).

On the surface, it is easy to label all religions as manifestations of
the same spiritual longings in men, leave the situation there, and
conclude that all religions have the same value---no more, no less.
Many have done that. This is the foundation of much "comparative
religion."

But can we really declare that the visions and goals of an Isaiah, or
a Buddha, or a Mohammed, or a Teresa of Avila, or an Ayatollah
Khomeini or a Jim Jones are all of the same quality? Clearly throughout history, religious motivations have highlighted both the most
sublime heights and the most despicable depths that man can reach.
Those who claim that all religions are the same really include in their
claim only a few "revealed" religions.[1] But if all religions are truly the

same, we must include Jim Jones and the People's Temple, the Church of Satan, and even the cannibalistic practices of South American Indians.

It is also easy to become cynical and disparage all religions as equally worthless. Many have also done that.[2] Those who have done so have ignored the good that religions have done. They have also ignored the evil that the non-religious have done. Basically, they close their eyes to the nature of man.

But we dare not ignore such a widespread historical testimony[3] not only to religious needs and deeds, but to a spiritual realm beyond our own. The testimony is so widespread and substantial throughout all history, that we are forced to acknowledge that another realm exists besides the visible.

Neither of these approaches to religion does it justice. The third approach, which we have followed in this book, is that there is one religious tradition which is correct, meaning the others systems are based on error. How did we determine that? With so much evidence for each religion, how do we sort it all out? As we examine the different religions, there are a number of sharp distinctions that must be accounted for. Only after evaluating these distinctions were we able to develop the overall picture of religious development that we premised at the beginning.

The Value of the Evidence

As we look at historical evidence, we realize that not all evidence is of equal value. The task of the historian is to weigh the evidence and determine validity accordingly. There is a vast difference between a historical event verified by witnesses, and the unsupported statement of an independent authority, whether the issue is secular or religious.

Religious revelation may be divided into two types. The most common is termed "religious experience," or personal revelation.[4] It is personal and subjective. You cannot deny my experience, but neither can I deny yours.

We face a serious problem, however, when my experience and your experience do not correlate. That is when we need a basis to evaluate, and a standard to corroborate one or the other. This, historically, has been the problem when evaluating the "cults." When the *Book of Mormon* contradicts *Science and Health*, which do you follow? When both contradict the Bible, which do you follow? The problem has crystallized within the New Age Movement where new revelation is given daily by an assortment of channelers. When different channelers give varying and even contradictory revelation, whom do you follow?[5]

Sometimes, the character (or integrity) of the one claiming the revelation is suggestive.[6] In the 1970's Jim Jones set himself up as a miracle worker, and a would-be messiah (specifically a reincarnation of both Jesus and Lenin). After the Jonestown tragedy, careful investigation revealed his chicanery and fraudulent methods.[7] The one thing that Jones could not stand was investigation into his authority and validity. As soon as some question arose about his system, he fled with his followers to Jonestown in Guyana. When pursued there in 1978, he forced a mass murder/suicide. Anyone who carefully investigated Jim Jones (before or after Guyana) saw him a fraud.

This type of investigation draws us into the realm of the second type of revelation--that of historical events. This revelation takes place within the space-time continuum. Historical events are observed by witnesses, and are subject to verification by historical research, even as are other events of the same era.[8] Historical revelation permits, nay demands verification. While I cannot deny your personal revelation, I can certainly examine the historical record of your accomplishments. This gives me a basis on which to evaluate the revelation you claim.

Few religions claim extensive historical revelation. Buddhism is founded on the teachings of Gautama the Buddha--expressions of his personal revelation. Hinduism is based on the *Vedas* and the *Upanishads*--anonymous personal revelations. Islam is based on the teachings of Mohammed--an expression of his personal revelation. Mormonism is based on a book of Joseph Smith, which no-one else ever saw in a physiological sense. Taoism, Confucianism, Baha'i, Christian Science, and Jehovah's Witnesses are based on the teachings of their founders--their personal revelation. Historical events are incidental to the teachings.

In contrast, Judaism is based on the Exodus. The Exodus was a historical event experienced by thousands--and anchored in space-time history.[9] The primary foundation of the Jewish religion is that event which demonstrated and demanded a relationship between the nation and its Creator. The teachings of Moses and later prophets (their personal revelations) derive from that event, and depend upon that event for their validity. This is the central argument of the Old

Testament.

Likewise, Christianity is based on the death, burial, and resurrection of Jesus Christ, an event witnessed by hundreds, and again anchored in space-time history.[10] Again, the teachings of Jesus and then the Apostles (their personal revelation) hinge on the reality of the resurrection event. The claims of both the Old Testament and New Testament are that these personal revelations are rooted in and authenticated by the space-time history surrounding them.[11]

Jesus challenged His critics to examine His authority and His validity. He proclaimed in advance His resurrection (e.g., John 2:19-21). The Jewish leaders knew that and took *extensive extra precautions* to prevent it (Matt 27:62-66). After the resurrection, all they had to do was to prove that it had not occurred (e.g., produce the body), and Christianity was stopped. In fact, Paul, the Jew who first repudiated and then embraced the Messiahship of Jesus, declared that if the resurrection had not occurred, Christianity was worthless.[12]

We also contrast the authority of a Jim Jones with that of Jesus Christ by examining their lives. Jesus worked in public view. He performed miracles, but not for show, and the results were unquestionable. Mary Baker Eddy, or Jim Jones at their best could occasionally cause psychosomatic healing. At their worse they performed outright fraud.

Jesus performed actual healing from independently verifiable physical problems such as leprosy and hemorrhaging. He demonstrated power over the natural world, including bread and meat, the wind and rain, and even clinically verified death. And his power and acts were validated by even His opponents.

While many questioned His powers before they observed Him, *no witness denied the reality of what He did*. While they did not question his power, they did question the source of His power.[13] The records also indicate that He often told the individual receiving help not to tell anyone pointing out that His work was not for show. Of course the final miracle was His own resurrection, which has been described as a declaration with power of His position as the Son of God (Romans 1:4).[14]

The Variety of Sources

If there is only one true religion, then how do we explain the multiplicity of religious experience. After careful examination, we feel that there is only one explanation which accounts for all the data and claims of religious evidence. The Bible presents three possible sources for religious "truth" or "revelation." Religious "revelation" may come from the true God. It may be a counterfeit from a spiritual being disguising itself as either the true God or a representative of the true God. It may be a counterfeit from the mind of men. It is our individual responsibility to sort out the evidence and make a choice.

Religious history demonstrates all three sources. In the case of a counterfeit, it may be extremely difficult to determine whether it is a product of a disguised spiritual being or of men. When a religious leader claims to have had a revelation, it is difficult to determine whether he or she is telling the truth. It is critical to remember, however, that even if he had an actual revelation, it does not mean that it came from the true God.

"Revelation" does come from the minds of men. An example from the Old Testament is seen in 1 Kings 12:25-33. After successfully rebelling against Rehoboam, Solomon's son, Jeroboam, the newly crowned king of the nation of Israel (the Northern Kingdom), instituted a new religion purely to insure that the people not be attracted to the Southern Kingdom, Judah. The 1 Kings passage notes how carefully Jeroboam counterfeited the worship centered in Jerusalem to turn the people away from the true God.

A more recent example might be Scientology. When originally published in 1950, "Dianetics" was touted as a "science," but when various health organizations took issue, it was organized as a religion.[15] L. Ron Hubbard claimed to have "discovered, developed, and organized" psychological thought from the past 400 years to produce Scientology.[16] The Church of Scientology has been the center of a number of tax evasion court cases, which have focused attention on U.S. Constitutional First Amendment issues (i.e., freedom of religion and speech).

More often, a religion claims as its source some type of spiritual or personal revelation. This is the pattern we have seen throughout our study. This personal revelation becomes the authority for the group.

The Goals of Religion

If the historicity of the Judeo-Christian tradition is true, then why is there so much effort in both the spiritual and human realms to supplant or deny it? The answer lies back in the initial state of mankind as a result of the fall.

God warned Adam and Eve that if they disobeyed, they would die (Gen. 2:17). When they disobeyed, they began dying physically, but immediately they suffered spiritual death, i.e., they were separated from God. Man has always had spiritual needs. They were highlighted when the fall produced what has been termed a "God shaped vacuum in men's hearts." Satan has been trying to fill that vacuum ever since.

His process involves a number of lies. John places these in three categories--the lust of the flesh, the lust of the eyes, and the pride of life (1 John 2:16). A number of people have observed that these also characterize the key lies that Satan used against Eve in the garden (see below). In an effort to fill that emptiness resulting from separation from God, men and women buy into the various lies.

Counterfeit religions then become means to that same end, whether originated on the spiritual or the human level. While in many cases they serve as placebos to dull the ache of a spiritually dead heart, they may also be used as tools or means to other ends. They may produce power. They may produce wealth. They may produce prestige. The key is that they can be effective for many purposes, but they cannot fulfill the primary and only *critical* purpose of religion. They cannot restore men to God.

The Process of Perversion

Of course, religion does not have to come from false sources to be perverted to these ends. We see this throughout history, and even throughout the Bible. Men had the truth, but rejected the implications and bought into lies for their personal aggrandizement, even while retaining the trappings of the truth.

Eli's sons were judged of God in 1 Sam 2:12-36. They were judged because they served as priests in classic Judaism, but "they did not know the Lord." Rather, they used their position for their own advantage, stealing the best of the meat offered to sacrifice, and seducing women. These perversions demonstrate the fallen nature of man explicated in Genesis and the rest of Scripture.

While many use existing religions to advance their own purposes, "new revelations" are often used to justify the selfish actions. Again we see this in the Bible. In 1 Kings 22, King Ahab desired to attack Ramoth-Gilead which was occupied by the Syrians. Ahab asked Jehoshaphat (King of Judah) to join him in the attack. Jehoshaphat asked for verification from God. Ahab's prophets immediately assured them that God would give them victory. Jehoshaphat (not trusting Ahab's prophets since they followed the break-off religion created by Jeroboam) asked if there wasn't a prophet of the *true* God left. Ahab reluctantly admitted that Micaiah was in the region, but he didn't like Micaiah because Micaiah wouldn't prophesy good things.

Jehoshaphat insisted, and Micaiah was called. True to Ahab's fears, Micaiah's prophecy was of defeat in the upcoming battle. Further, Micaiah pointed out how God allowed a "deceiving spirit" to give Zedekiah and the other prophets of Ahab false information regarding the future. As Micaiah prophesied, Israel was defeated, and Ahab was killed in the battle, even though he disguised himself. The validity of Micaiah's prophesy over that of Zedekiah was proven by the subsequent historical event.

The "deceiving spirit" that Micaiah described illustrates the primary process whereby false religions begin. Zedekiah claimed to be a prophet of God. His willingness to prophesy whatever the king desired rather than truth demonstrates that he really wasn't God's prophet. This fact is substantiated by Jehoshaphat's demand that a real prophet of the true God be consulted. It is probable that Zedekiah was a prophet of the syncretistic school of Jeroboam. As such, he had already intellectually rejected the validity of God's word and God's demand that worship of Him be absolute. As such, he had given another authority higher place. Given the background of the current incident (Ahab's wife was Jezebel, who introduced Baal worship into Israel) it is likely that Zedekiah in his syncretism had also bought into Baalism.

What is key is the fact that Zedekiah claimed that he had supernormal revelation. From Micaiah's testimony, we are given insight that Zedekiah's claim was valid. However, it was not from the source that he avowed.[17]

Characteristics of Counterfeits

The purpose of a false religion or a counterfeit is to draw man away

from worship of the true God. To do that, it must do two things. It
must appeal to man and it must have an appearance of truth (i.e., it
must be a passable counterfeit). The issues that counterfeits address
are real issues. The problem is that the solutions they offer, while
helpful, are not adequate. They deny some aspect of the nature of
God, or of man, or of both.

The Appeal of Counterfeits

It has been our contention that all false religions are subversions and
denials of the truth. We have seen the process by which it works. But
what is it that attracts men to the false rather than the true? We have
observed how there is a consistent tradition throughout the world
reflecting back to one God. We have suggested that this is a faint
memory of the true God Who was once worshipped by the ancestors of
all men. He was displaced as other spiritual beings usurped the
worship and authority which belongs to Him. Why?

Men follow a given religion for a variety of reasons. While some
honestly seek communion with God, others use religion for their own
advantage. Religion often is used as a tool to acquire power, prestige,
or wealth. Consequently, counterfeits consistently repeat the three lies
Satan made to Eve.

The first lie is: *"You will not surely die."* This lie denies God's
judgment. It also denies man's resulting mortality. We have already
noted how several religious founders (e.g., Mary Baker Eddy and
Charles Russell) struggled with the issue of God's judgment. Reading
Mary Baker Eddy's authorized biography, one is struck with this
underlying premise to her thinking--"I cannot accept a god who
judges."

Mohammed promised immortality. Hinduism promises re-incarnation. In either case, the lie is, "You will not surely die."

The second lie is: *"You shall be as gods."* This lie denies God's
authority. It also denies man's finiteness. It is a promise of power,
which may lie in two realms.

Physical power is resident within the visible religious hierarchy.
Positions of authority are heady. Jim Jones wielded this kind of power.
So did Joseph Rutherford. The bishop of Rome and the patriarch of
Constantinople bickered over power in the physical realm.

Spiritual power denies man's finiteness and his fall--it makes him out to be part of (or have authority over) the supernormal realm. Power in the spiritual realm is part of the appeal of the Eastern religions where man is viewed as part of the universal god. It is a basic tenet of the New Age movement. But it also shows up in Mormonism. One of the key doctrines of Mormonism is the lie that men will become gods.[18]

The third lie is: *"Your eyes shall be opened."* This lie denies God's goodness and wisdom. It portrays God as a God Who has arbitrarily hidden something from us, perhaps because we are not good enough, or powerful enough.

As a religious foundation, this lie promises greater knowledge or higher consciousness. This is one of the principles of early Christian Gnosticism. It is also the foundation of many of the more esoteric groups such as the Rosicrucians[19] and the Freemasons,[20] and the New Age.[21] In all of these, the lie is, "your eyes shall be opened."

The appeal of the lie depends on the person. This is one reason why there are so many counterfeits--surely there is something that will appeal to each of us.

A Passable Counterfeit

A passable counterfeit must have some degree of truth. That is why most counterfeits probably originate in the fallen spiritual hierarchy. It comes from a supernormal source, i.e., a "god" or an "angel." It can be supported to a degree by supernormal power. However, since this supernormal power is under the ultimate veto of the true Creator God, it is inevitably very limited and erratic.

Still, originating the revelation in the supernormal realm provides more flexibility. The counterfeit does not need to resemble the truth that closely, especially if it is attractive to the one to whom it is presented. The New Testament characterizes the spiritual hierarchy and its world system as fulfilling three categories of lusts--the lust of the eyes, the lust of the flesh, and the pride of life (1 John 2:16-- Satan's three lies to Eve fall into the same categories). Lust overrides caution.

As such, it is not surprising that most religions (of the thousands that have appeared in history) do not espouse, let alone live up to, the ethical standards once touted as the evidence of the highest "revealed" religions.

What is surprising is that these standards should retain their value in a fallen world. They serve to remind us of man's being created in the image of God, and a perfection he no longer has. As such, they are part of the truth that the better counterfeits do attempt to copy. But religions usually attract the adherent by appealing to his or her lusts. Lust often begins in valid physical and psychological needs. After man fell and lost his relationship with God, he also was estranged from his fellow men, and even from himself. The world was put under a curse, and subsequent life has left a sense of futility. As a result, man has many needs. But he also has many wants, and in his fallen self-centered state he often confuses the two.

Men attempt to satisfy these losses in a variety of ways--which ultimately do not satisfy. Out of this emptiness men turn to religion.

Again, we look at the People's Temple for an example. Jim Jones attracted people who had real needs. If a man was hungry, Jones provided a meal. If he needed a job, Jones provided a job-placement service. But much of what he promised was an empty facade. He knew how to inspire a false hope in those who had no hope. As Mel White puts it: "When you give the people hope in practical ways--even if that hope is built on lies--the people fill the church."[22]

This is the core of all counterfeits--they provide a hope. It may be remote. It may cost dearly. It may be built on lies. But it's better than hopelessness. So the lie is believed, and the counterfeit passes for the real thing.

Competition Between Counterfeits

We have noted how the number of gods tend to proliferate. Our contention is that this demonstrates the spiritual hierarchy behind the scenes. Different spiritual beings would present themselves to men in differing ways. In the process, they used their powers as spiritual beings to demonstrate their superiority.[23]

By the nature of the hierarchy, some "gods" were greater than others--e.g., a fallen angel was more powerful than a demon. Eventually, men in a given culture would compare notes and incorporate these different manifestations into a pantheon. The evidence also suggests actual reports of in-fighting going on behind the scenes.

But there is also evidence to suggest already established national hierarchies. We have already seen how spiritual beings are the powers behind the thrones. There is every reason to believe that subordinate beings assisted the key national power, e.g., the prince of Persia, and thus presented themselves as a cultural pantheon. Of course, this prince would be subject to Satan, and this merely part of the overall spiritual hierarchy.

The multiplicity of cults also demonstrates the *nature* of the spiritual hierarchy behind the scenes. While Satan is in control, he achieved this position by the fact of his greater power as an anointed cherub before his fall (Ezek 28:14). Satan fell by maintaining that he would displace God (Is 14:13-14), that is, by seeking to advance his own interests. In the process, he took one third of the angels of heaven with him who seem to have had similar goals (Rev 12:4). His current titles include "ruler [or prince] of demons" (Matt 9:34), "ruler [or prince] of this world" (John 12:31), and "god of this world" (2 Cor 4:4).

Still, Satan is finite and limited--and deluded in his dreams of godhood. And like Satan, each subordinate fallen angel and demon has the dream of displacing those over them as they try to advance their own interests. Thus, behind the scenes there is an internal conflict going on as angel and demon fight angel and demon. This often manifests itself in the visible realm by wars and conflicts.

A Better Counterfeit

We have noted that some counterfeits are "better" than others, i.e., they appeal more to fallen men than others. As we look at the major counterfeits, we realize that it is not just a matter of how closely they replicate the truth. Rather, several other factors determine how successful the counterfeit is.

Timing is a factor. We do not feel that it was an accident that most of the *major* world religions date their source to the century that the nation of Israel was in exile as punishment from God. As we have seen, four key men and the writers of the Rig Veda were contemporaries of Daniel the prophet in exile. Satan appears to have taken advantage of God's judgment on Israel to deploy his forces for this purpose.

The *strength* of the behind the scenes spiritual being is a definite factor. Some counterfeits were backed by stronger forces than others. They spread through the means of military-political conquest. Islam's initial phenomenal growth illustrates this method.

It would also appear that Satan and his subordinates, as finite beings limited by God's ultimate veto, have had to experiment in their attempts to counterfeit. As a result, some counterfeits have a *broader appeal* than others.

Since man, created in the image of the true God to have fellowship with Him, has certain innate traits, any counterfeit must provide at least some answers to some of the basic questions of life. For example, men have certain moral traits such as a sense of justice and compassion (although greatly distorted in the fall).

Passable counterfeits must either fulfill those needs for a moral standard, or provide a plausible reason for suppressing them. Suppression requires a system that appeals to the selfish motives (e.g., personal power and self-advancement in place of any consideration of others). This suppression works overtly only with someone who has already denied the rights of others in his own mind. However, because suppression also produces victims, it also produces resentment, and ultimately retribution. For such a system to work it would require strong repression. This has been seen this century in Naziism, Communism, and Satanism. It is extremely interesting that any overt portrayal of the spiritual hierarchy even in fiction, produces a repulsive picture.

Since repressive counterfeits tend to be counter-productive, other counterfeits have been developed which appeal to man's innate ethical standards. However, it is done is such a way that subtly rationalizes a appeal to selfish motives, e.g., by doing enough good, a man can become acceptable to God. Here is where Satan disguises himself as an angel of light.[24] Paul observed this battle early and several of his letters address the issue. He warned of the spiritual conflict in Eph 6:12. He warned of Satan's ability to disguise himself in 2 Cor 11:14. He even warned that angels would present other gospels in Gal 1:8-9.

These gospels are counterfeit because they leave the true God out of the picture and provide a substitute god who is presented as a slave whose purpose is to prosper the worshiper. In reality, the relationship is reversed as so many find out after they have been ensnared.

The Ultimate Counterfeit

We have observed how man lost control of his world in the fall. We have noted the spiritual hierarchy behind the scenes that currently has control. We have seen how a multitude of counterfeit religions have appeared over the centuries to draw men away from God. We have also seen how Jesus Christ proclaimed Himself the promised Messiah and Redeemer to reconcile men back to God, and how He validated His claim in the resurrection. Further, we have noted how the behind the scenes battle continues, with new counterfeit religions and gospels arising regularly. But where do we go from here? What will be the ultimate outcome?

The book of Revelation talks of a final battle between Christ and Satan. As a precursor to this battle there will be a final false world religion which follows a counterfeit messiah. It is tempting to look for the groundwork for this religion among today's world religions. Last century some looked for it in the Catholic Church.[25] In recent years, many have looked for it in the New Age movement.[26] With the recent troubles in Iran and Operation Desert Storm in Iraq, some have looked for it in Islam.[27]

Revelation 13 seems to indicate that it will be a new counterfeit created in that time, after the removal of the restraint of the Holy Spirit from the world (2 Thes 2:7). It will be an effective counterfeit of the true religion (v. 11--"two horns like a lamb") but will be distinctly Satanic (v. 11--"he spake as a dragon"). The focus of its worship will be a counterfeit of Jesus Christ (v. 3--and its reference to a fatal wound which was healed). It will become a worldwide religion which will stand in direct opposition to Christianity, the following of the true Christ (v. 3 and 7).

A second "beast" will rise up in support who will become a false prophet. He will focus worship on the counterfeit christ (v. 12) and perform a number of miracles during that timeframe (v. 13). The final miracle will be the ultimate in idols--a replica of the counterfeit christ that speaks.

But the ultimate counterfeit will be Satan's last hurrah during this age. This final false religion will no more be in place that the True Christ, the Crucified and Resurrected One will come the second time.

After defeating the gathered forces of Satan, this time He will seize the counterfeit christ and his false prophet and cast them into the lake of fire (Rev. 19:20). Only after this time will there be but one world religion, that of the true God. In the words of the prophet Jeremiah: "'And they shall not teach again, each man his neighbor and each man his brother, saying, "Know the Lord," for they shall all know Me,

from the least of them to the greatest of them,' declares the Lord, 'for
I will forgive their iniquity, and their sin I will remember no more (Jer
31:34).'"

Notes

[1] Cf. Huston Smith in his "Introduction" to Frithjof Schuon's *The Transcendent Unity of Religions*, pp. xiii and xix.

[2] One of the most notable was Bertrand Russell who declares "My own view
on religion is that of Lucretius. I regard it as a disease born of fear and as a
source of untold misery to the human race (*Why I Am Not A Christian*, p. 24)."
Russell takes the view that all evil done by an adherent of a religious belief is
a direct result of the belief. Based on this logical fallacy he castigates all
religion. It is clear, however, from our study of current history, that while
religious adherents have committed innumerable evil deeds, "enlightened,"
"modern," "secular," men have committed evils far greater. The reports of
atrocities that have seeped out from behind the Iron and Bamboo curtains
demonstrate that the malaise actually infects the entire human race. Interestingly, Dr. Martin Marty, a scholar at the University of Chicago, commented on
a recent opinion poll conducted by the City University of New York (reported
in the *Dallas Morning News*, April 10, 1991): "[it is] 'astonishing that in a
high-tech, highly affluent nation, we have 90 percent who identify' themselves
as religious."

[3] We use the term "historical testimony" to denote the type of evidence
which is available. Since the late 19th century, we have become more and
more in tune with the scientific method, and the "proofs" of science.
Unfortunately, as a result, many have developed the mind-set that something
is not true unless "proven" by science. There are several areas where we
function daily that "scientific proof" is not only unavailable, but impossible.
Scientific proof requires reproduction of a given process under controlled
conditions with similar results. Our media could not operate if it were required
to prove each event by scientific means. Our legal system could not operate
if it were required to prove the guilt or the innocence of any individual by
scientific proof. Likewise, our historians could not function under these
conditions. All three use eyewitness reports. We call this alternative form of
proof the legal-historical method. In the process we use three basic types of
evidence—oral testimony, written documents, and artifacts. From these,
through deductive reasoning, we arrive at conclusions, hopefully "beyond a
reasonable doubt." Many historical events are still highly debated because the
evidence is not sufficient to put the conclusions in that category. A prime
example is the assassination of John F. Kennedy. After 25 years of intensive

study, the question of the number of assassins is still highly disputed.

⁴ Religious experience is used here to denote a wide variety of phenomena. Ninian Smart (*The Religious Experience of Mankind*, p. 15) defines the term when he states: "religious experience involves some kind of 'perception' of the *invisible* world, or involves a perception that some visible person or thing is a manifestation of the invisible world." According to this definition, a person may actually behold an event or person revealing the "invisible" world, but not perceive it as a manifestation. Thus, for example, a person could accompany Paul along the road to Damascus, see the light, see Paul's reaction, but be unaware of what was really going on (cf. Acts 9:7).

⁵ Even so, adherents of the New Age evaluate the experiences of others in the movement. Robin Westin (*Channelers: New Age Directory*, p. 87) records that those who claim to channel cover a wide spectrum. From an interview, he quotes Jack Pursel, a channeler for a being called Lazaris. Pursel states: "Within the channeling field there is a broad range of participants. At one end there is charlatanism and chicanery. The middle range includes those with good intentions, but little contact, to those who have a strong contact but little insight. Then there are those who are channeling powerful energies with wonderful insights." The question that is not asked nor answered is "how do you know?"

⁶ This is part of the reason that we examine the character of the founders of different cults so carefully. While we recognize the sinful nature of all men, and we don't necessarily expect them to be perfect, we do expect their lives to correlate with their claims. Thus, a religious leader should live up to certain minimal standards which are higher than the average man. If the leader claims to be god, then we do expect perfection.

⁷ Mel White (*Deceived*) discusses the methods that Jim Jones used to deceive and brainwash his followers. White discusses the methods that Jones used to fake miracles (pp. 42-43, 58-61), and to win allegiance (pp. 17-31). He especially notes how Jones carefully picked those he would allow to join his group (pp. 49-51) and manipulated the press (pp. 35-37).

⁸ This last qualifier must be emphasized. Often higher standards of verification of so-called "religious" events are exacted than for other events of the same period. Because of the significance religion has for life, this may be beneficial--as long as the standards are not impossibly high. For example, Julius Caesar lived a few decades before Jesus Christ. We have 10 copies of Caesar's "Gallic Wars," the earliest dated a 1000 years after his death. In comparison, we have 5000 Greek manuscripts (not to mention manuscripts in Latin, Syriac, and other languages) containing portions of the New Testament, and thus testifying to Jesus Christ. The earliest of these date to within 100 years of His death. With 500 times the manuscript evidence and one tenth the time gap, it would seem obvious that we would be *more* confident of the

historicity of Jesus Christ than of Julius Caesar. Unfortunately, there is an entire school of thought which suggests that because we do not have a signed original document, then the entire New Testament testimony falls in the category of myth--although the same individuals accept Julius Caesar without question.

⁹ All the events leading up to and including the Exodus were performed in public, not only before the yet-future nation of Israel, but pharaoh and his people. After the assembly of Israel arrived at Sinai, Moses did receive the law independently on the mountain, but during the period, the entire nation had seen the manifestation of God and heard His voice--and then decided to let Moses copy the Law for them (cf. Deut 5:22-31). Further, early in the period, Moses, Aaron (with two of his sons), and seventy leaders of the nation had seen God (Ex 24:9-12 [from the New Testament, we understand this as a vision of the pre-incarnate Jesus Christ]). After the giving of the law, the entire nation experienced the forty years of wandering and then the conquest. Even a casual reading of the Old Testament is challenging as one is confronted over and over by the phrase, "when I brought your fathers out of Egypt," or a similar reference to that event. It is then no accident that some "modern" scholars who have tried to undermine the Judeo-Christian belief system *began* with a denial of the historicity of these events (cf. Julius Wellhausen, *A Prolegomena to the History of Ancient Israel*, p. vii). However, unable to deny the magnitude of reference to the Exodus, they have attempted to redefine it so that becomes primarily a religious event based at best on a kernel of "true" history which was reinterpreted after the event to show God's guidance [i.e., it then becomes a "personal revelation"] (cf. Bernhard W. Anderson, *Understanding the Old Testament*, pp. 17-19). Likewise, it should not be surprising that people deny the historicity of both the Exodus and the Resurrection, given the issues at stake. After all, we have people today denying the holocaust, which not only had a thousand-fold more witnesses (many of whom still are alive), but also photographic evidence. When we recall the primary focus of the holocaust, this denial not only fits our pattern, but corroborates our position.

¹⁰ We must emphasize here that the issue of miracles is not a historical problem, but a philosophical problem. As Josh McDowell points out (*Evidence That Demands a Verdict*, p. 8) the modern historical method rests on a rationalistic presupposition that miracles *could not* occur, and that Christ *could not* have been resurrected, therefore any evidence that supports those points must, by definition, be invalid. John Warwick Montgomery (*History and Christianity*, p. 20) notes that this is the logical fallacy termed "begging the question." Sound scholarship demands that the evidence be examined *prior* to the decision of the validity of the event.

¹¹ That is one reason why the Old Testament is so dogmatic regarding the requirement that a prophet be one hundred per cent accurate. An interesting

illustration of this premise is in the Gospel accounts of the life of Jesus. In Mark 2:1-12 (paralleled in Matt. 9:2-8 and Luke 5:18-26) a paralyzed man is brought to Jesus. Instead of healing the man, Jesus tells him that his sins are forgiven. Immediately the crowd proclaimed the statement blasphemy because it assumed the prerogatives of God. Jesus then demonstrated His authority to forgive sins by healing the man.

[12] While Paul's vision on the road to Damascus could be construed as a "personal revelation," Paul uses it to add himself to the list of eye-witnesses. The resurrection is proclaimed a historical event, and the entire New Testament is written on that foundation. In 1 Cor 15:14-17, Paul stated: "And if Christ has not been raised, then our preaching is vain, your faith also is vain. Moreover we are even found to be false witnesses of God, because we witnessed against God that He raised Christ, whom He did not raise, if in fact the dead are not raised." It was C.S. Lewis, another person who became a Christian against his own intentions, who declared that we have but three choices regarding Jesus and His claims. We can view him as a Lunatic, a Liar, or the Lord of all creation (*Mere Christianity*, pp. 40-41).

[13] For example, see John 10:20, where Jesus had just healed a man who had been blind from birth. John spends two chapters relating this episode and it reveals the process the Jewish leaders followed (John 9:13-34). They interrogated the man. They interrogated witnesses. They interrogated the parents of the man, now an adult. They questioned the testimony of the witnesses, but the conclusion was that the man had been born blind, and was now able to see. They did not have a problem with the healing, per se. The problem in their mind was that he was healed on the Sabbath, a violation of their understanding of the law. The Jews had already decided the character of Jesus, and now they were trying to make the evidence fit their conclusions. Some of the observers accused Jesus of healing through the power of a demon (which others refuted saying that demons didn't have *that* kind of power). Similar accusations were made in John 8:48; Matt 9:24, and 11:18; Mark 3:22; and Luke 11:15; et al.

[14] See 1 Corinthians 15:1-9. For further discussion of the historicity of this event see Josh McDowell, *Evidence that Demands a Verdict*; John Warwick Montgomery, *History and Christianity*; J.N.D. Anderson, *Christianity, the Witness of History*; or Frank Morison, *Who Moved the Stone?*, among many others.

[15] The initial motives of its founding are problematic. It was founded by L. Ron Hubbard, a science fiction writer of the 1940's who declared "If a man really wants to make a million dollars, the best way would be to start his own religion" (Eugene H. Methvin, "Scientology: Anatomy of a Frightening Cult," *Reader's Digest* May 1980, p. 86). He published his book *Dianetics: The Modern Science of Mental Health* in 1950. He established the first Church of Scientology four years later in Washington DC. This cult is supposedly based

on secret teachings that 75 million years ago earth was one of 90 planets ruled by Xemu. Earth's problems stem from Xemu's efforts to control over-population by killing off a number of beings, but ended up freeing their spirits, who affect (or who willfully incarnated themselves into) mankind. These problems show up as "engrams," supposedly painful experiences either from this life or an earlier incarnation. "E-meters" (a type of lie detector) are used to detect these engrams. The Food and Drug Administration has investigated the use of these and labeled them fraudulent. The Internal Revenue Service has investigated the organization and its leaders several times for tax fraud. Its activity subsided after 8 leaders were convicted in 1981 of burglarizing the IRS and stealing government documents (*U.S. News and World Report*, July 5, 1982). Hubbard died in 1986. Subsequently the organization lost several court cases and agreed to pay several million in out of court settlements.

[16] Cf. the introductory note and introduction to *Scientology: The Fundamentals of Thought* by L. Ron Hubbard. The editor's note states: "Scientology was discovered (found), not invented (created) [p. 17]." But no source for the discovery is given and the characteristics of the "religious philosophy" are credited *solely* to Hubbard.

[17] Why did God allow a deceiving spirit to go to Zedekiah? The answer is not entirely clear, however, this was the time of God's judgment on Ahab. As a result of this revelation, Ahab went into the battle and was killed in a manner which fulfilled other prophecies. We also see here that the spiritual hierarchy. which rules the world faces limitations. When it comes to the affairs of men, this hierarchy is limited in what it is allowed to do. While within limits it has a large degree of autonomy, even Satan, who Jesus characterized as the ruler of this world, had to ask God's permission before he acted against Job, one who belonged to God (Job 1:11-12 and 2:5-6).

[18] According to Mormon doctrine, the fall allowed Adam and Eve to have children, which ensured that the "offspring of God should leave the scenes of their primeval childhood and enter the school of mortal experience" (i.e., be born into the physical world) with the ultimate goal that "by the proper use of which knowledge [of good and evil] man may become even as the Gods" (James E. Talmage, *A Study of The Articles of Faith*, 3:2). These doctrines are derived from *Doctrines and Covenants* and *The Pearl of Great Price*, a later revelation of Joseph Smith, and clarified by "revelation" from Brigham Young's *Journal of Discourse*.

[19] Rosicrucianism was supposedly derived from Egyptian mysticism during the XVIII dynasty begun under Ahmose I (1567-44 BC--cf. H. Spencer Lewis, *Rosicrucian Questions and Answers*, p. 39). The earliest historical reference is in the early 17th century, which tells of a Christian Rosenkreuz who journeyed throughout the Middle East where he learned much "secret wisdom." Upon his return to Germany he passed this on to others and founded the order.

[20] Freemasonry apparently began originally as an association of craftsmen,

but became a secret organization with mystical rituals in the 18th century. Again, the secret knowledge supposedly dates back to the times of the Egyptians (cf. C.F. McQuaig, *The Masonic Report*). Paul deParrie (*Ancient Empires of the New Age*, p. 166) argues however, that the Freemasons date back to the eighth century as a mystical secret society, which was revived by the Rosicrucians who used the craftsman association as a front of respectability.

[21] One of the arguments of the New Age is that they possess secret teachings which the church "expurgated" from the Bible, e.g., reincarnation. These allegations vaporize after a historical investigation when it is shown that many Biblical manuscripts which omit these teachings predate the date of the supposed expurgation. However, if one is willing to accept such basic concepts, *then* the New Age teachers will go on to show new revelations. I.e., deny the validity of God's Word, and then you will be open to other teachings.

[22] Mel White, *Deceived*, p. 32.

[23] Job 1 and 2 demonstrate that Satan has certain super-normal powers. When God allowed it, he was able to instigate foreign forces to attack, send down fire from the heavens, and manage the winds to destroy Job's family and possessions. He was also able to physically attack Job with boils. It must greatly gall Satan, however, that these powers are limited to *what God allows*. This is probably a key reason that "magic" is so problematic—the spiritual forces which are called upon to perform it are finite and restrained.

[24] For example, George Otis, Jr. (*The Last of the Giants*, p. 77), quotes a Muslim imam who states, "Islam offers a way for emasculated men to become something. Christianity, on the other hand, is a welfare religion—Jesus paid it all—and my people don't need that."

[25] Cf. Alexander Hislop, *The Two Babylons or The Papal Worship*. Hislop bases his arguments on the history of the mother-goddess cult.

[26] Cf. Dave Hunt, *Peace, Prosperity and the Coming Holocaust*. Hunt presents a compelling argument based on his studies of the New Age, history, and prophecy (notably Ezek 38-39 and Rev 13). While he shows the role of the spiritual hierarchy in the New Age movement, he limits or ignores its role in the other world religions, weakening his argument.

[27] Cf. George Otis, *The Last of the Giants*. Otis presents a logical argument based on Ezek 38-39 and Rev 13 and 17, drawing extensively on recent events, especially Desert Storm, as supporting data. Otis' work, published shortly after the current study was initially written, takes a similar view regarding the behind the scenes spiritual hierarchy, although he applies the principles in a geographical and prophetic, not historic sense.

Bibliography

There is an amazing amount of material available in the field of comparative religions. The most detailed material focuses on one religion or area, although there are several good surveys. A number of general works use either an anecdotal (stories or practices taken out of context) or a proof-text (comparison of incidental practices from widely separated groups to prove a point) approach. These are much less helpful. There is not nearly as much material available on the history of religions, and most of that available either follows an evolutionary view of development, or focuses on one religious tradition. The following works are but a portion of the material used in the development of this study, and merely represent the types of material that are available regarding religious history. It will be noted that works presenting various points of view are included. This list was designed to give some initial guidance to anyone desiring further research in a given area and *is not to be viewed necessarily as an endorsement for views of the works included.*

General Religion

Albright, William Foxwell. *From the Stone Age to Christianity.*
Garden City: Doubleday and Company, Inc., 1957.
Covers Ancient Near Eastern religious thought focusing on the available data. Attempts to integrate the early evidence for monotheism with an evolutionary view of religion.

Beaver, R. Pierce and others, editors. *Eerdmans' Handbook to the World's Religions.* Grand Rapids: Wm. B. Eerdmans Publishing Co., 1982.
Excellent reference tool covering all the major religions as well as many others, written from a somewhat conservative perspective. Dates founding of Judaism after exile and is ambivalent regarding source of early religion.

Campbell, Joseph. *The Hero with a Thousand Faces.* Second Edition. Princeton: Princeton University Press, 1968.

Uses archetypal literary criticism for analysis of mythology. Catergorizes all religious teaching as myth which Campbell attempts to demythologize.

Custance, Arthur C. *The Doorway Papers* 10 volumes, Grand Rapids: Zondervan Publishing House, 1975-1980.
A collection of essays on a variety of subjects in the overall field of early Biblical studies. Volume 2 has several essays on primitive cultures, volume 1 discusses primitive monotheism and the origin of polytheism.

Frazer, James G. *The Golden Bough*. London: Macmillan, 1890. One volume abridged edition. New York: Crown Publishers, Inc., 1981.
Takes an evolutionary view of religion. Although considered a "classic," most of his "evidence" is anecdotal taken arbitrarily from different primitive cultures.

Hislop, Alexander. *The Two Babylons*. Neptune, NJ: Loizeaux Brothers, 1959.
Examines history of "mother-goddess" cult which appears over a wide spread area. Very thorough, but somewhat dated (first published in 1916).

Karrer, Otto. *Religions of Mankind*. New York: Sheed and Ward, Inc., 1936.
Study of the concept of religion as a universal phenomenon. Discounts the evolution" of religion, but takes a low view of primitive man. Argues for superiority of Christianity (written from a Roman Catholic perspective).

Malinowski, Bronislaw. *Magic, Science and Religion*. Garden City: Doubleday Anchor Books, 1955.
Study of religion in primitive societies from a sociological perspective. Takes a "functionalist" perspective for origin of religion.

Miceli, Vincent P. *The Gods of Atheism*. Harrison, New York: Roman Catholic Books, 1971.
Excellent study of various anti-theistic philosophies of past two centuries. Points out how atheism merely substitutes another god

in place of God.

Ohmann, Richard M. *The Making of Myth*. New York: G. P.
Putnam's Sons, 1962.
A collection of "controlled essay materials" designed to further the
idea that mythology and by inference religion comes from the same
human source—a "primitive" mindset.

Schuon, Frithjof. *The Transcendent Unity of Religions*. Wheaton:
The Theosophical Publishing House, 1984.
Looks for a basic unity in all religions in their seeking God.
Places unity in the transcendant realm (i.e., spiritual) thus ap-
proaches a monistic concept.

Wellhausen, Julius. *Prolegomena to the History of Ancient Israel*.
Reprint edition. Goucester, Mass.: Peter Smith, 1973.
Primarily a supposed history of Israel and Judaism, but is
significant in an overall sense because of its emphasis on the
evolution of religion. Foundation of most liberal interpretation of
the Bible.

Comparative Religion

Anderson, J. N. D. *The World's Religions*. Grand Rapids: Wm. B.
Eerdmans Publishing Co., fourth edition (completely revised,
1975).
Essays cover animism and major non-Christian religions. Each essay
briefly covers origins and major doctrines. Excellent reference work.

Bouquet, Alan Coates. *Comparative Religion*. Reprint edition,
Baltimore: Penguin Books, 1969.
Seeks a naturalistic explanation for all religions, e.g., extra-
sensory perception is behind prophecy and miracles (the author put
great hope in Duke University experiments which have since
fizzled out). Assumes evolutionary development, although he
acknowledges that not enough credence' has been given to the
evidence of early monotheism.

Hutchison, John A. *Paths of Faith*. New York: McGraw-Hill Book
Company, 1981.
Excellent basic text book of comparative religion. Concentrates

on beliefs and practices, but give brief account of origin of individual religions. Follows overall evolutionary view and deems each relgion equally valid.

McDowell, Josh M. and Stewart, Don. *Handbook of Today's Religions*. San Bernadino: Here's Life Publishers, 1983.
Good summary of beliefs of religions in world today and their current beliefs. Contrasts other religions with Biblical Christianity.

Neill, Stephen. *Christian Faith and Other Faiths*. Downers Grove: InterVarsity Press, 1984.
Contrasts Judaism, Hinduism, Buddhism, and Islam with Biblical Christianity.

Ridenour, Fritz. *So What's The Difference?* Glendale Ca:　G/L Publications, 1967.
A basic (written primarily for youth) comparison of Biblical Christianity with both the four major non-Christian religions and four major cults (Unitarianism, Jehovah's Witnesses, Christian Science, and Mormonism). Examines Roman Catholicism from a Biblical base and views it as "non-orthodox Christianity."

Schipper, Earl. *Religions of the World*. Grand Rapids: Baker Book House, 1982.
Begins with Biblical Christianity, then examines the four major non-Christian religions. While rejecting their validity, argues that they have a role as aspects of God's "Common Grace" restraining sin in the world. Useful as a springboard for further study of these religions.

Smith, Huston. *The Religions of Man*. New York: Harper and Row, 1965.
Considered somewhat of a classic by many. Focuses on the positive values of each religion and its worth to its adherents (beginning with the premise that all religions are essentially of equal value). Concentrates on the basic current practices of each religion while downplaying the historical data (including the bodily resurrection of Jesus Christ).

History of Religion

Bierer, Everard. *The Evolution of Religions*. New York: G. P. Putnam's Sons, 1906.
     As noted by title, takes an evolutionary view. While very much out of date, it is a very clear delineation of this essentially passé view.

Eliade, Mircea. *History of Religious Ideas*. 3 volumes. Translated by Willard R. Trask. Chicago: University of Chicago Press, 1978.
     Considered a key work in the field. Primarily relates mythological themes. Takes an overall evolutionary view. Extensive critical bibliography to assist more in-depth studies.

Parrinder, Geoffrey, ed. *World Religions: From Ancient History to the Present*. New York: Hamlyn Publishing Group, 1984.
     A semi-historical presentation (e.g., covers Aztec and Mayans before Mesopotamia, Egypt, Greece and Rome). Denies historicity of resurrection, puts all religions on same basis. Some historical data questionable on early periods.

Schoeps, Hans-Joachim. *The Religions of Mankind: Their Origin and Development*. Garden City: Doubleday and Co., 1968.
     Historical survey which covers extinct religions by region and then the major world religions. Acknowledges Biblical accounts of resurrection, but places this event in realm of "religious history" not subject to research (i.e., a matter of belief, not historicity).

Schmidt, W. *The Origin and Growth of Religion: Facts and Theories*. New York: Cooper Square Publishers, Inc., 1971 reprint.
     Survey of the evidence of an original monotheism in primitive cultures. Concludes that *all* cultures show traces of an original monotheism.

Sharpe, Eric J. *Comparative Religion: A History*. LaSalle, IL: Open Court, 1986.
     Good extensive survey of the history of comparative religious studies. Begins from a rationalistic perspective, although it has a balanced approach. Excellent reference tool.

Smart, Ninian. *The Religious Experience of Mankind*. New York:

Charles Scribner's Sons, 1969.

One of the more thorough surveys. Recognizes the historical base of Judaism and Christianity, although it questions the nature of the resurrection and builds on Wellhausen's ideas. Notes the relationship of religion with the "invisible" world. Includes humanism as a modern religious phenomenon.

Toynbee, Arnold. *An Historian's Approach to Religion*. London: Oxford University Press, 1956.

Written by noted historian. Primarily is a study of religious practices in their historical context, but does not look at beliefs or claims. Depreciates the claims of Jesus and reduces Christianity to merely a higher philosophical expression of universal longings, ignoring the historical evidence.

Ancient Near Eastern Religions

Brandon, S. G. F. *Religion In Ancient History*. New York: Charles Scribner's Sons, 1969.

A collection of essays on different religious aspects. Follows liberal view of Old Testament and its culture, and assumes evolutionary views with regard to religion in general. Denies historicity of Passover/exodus and essentially ignores the Resurrection.

Breasted, James Henry. *The Dawn of Conscience*. New York: Charles Scribner's Sons, 1933.

Investigates origins of morality based on an evolutionary world view. While recognizing ties between Mesopotamia and Egypt, ignores Mesopotamia and argues for origin of religion and ethics in early Egypt.

Budge, E. A. Wallis. *Egyptian Magic*. New York: Dover Publications, 1971.

Examines the relationship of magic and Egyptian religious beliefs. Primarily anecdotal.

_____. *From Fetish to God in Ancient Egypt*. London: Oxford University Press, 1934. Reprint edition. New York: Dover Publications, 1988.

Attempts to evaluate the various strains of religious thought as

developed in early Egypt. Deals primarily with key aspects of
religious worship noting the lack of a coherent theology. Somewhat dated.

Frankfort, Henri. *Ancient Egyptian Religion.* New York: Harper
Torchbooks, 1961.
Discusses religious aspects, but does not attempt to systematize
the religion. Covers entire period of Egyptian history as a "static"
or homogeneous whole.

Frankfort, Henri and others. *The Intellectual Adventure of Ancient
Man.* Chicago: University of Chicago Press, 1946. Reprint
edition, 1977.
Collection of essays which examine the thought process of
ancient man based upon available documents. Notes the high
intellectual ability of early man and his high awareness of the
world around him, but denigrates early man's correlation of the
spiritual/physical realms.

Faulkner, R.O., trans. *The Ancient Egyptian Book of the Dead.*
Austin: University of Texas Press, 1990.
Translation of the collection of Egyptian texts which is known as
"The Book of the Dead." Provides insights into the Egyptian view
of the afterlife.

Gray, John. *Near Eastern Mythology.* London: Hamlyn Publishing
Group, 1969.
Well-illustrated, popularly written summary and background of
Ancient Near Eastern mythology. Assumes that Old Testament is
a borrowing of earlier myths and unquestioningly follows argu-
ments of Wellhausen.

Heidel, Alexander. *The Babylonian Genesis.* Chicago: The
University of Chicago Press: 1963.
Translation of various Babylonian creation myths with a study of
the parallels with the Old Testament. After very careful and highly
technical examination, notes that the similarities are not as close as
expected, and concludes that any question of relationship must be
left open.

Hooke, S. H. *The Origins of Early Semitic Ritual.* London: Oxford

University Press, 1938.
  Compares Old Testament religious practices with Babylonian and
Canaanite practices. Assumes that a similar ritual demands the same
source, and confuses prophetic warnings against abuse with a condemna-
tion of all religion.

Jacobsen, Thorkild. *The Treasures of Darkness.* New Haven: Yale
University Press, 1976.
  Study of Mesopotamian literature for religious concepts.
Proposes a historical development of concepts based on internal
data of late copies.

James, E. O. *Prehistoric Religion.* N.p., 1957. New York: Barnes
and Noble, 1962 reprint edition.
  Study of religious evidences based on examination of prehistoric
burial sites, and beliefs and practices of modern primitive tribes.
Sees the early High God in background of many cultures, but
hesitates to view this as true monotheism.

Kramer, Samuel Noah. *History Begins At Sumer.* Third Edition.
Philadelphia: University of Pennsylvnia Press, 1981.
  Collection of essays which cover various "firsts" (including
religious) recorded in the tablets recovered from Sumer.

_____. *Mythologies of the Ancient World.* New York: Doubleday
and Co. Anchor Books, 1961.
  Study of ancient mythologies arranged by culture. Each
culture's study is written by an expert in that field. More theoretical regarding the mindsets than explanatory of myths or religious
beliefs.

_____. *Sumerian Mythology.* Philadelphia: University of
Pennsylvania Press, 1972.
  Expostion and study of key myths from Sumeria. Explains
stories from Sumer with brief excerpts to show points. Discusses
relationship of Sumerian mythology to Near Eastern studies.

Pritchard, James B. *Ancient Near Eastern Texts Relating to the Old
Testament.* Princeton: Princeton University Press, 1969.
  Standard in field. A compilation of various source documents
which provide background to Old Testament studies, translated and

introduced by experts in each specific field.

Ringgren, Helmer. *Religions of the Ancient Near East*. Translated by John Sturdy. Philadelphia: The Westminster Press, 1973.
    Good survey of what is known about Ancient Near Eastern religion, comparing pantheons, mythology, and ritual for Sumeria, Babylonia/Assyria, and the Western Semitic region. Generally cautious in interpretation of data, although it assumes an evolutionary perspective.

Watterson, Barbara. *The Gods of Ancient Egypt*. New York: Facts on File, 1984.
    Anecdotal studies of thirty major gods with brief introduction. No overall cosmology.

Wohlstein, Herman. *The Sky-God An-Anu*. Jericho, NY: Paul A. Stroock, 1976.
    Scholarly compilation of various Ancient Near Eastern documents which refer to *An*. Documents the changing view of this god's status based on context and attributes.

Baha'i

Esslemont, J. E. *Baha'u'llah and the New Era*. Wilmette IL: Baha'i Books, 1970.
    History of Baha'i religion from origins to mid-twentieth century and survey of teachings focused around numerous extracts from writings of Baha'u'llah and successive leaders.

Hatcher, William S. and Martin, J. Douglas. *The Baha'i Faith: The Emerging Global Religion*. San Francisco: Harper and Row, 1985.
    Fairly objective overview of the history and teachings of this group, although written from an insider's perspective.

Holley, Horace. *Religion for Mankind*. Wilmette IL: Baha'i Publishing Trust, 1956.
    Exposition of the teachings of Baha'i with an emphasis on its universalistic perspective.

Townsend, George. *The Glad Tidings of Baha'u'lluh*. Oxford:

George Ronald, 1978.
Summary of Baha'i teachings centered around extracts from
writings of Baha'u'llah.

Buddhism

Byles, Marie Beuzeville. *Footprints of Gautama the Buddha*.
Wheaton: Theosophical Publishing House, 1957.
Story of the founder of Buddhism in light of author's journeys
through the area where he lived.

Carus, Paul and Nyanatiloka. *Buddha: His Life and Teachings*. New
York: Crescent Books, n.d.
Biography compiled by extracting material from Pali canon.
Also contains a summary of basic teachings of Buddhism.

Conze, Edward, translator. *Buddhist Scriptures*. Baltimore: Penguin
Books, 1959.
Extracts from Pali canon and other Budhist texts. Covers
aspects of life of Gautama and his teachings.

Deshimaru, Taisen. *The Ring of the Way*. New York: E. P. Dutton,
1983.
One modern school of Zen Buddhism, consisting of the teachings
of Taisen Deshimaru.

Evans-Wentz, W. Y., ed. *The Tibetan Book of the Dead*. London:
Oxford University Press, 1960.
Translation with commentary of Tibetan book explaining the
process of reincarnation from the perspective of the "soul" as it
proceeds through the forty-nine days between incarnations.

Gard, Richard A. *Buddhism*. New York: George Braziller, 1962.
Biography compiled from Pali canon and early legends. Includes
summary of basic teachings. Good overview of various Buddhist
schools.

Humphreys, Christmas. *Buddhism: An Introduction and Guide*.
Third edition. Harmondsworth: Penguin Books, 1962.
Short biography of Gautama the Buddha and extensive explana-
tion of Theravada teaching with brief summary of other schools.

Khantipalo, Phra. *Buddhism Explained.* Bangkok: Mahamkut Rajavidyalaya Press, 1989.
Survey of Theravada school of Buddhism as practiced in modern Thailand.

Lester, Robert C. *Buddhism: The Path to Nirvana.* San Francisco: Harper and Row, 1987.
Summary of life and teachings of Buddha with a comparison of practice in Japan and Thailand.

Rockhill, W. Woodville. *The Life of the Buddha and the Early History of his Order.* London: Kegan Paul, Trench Trubner, and Co., 1884. Reprint edition, Petaling Jaya: Mandala Trading, 1987.
Translation of Tibetan traditions regarding life of Buddha and his teachings.

Ross, Nancy Wilson. *Buddhism: A Way of Life and Thought.* New York: Random House, 1981.
Brief biography of Buddha. Excellent comparison of Theravada, Zen, and Tibetan schools. Good differentiation of the various modern sects of these three major schools.

Schumann, H. W. *The Historical Buddha.* London: Arkana, 1989.
Well-researched history of Buddha, incorporating background material for the period of his life.

Suzuki, D. T. *An Introduction to Zen Buddhism.* New York: Grove Press, Inc., 1964.
Survey of the Zen school by the noted Japanese scholar who is credited with introducing Zen Buddhism to the Western world.

Watts, Alan W. *The Way of Zen.* New York: The New American Library, 1957.
Survey of the Zen school by an western (English-American) convert and scholar.

Yu, Chai-Shin. *Early Buddhism and Christianity.* Delhi: Motilal Banarsidass, 1981.
Examines the early periods of these two religions from a Buddhist perspective. Concentrates on similarities, noting several common religious practices while downplaying the role of doctrine.

Talks of resurrection as Christ's source of authority, but views
resurrection as an item of faith, not historical fact.

Christianity

Ahlstrom Sydney E. *A Religious History of the American People*.
Garden City, NY: Doubleday and Co., 1975.
Well-researched two volume history of Christianity in the United
States, including the colonial period.

Bainton, Roland H. *Christendom*. New York: Harper and Row,
1966.
Good basic survey of history of Christianity up to Reformation
focusing on its impact on Western Civilization.

_____. *The Age of the Reformation*. Princeton: D. Van Nostrand
Co., Inc., 1956.
Good study of the background and spread of the Prostestant
Reformation.

Cairns, Earle E. *Christianity Through the Ages*. Grand Rapids:
Zondervan, 1967.
Good survey of history of Christianity from a conservative
perspective.

Chadwick, Henry. *The Early Church*. Baltimore: Penguin Books,
1970.
Part of Pelican History of the Church series. Covers developments up to Augustine.

Cragg, Gerald R. *The Church and the Age of Reason: 1648-1789*.
Baltimore: Penguin Books, 1970.
Part of Pelican History of the Church series. Covers the Church
in Europe from the Peace of Westphalia to the French Revolution.

D'Aubigne, J. H. Merle. *History of the Reformation of the Sixteenth
Century*. London, n.p., 1846. Reprint edition Grand Rapids:
Baker Book House, 1976.
Classic, in-depth, study of the background and events leading up
to the Reformation.

Fremantle, Anne. *The Papal Encyclicals in their Historical Context*. New York: The New American Library, 1963.
Study of teachings of Popes up to John XXIII (1963) including social, political, and historical issues involved.

Hefley, James C. *The Conservative Resurgence in the Southern Baptist Convention*. Hannibal: Hannibal Books, 1991.
Excellent survey of past twelve years in the largest protestant denomination in the U.S. Illustrates the problems which result when the basic authority of the Bible is rejected, and relates how this denomination has fought to regain that authority.

Hillerbrand, Hans J. *The World of the Reformation*. New York: Charles Scribner's Sons, 1973. Reprint edition, Grand Rapids: Baker Book House, 1981.
Study of European society in the sixteenth century with interaction of events of the Reformation.

Hurlbut, Jesse Lyman. *The Story of the Christian Church*. Grand Rapids: Zondervan, 1970.
Essentially an expanded outline of key events, movements, and individuals, but provides an excellent basic "big picture."

Lautourette, Kenneth Scott. *A History of Christianity*. Two volumes. New York: Harper and Row, 1975.
An intermediate depth history of Christianity by noted scholar. Good presentation.

_____. *A History of the Expansion of Christianity*. Seven Volumes. Grand Rapids: Zondervan, 1970.
An exhaustive history of how Christianity moved throughout the world. Focuses on outreach and expansion to expense of internal developments.

Southern, R. W. *Western Society and the Church in the Middle Ages*. Baltimore: Penguin Books, 1970.
Part of Pelican History of the Church series. Covers period from Augustine to start of the Reformation.

Tavard, George H. *The Catholic Approach to Protestantism*. New York: Harper and Row, 1955.

One Catholic writer's view of Protestantism and a proposed
process of ecumenicalism.

Torbet, Robert G. *A History of the Baptists.* Valley Forge: The
Judson Press, 1963.
Class study of Baptist history (all strains), surveying theories of
origins and documenting known history.

Christian Science

Eddy, Mary Baker. *Miscellaneous Writings.* Boston: Christian
Science Publishing Co., n.d.

_____. *Science and Health.* Boston: Christian Science Publishing
Co., n.d.
These two books contain the basic teachings of this movement.
The latter was revised numerous times by the author including
seven major revisions.

Gottschalk, Stephen. *The Emergence of Christian Science in American
Religious Life.* Berkeley: University of California Press, 1973.
Critical study of background, founding, and history of the move-
ment, noting the deviations of founder from Orthodox Christianity.

John, DeWitt. *The Christian Science way of life.* Boston: The
Christian Science Publishing Society, 1962.
Survey of Christian Science teachings written by a member of
the Christian Science Board of Directors. Clearly expounds the
teachings of the group, including showing where they deviate from
orthodox Christianity.

Kirban, Salem. *Christian Science.* Chicago: Moody Press, 1974.
Critically compares Christian Science beliefs with the Bible.
Best of this series by Moody on the cults.

Wilbur, Sibyl. *The Life of Mary Baker Eddy.* Boston: Christian
Science Publishing Co., 1913.
Officially sanctioned biography of the founder of Christian
Science. Plays down outside influences.

Confucianism

Blofeld, John, translator. *I Ching: The Book of Change.* London Books: Unwin Paperbacks, 1989.
Translation of this basic source book for several Eastern religions. Key work for Confucianism. Includes introduction which explains the theory and practice.

Kelen, Betty. *Confucius: In Life and Legend.* New York: Thomas Nelson, Inc., 1971.
Basic, brief, biography of the man Confucius. Reviews the legends about him and concludes that he was a historical figure and that arguments to the contrary have no weight.

Smith, D. Howard. *Confucius.* New York: Charles Scribner's Sons, 1973.
Focuses on role of Confucius in Chinese thinking. Argues for the historicity of the man. Maintains that the system he founded was not a religion, but became a religion as a result of interplay with Buddhism and Taoism.

Ware, James R., translator. *The Sayings of Confucius.* New York: The New American Library, 1955.
Topical arrangement of sayings attributed to Confucius, translated into English. Introduction includes brief biography and background.

Yeh, Theodore T. Y. *Confucianism, Christianity and China.* New York: Philosophical Library, 1969.
Examination of interaction of these two faiths in modern China by scholar who studied in both lands. Topically arranged. Evaluates the teachings of Confucius from both Western and Christian bases.

Cults

(See also Christian Science, Jehovah's Witnesses, Mormonism, and Mysticism/New Age).

Ankerberg, John and Weldon, John. *The Secret Teachings of the Masonic Lodge.* Chicago: Moody Press, 1990.

Extensive evaluation of Masonic teachings based on study of
many Masonic works and interviews with both current and former
masons. Views Freemasonry as a religious cult with secret
teachings and explanations varying for different levels. These
"deeper" teachings tie Freemasonry into the occult and spiritism.

Boa, Kenneth. *Cults, World Religions and You*. Wheaton: Scripture
Press, 1984.
   Survey of a wide number (27) of religions, cults, and move-
ments. Very brief in treatment of each, but provides an excellent
Biblical evaluation and personal application.

Gruss, Edmond C. *Cults and the Occult*. Phillipsburg: Presbyterian
and Reformed Publishing Co., 1974.
   Brief survey from a Biblical perspective, but more inclusive than
most surveys. Good selection of Biblical passages which relate to
each cult. Primary value as a source for further study material.

Hubbard, L. Ron. *Dianetics: The Original Thesis*. Los Angeles:
The Church of Scientology of California, 1976 revised edition.
   Hubbard's orginal outline which led to Dianetics. It is built on
the idea that the mind has an analytical part (the human) and a
reactive part (the animal). Maintains that a rational mind is a
happy mind, therefore, unhappiness is the result of some irrational-
ity (or dominance of reactive mind), often as a result of some
unrecalled trauma from the past.

_____. *Scientology: The Fundamentals of Thought*. Los Angeles:
The Church of Scientology of California, 1973.
   Systematic summary of Scientology's basic teachings as set forth
by the founder of the movement.

Hutchinson, William. *The Spirit of Masonry*. Wellingborough,
England: The Aquarian Press, 1987.
   Reprint of 1775 work which was instrumental in giving Free-
masonry a degree of respectability.

Incognito, Magus. *The Secret Doctrine of the Rosicrucians*. N.p., n.d.
Reprint edition. New York: Barnes and Noble, 1993.
   Book written under pseudonym, apparently early this century.
Purports to reveal hidden doctrines, but limited in what it "re-

veals." Clearly shows the eastern mystic origins of this group.

Lewis, H. Spencer. *Rosicrucian Questions and Answers with Complete History of the Rosicrucian Order*. San Jose: Supreme Grand Lodge of AMORC, 1941.
Explanation of Rosicrucianism from an insider's perspective. As an official explanation, it is limited in what it divulges.

Macoy, Robert. *A Dictionary of Freemasonry*. New York: Bell Publishing Co., 1989.
A combination of dictionary or encyclopedia of freemasonry terms, symbols, etc., preceded by a history which supposedly traces the movement back to the time of Moses.

Martin, Walter. *The Kingdom of the Cults*. Minneapolis: Bethany Fellowship, 1974.
In depth analysis and evaluation of about fifteen cults of significance in the United States at time of writing. Thorough and well-documented. Extremely useful still, although somewhat dated.

McQuaig, C. F., *The Masonic Report*. Norcross GA: Answer Books and Tapes, 1976.
Exposition of the religious nature of freemasonry by a former high-ranking mason.

Steiner, Rudof. *Theosophy*. London: Rudolph Steiner Press, Revised edition, 1965.
Claims to write independently of Blavatsky's Theosophical Society, but proposes similar views of man in a process of reincarnation.

Staff of the Church of Scientology of California. *What Is Scientology*. Los Angeles: The Church of Scientology of California, 1978.
Summary of history, doctrines, and ritual of Church of Scientology written by insiders. Format is highly promotional and avoids controversial issues.

Van Baalen, Jan Karel. *The Chaos of the Cults*. Grand Rapids: Wm. B. Eerdmans Publishing Co.,
Biblical evaluation of about fourteen major cults of mid-century America and the concept of cults. Dated, but still very useful.

White, Mel. *Deceived*. Old Tappon: Fleming H. Revell Co., 1979.
Written shortly after the Jonestown, Guyana tragedy. Examines
the position of the People's Temple in the American community to
determine what attracted its followers and led to its outcome.

Demons and Satan

Barnhouse, Donald Grey. *The Invisible War*. Grand Rapids:
Zondervan Corporation, 1965.
Popularly written examination of the hidden spiritual heirarchy
which is in control of this world and the spiritual warfare as
explained in Scriptures.

deParrie, Paul. *Satan's Seven Schemes*. Brentwood, Tenn: Wolge
muth and Hyatt, Publishers, Inc., 1991.
Analyzes the dialog between Satan and Eve to derive seven
strategies which characterize Satanic deception. Shows how these
same strategies are evident in society today, although he may be a
bit overzealous in his sweeping identifications.

Dickason, C. Fred. *Angels, Elect and Evil*. Chicago: Moody Press,
1975.
Solid basic study of Biblical revelation regarding angelic beings,
their nature, and their role in world affairs.

Lindsey, Hal. *Satan is Alive and Well on Planet Earth*. Grand Rapids:
Zondervan Publishing House, 1972.
Popularly written study of Satan from a Biblical perspective.
Examines the issue of spiritual warfare in U.S. society in the
1970's.

Paine, Lauran. *The Hierarchy of Hell*. New York: Hippocrene
Books, Inc., 1972.
Undiscerning amalgamation of ideas from a wide spectrum of
myths and extra-biblical writings. Views hell and its denizens as
a concept of men's imaginations with every culture borrowing from
elsewhere (but does not explicate any ultimate source).

Pentecost, J. Dwight. *Your Adversary the Devil*. Grand Rapids:
Zondervan Publishing House, 1969.
Thorough Biblical study of Satan and his role in spiritual warfare.

Solid study of the Biblical data.

Schlink, Basilea. *The Unseen World of Angels and Demons.* Old
Tappon NJ: Fleming H. Revell Co., 1985.
English translation of German work on Biblical presentation of
Satan, Angels, and the spiritual realm. Good basic work.

Unger, Merrill F. *Biblical Demonology.* Wheaton: Scripture Press,
1952.
Key study of the Biblical data regarding the role of angelic
beings in the world system.

Eastern Religions

(See also individual religions)

Bancroft, Anne. *Religions of the East.* New York: St. Martin's
Press, 1974.
Good overview of eastern mystic religions, including Hinduism,
Buddhism, and Taoism. Includes major sections on Tibetan Tantric
Buddhism, Zen Buddhism, and Sufism, areas often overlooked.

Blofeld, John, translator. *I Ching: The Book of Change.* London
Books: Unwin Paperbacks, 1989.
Translation of this basic source book for several Eastern
religions. Includes introduction which explains the process used
and the history as known.

Campbell, Joseph. *Oriental Mythology: The Masks of God.* New
York: Penguin Books, 1962.
Part of four volume set on mythology. Focuses on mythology
of Egypt and Asia (essentially, India, China, and Japan). Begins
with evolutionary views, but provides good, fairly detailed history
of myth and ritual backgrounds.

Capra, Fritjof. *The Tao of Physics.* Toronto: Bantam Books, 1984.
Surveys eastern religions along with an exposition of modern
physics. Argues that physics verifies premises of eastern religions.
Builds on several questionable assumptions, with conclusions that
do not follow (e.g., many of his premises only apply to the world
of sub-atomic physics).

256 To Serve Other Gods

Fenton, John Y. and others. *Religions of Asia.* New York: St. Martin's Press, 1983.
Comparative religion book focusing exclusively on what are commonly termed Eastern religions (ignoring the Southwest Asian origin of Judaism/Christianity/Islam). Very helpful in what it covers with information on several of the less well-known groups.

Ions, Veronica. *Indian Mythology.* New York: Peter Bedrick Books, 1983.
Well-illustrated, popular overview of the religious backgrounds of the Indian sub-continent. Includes a good overview of the pre-Vedic and early Vedic periods. Incorporates Hindu, Buddhist and Jain mythologies.

Keith, A. Berriedale. *Indian Mythology.* The Mythology of All Races, vol. vi., edited by Louis Herbert Gray. New York: Coopers Square Publishers, 1964
A general survey of mythological concepts in ancient India. Covers major traditions which lie behind Indian religions.

Rice, Edward. *Ten Religions of the East.* New York: Four Winds Press, 1978.
Good survey which cover a number of lesser known religions. Includes Jains, Zoroastrians, Sikhs, Taoism, Confucianism, Bon, Shinto, Cao Dai, Bahai'i, and Theosophy.

Yogi, Maharishi Mahesh. *Transcendental Meditation: Serenity without Drugs.* New York: The New American Library, 1968.
Basic work for TM. Clearly delineates TM as a religion which seeks to establish a means for the individual to contact the universal being (i.e., for atman to get in touch with Brahman).

Greco-Roman

Graves, Robert. *The Greek Myths.* Baltimore: Penguin Books, 1955.
Systematic retelling of various Greek myths citing various sources and versions. Attempts to explain the myths in light of modern anthropology and archaelogy (i.e., as part of the fabelism school).

Meyer, Marvin W. *The Ancient Mysteries: A Sourcebook.* New

York: Harper and Row, 1987.
Brief explanations of what is knon about the various mystery
religions of the Mediterannean world including Mithraism.
Translations of key documents that relate the limited information
available. Lumps all mystical strains as of one type.

Vermaseren, M. J. *Mithras, the Secret God*. Translated by Therese
and Vincent Megaw. London: Chatto and Windus, 1963.
Starting with Iranian beginnings, follows spread of worship of
Mithras through the Roman Empire. Covers various legends and
information available on ritual.

Hinduism

Basham, A. L. *The Origins and Development of Classical Hinduism*.
New York: Oxford University Press, 1989.
Excellent survey of the field by an acknowledged expert in the
field. Points out the tenuous foundation for any early dating of
Hinduism (prior to 6th century BCE).

Danielou, Alain. *Hindu Polytheism*. New York: Pantheon Books,
1964.
Survey of Hindu thought followed by discussions of the principle
gods. Good reference tool which discusses the symbolism in the
standard portrayals of various gods and goddesses.

Dhavamony, Mariasusai. *Classical Hinduism*. Rome: Universita
Gregoriana Editrice, 1982.
Study of Hindu traditions, focusing on the period between the
completion of the Upanishads and the composition of the Puranas
(6th century BC to 8 century AD).

Jain, K. C. *Prehistory and Protohistory of India*. New Delhi: Agam
Kala Prakashan, 1979.
Study of archaeology of sub-continent with extensive work on
the Harappan culture, including prescursors of Hindu religion.

Mascaro, Juan, translator. *The Bhagavad Gita*. Harmondsworth:
Penguin Books, 1962.
Basic translation of this epic poem, which is near heart of Hindu-
ism.

Morgan, Kenneth W. *The Religion of the Hindus*. New York: Ronald
  Press Co., 1953.
    Collection of essays written by Hindu scholars. Includes summa-
    ries of major sacred literature as well as explanations of religion.

Nikhilananda, Swami. *The Upanishads*. New York: Harper and
  Row, 1964.
    One of the better translations of these works. Abridged from
    writer's four volume work published by same publisher. Good
    survey of Hindu thought in introduction. Includes good explanato-
    ry footnotes.

O'Flaherty, Wendy Doniger. *The Rig Veda: An Anthology*. Balti
  more: Penguin Books, 1981.
    Translation of 108 of the Rig Vedic poems. Arranged by subject
    with introduction and explanatory footnotes.

Richards, Glyn. *A Source-Book of Modern Hinduism*. London:
  Curzon Press, 1985.
    Selections from works of various Hindu leaders since the 18th
    century. Good survey of modern Hindu thinking.

Sastri, Gaurinath. *A History of Vedic Literature*. Calcutta: Sanskrit
  Pustak Bhandar, 1982.
    An attempt to arrange the Vedic literature in a historical manner.
    Excellent explanation of material.

Torwesten, Hans. *Vedanta: Heart of Hinduism*. Adapted by Loly
  Rosset from a translation by John Phillips. New York: Grove
  Weidenfeld, 1991.
    Good overview of Hindu thought by a German scholar. Less
    successful in the comparisons with Biblical issues and Christian
    tradition (assumes a somewhat "easternized" view of Bibli-
    cal/Christian thought).

Islam

A'la Maududi, Sayyid Abul. *Finality of Prophethood*. Lahore:
  Islamic Publications, 1981.
    Argues that Mohammed was the final prophet in the line
    stretching through the Old and New Testaments. Somewhat

strained and very subjective in its conclusions.

Ayub, Hassan. *Islamic Belief.* Dehli: Hindustan Publications, 1984.
Good summary of basic Muslim beliefs. Excellent reference
tool.

Baagil, H. M. *Christian Muslim Dialogue.* N.p., n.d.
More of a monologue against a strawman Christianity. Represents an attempt to proselytize Christians. Given to troops in
Persian Gulf at same time that Muslim governments placed severe
limits on Christians in coalition forces.

Bassiouni, M. Cherif. *Introduction to Islam.* Chicago: Rand McNally
and Co., 1988.
Explanation of Islamic teachings and practices, written specifically for a non-Muslim. Brief, but covers many specifics not included
in larger works (e.g., how to convert Islamic calendar to western).

Denny, Frederick Mathewson. *An Introduction to Islam.* New York:
Macmillan Publishing Co., 1985.
Good, thorough study of practices and beliefs. Begins with in-
depth background of Middle-Eastern religion. Contrasts Islam with
both Judaism and Christianity.

Haeri, Shaykh fadhlalla, *The Elements of Sufism.* Longmead: Element
Books, 1990.
Excellent overview of this mystical strain of Islam. Gives brief
history, outlines key teachings and practices held in common by the
various groups, and gives brief biographies of major historical
figures.

Haykal, Muhammad Husayn. *The Life of Muhammad.* Delhi:
Crescent Publishing Co., 1978.
Biography of the founder written from a Muslim perspective.
Does not critically evaluate a number of legends which have
accrued, as compared to other Muslim works.

Ibrahim, Sliman Ben and Dinet, Etienne. *Life Of Mohammed.*
Secaucus NJ: Charatwell Books, 1990.
Extensive biography of the founder written from a Muslim
perspective.

Otis, George, Jr. *The Last of the Giants*. Tarrytown, NY: Fleming H. Revell Co., 1991.
> Survey of modern Islam and its role in Biblical prophecy. Concludes that Islam is the religious beast of Revelation. Very interesting section on spiritual strongholds and the implications for missions.

Payne, Robert. *The History of Islam*. New York: Dorset Press, 1990.
> Well-written history of Mohammed and the military expansion of the Muslims.

Pickthall, Hohammed Marmaduke. *The Meaning of the Glorious Koran*. Mecca Al Mukarramah: Muslim World League, 1977.
> English translation of the Koran by English convert to Islam.

Williams, John Alden. *Islam*. New York: George Braziller, 1962.
> Presentation and explanation of three main sources of Islamic doctrine (Koran, Hadith, and Shari'a) including extracts. Good survey of several of the most significant sects.

Jehovah's Witnesses

Duggar, Gordon E. *Jehovah's Witnesses*. Grand Rapids: Baker Book House, 1989.
> Well researched and written personal account of a couple who spent a number of years in the movment then left.

Hoekema, Anthony A. *Jehovah's Witnesses*. Grand Rapids: Wm. B. Eerdman's Publishing Co., 1963.
> An in-depth examination of the movement as a cult by a recognized theologian.

Horowitz, David. *Pastor Charles Taze Russell*. New York: Philosophical Library, 1986.
> Presents a Jewish perspective of Russell, the founder of the Jehovah's Witnesses, as a Zionist and supporter of the Jewish people.

Kirban, Salem. *Jehovah's Witnesses*. Chicago: Moody Press, 1972.
> Critically compares Jehovah's Witnesses' beliefs with the Bible.

Stroup, Herbert Hewitt. *The Jehovah's Witnesses.* New York: Columbia University Press, 1945.
  In depth sociological study of movement. Dated in some respects, but conclusions are worth noting.

Watchtower Society. *Babylon the Great Has Fallen!* Brooklyn: Watchtower Bible and Tract Society, 1963.
  Explanation of Biblical prophecy from a Jehovah's Witness point of view. Uses an allegorical approach to which only the JW's have the correct key of interpretation.

_____. *This Means Everlasting Life.* Brooklyn: Watchtower Bible and Tract Society, 1950.
  Official exposition of Jehovah's Witnesses' doctrine and teaching put out by the Watchtower Society.

Judaism

Bokser, Ben Zion. *The Jewish Mystical Tradition.* Northvale NJ: Jason Aronson, Inc., 1993.
  Traces history of mystical elements in Judaism from Biblical prophets through the Talmud to modern times. Strongest focus is on Hasidism.

Epstein, Isdore. *Judaism: A Historical Presentation.* Baltimore: Penguin Books, 1959.
  Excellent history of Judaism written by noted Jewish scholar. Takes conservative view of historical records.

Gaster, Moses. *The Samaritans.* London: The British Academy, 1925.
  Studies the Samaritans within their historical context, but views them as a Jewish sect without any syncretism. Opts for Samaritan traditions over Biblical accounts.

Hereford, R. Travers. *The Pharisees.* New York: The MacMillan Co., 1924.
  In-depth study of the Pharisees, including their origin and their teachings. Concludes that Pharisees are forerunners of Rabbis.

Kemelman, Harry. *Conversations With Rabbi Small.* New York: Fawcett Crest, 1981.

Apologetic for Judaism as understood by this well-known Jewish
writer. Written in the form of a series of discussions between the
fictional Rabbi Small, a would-be convert, and her non-observant
Jewish fiance.

Merrill, Eugen H. *Kingdom of Priests.* Grand Rapids: Baker Book
House, 1987.
Excellent survey of Old Testament history (e.g., early or pre-
Mishnaic Judaism) from a conservative perspective.

Neusner, Jacob. *The Pharisees: Rabbinic Perspectives.* Hoboken:
KTAV Publishing House, Inc., 1973.
Condensation of 3 volume work. Technical examination of
traditions of origins of the Pharisees up to the destruction of
Jerusalem.

Parfitt, Tudor. *The Thirteenth Gate: Travels among the Lost Tribes
of Israel.* Bethesda MD: Adler and Adler, 1987.
Account of a series of journeys in the 1980's by the author
among various Jewish communities throughout Asia which claim
to be descended from the exiled nation. Includes group in
Bombay, India which traces its ancestry to Assyria.

Saldarini, Anthony J. *Pharisees, Scribes, and Sadducees in Palestinian
Society.* Wilmington: Michael Glazier, 1988.
Examines positions of these three groups in Jewish society at the
time of Jesus.

Scholem, Gershom, ed. *Zohar: The Book of Splendor (Basic
Readings from the Kabbalah).* New York: Schocken Books,
1949.
Several extracts from the Zohar translated into English with a
short historical introduction.

_____. *Kabbalah.* New York: Dorset Press, 1974.
Very good reference work. Contains several sections which
cover different aspects of the movement, including a detailed
history of the development, basic ideas involved, various key
topics, and brief biographies of significant individuals.

Shapiro, Sidney. *Jews in Old China.* New York: Hippocrene Books,

1984.
   Summary, including partial translations, of the works of several
   Chinese scholars on the history of Jews in China. Common
   consensus is that the Jews left the Middle East about the 3rd
   century BC, settled in Bombay, and then moved on to China about
   AD 1000. Notes some indication of Jewish settlements in China
   before Christ.

Wouk, Herman. *This Is My God*. New York: Pocket Books, 1974.
   Summary of Jewish thinking as understood by this well-known
   Jewish writer. Contains excellent, in-depth critique of Julius
   Wellhausen based on an exhaustive examination of Wellhausen's
   sources.

Mormonism

Arrington, Leonard and Bitton Davis. *The Mormon Experience*. New
   York: Alfred A. Knopf, 1979.
   History of Mormonism focusing on the life of Joseph Smith and
   the migration to Utah. Written from a Mormon perspective.

Brodie, Fawn. *No Man Knows My History*. New York: Alfred A.
   Knopf, 1975.
   Biography of Joseph Smith written by a Mormon with access to
   church documents, but critical of Smith and his actions.

Cowdrey, Wayne L., Davis, Howard A., and Scales, Donald R. *Who
   Really Wrote the Book of Mormon*. Santa Ana CA: Vision House
   Publishers, 1977.
   Examines the question of the origin of the Book of Mormon.
   Concludes that Smith used another person's work as the primary
   source of his work.

Kirban, Salem. *Mormonism*. Chicago: Moody Press, 1971.
   Critically compares Mormon beliefs with the Bible.

Smith, Joseph. *The Book of Mormon* Salt Lake City: The Church of
   Jesus Christ of Later Day Saints, 1986.

_____. *Doctrine and Covenants*. Salt Lake City: The Church of
   Jesus Christ of Later Day Saints, 1964.

_____. *Pearl of Great Price*. Salt Lake City: The Church of Jesus Christ of Later Day Saints, 1964.

These three works, which purport to be angelic revelation, form the foundation for the Mormon church and Mormon thinking. Most church doctrines derive from the latter two.

Talmage, James E. *A Study of the Articles of Faith*. Salt Lake City: The Church of Jesus Christ of Later Day Saints, 1961.

A thematic outline of official Mormon doctrine derived from the works of Joseph Smith and later church leaders.

Mysticism and New Age

Besant, Annie. *Esoteric Christianity or the Lesser Mysteries*. Adyar Madras, India: The Theosophical Publishing House, 1914.

Clear exposition of the gnostic foundation of Theosophy. Reads into the Biblical text "mystical" meanings which are supposed to show that Jesus was one of the touted ancient masters from Asia, and thus Christianity is a later mystery religion. A key foundation of New Age thinking.

_____. *Thought Power: Its Control and Culture*. Wheaton IL: The Theosophical Press, n.d. Reprint edition, 1953.

Shows the eastern mystical aspects of Theosophy. Clearly demonstrates that Theosophy and any spin-offs (including New Age) are from Eastern religious origins.

Blavatsky, Helen Petrovna. *The Key to Theosophy*. Adyar: The Theosophical Publishing House, 1953 reprint of 1889 book.

Somewhat superficial explanation of Theosophy by its founder.

Chandler, Russell. *Understanding the New Age*. Dallas: Word Publishing, 1988.

Well balanced presentation by religious editor of *Los Angeles Times*. Points out problems movement poses while not using scare tactics.

deParrie, Paul and Pride, Mary. *Ancient Empires of the New Age*. Westchester IL: Crossway Books, 1989.

Writer came out of the New Age movement. Traces New Age ideas back to the ancient cultures from which they came. Exam-

ines the characteristics and cultural context of those ideas, then
contrasts with Biblical Christianity.

Dowling, Levi H. *The Aquarian Gospel of Jesus the Christ.* N.p.,
   n.d. Reprint edition. Marina del Rey: DeVorss and Co., 1964.
   Purports to be a new revelation to "Levi," showing a ministry of
   Jesus in other parts of the world, including India. Basic work for
   New Age thinking.

Ferguson, Marilyn. *The Aquarian Conspiriarcy.* Los Angeles: J.P.
   Tarcher, Inc., 1987.
   Declaration of New Age goals and ideas written by an insider.
   Key work for bringing attention to New Age movement, and
   raising idea of conspiracy.

Gardner, Martin. *The New Age: Notes of a Fringe Watcher.* Buffalo:
   Prometheus Books, 1988.
   Collection of essays from *Skeptical Inquirer.* Writer takes an
   extremely cynical view of religion in general, and lumps conservative Christianity with the cults and charlatans. Overall tone is
   caustic. Title is a misnomer since he primarily focuses on
   purveyors of psychic phenomena with a few essays on Shirley
   MacLaine.

Hunt, Dave. *Peace, Prosperity and the Coming Holocaust.* Eugene:
   Harvest House Publishers, 1983.
   Views the New Age movement as the world religion beast of
   Revelation 13. Book mostly studies the occult/eastern mystic
   backgrounds of the New Age movement. Argues that time just
   prior to tribulation will be one of unprecedented peace and
   prosperity.

MacLaine, Shirley. *Out On A Limb.* Toronto: Bantam Books, 1983.
   Author's biographical account of her journey into New Age.
   Subtle indications of New Age movement's schisms from its
   Eastern Mystical background, e.g., one's *karma* is one's personal
   choice.

Martin, Walter. *The New Age Cult.* Minneapolis: Bethany House
   Publishers, 1989.
   Completed shortly before his death, explains why Martin had
   viewed the New Age and its antecedent thinking as a cult for 35

years.

Miller, Elliot, *Crash Course on the New Age Movement*. Grand
Rapids: Baker Book House, 1989.
Best book available on the subject. Writer came out of the New
Age Movement, but takes a balanced, critical perspective, noting
points where Christians would be co-beligerents with the New Age,
but more importantly, areas where Christians could be taken in.

Pearce, Joseph Chilton. *The Crack in the Cosmic Egg*. New York:
Crown Publishers, 1988.
Labeled a new age classic. The writer lauds what he calls a
non-logical or "autistic" thought pattern (i.e., the unstructured
thought patterns of a child) and establishes this as a goal to
transcend the physical world which he calls the cosmic egg.

Saraydarian, H. *The Hierarchy and the Plan*. Agoura: Aquarian
Educational Group, 1975.
Exposition of New Age hierarchy and conspiracy from a key
insider's perspective. Designed for teaching New Age ideas.

Primitive Religions

Bellingham, David. *An Introduction to Celtic Mythology*. Secaucus
NJ: Chartwell Books, 1990.
Collection of Celtic (Irish, Scottish, and Welsh) myths, inter-
spersed with sidebars which illustrate the myths' archaeological
background.

Campbell, Joseph. *The Power of Myth*. New York: Doubleday,
1988.
Confusing hodge-podge of bits and pieces taken from all over the
world, designed to support an Eastern Mystical worldview.

Carrasco, Davíd. *Religions of Mesoamerica*. San Franciso: Harper
and Row, Publishers, 1990.
Surveys the religions of the Mayan and Aztec cultures. Totally
downplays the human sacrifices and other cruel practices. Sees a
carry-over of some of the ideas into modern folk catholicism of
Central America.

Gimbutas, Marija. *The Goddesses and Gods of Old Europe*. Berkeley: University of California Press, 1982.
Archaeological study of Balkan cultures, correlating neolithic and calcolithic cultures with Minoan and later Greek cultures. Work is largely inferential, drawing primarily from later Minoan and Greek documents. Dating is very problematical. Illustrates problem of performing religious studies through archaeology.

Hultkrantz, Åke. *Native Religions of North America*. New York: Harper and Row, 1987.
Divides North American Indian religion into two general types called the hunting pattern and the horticultural pattern. Uses Shoshone and Zuni religions as types of the two, emphasizing diversity but also pointing out underlying similarities, including belief in a Supreme Being or Most High God behind the religious trappings.

Lawson, E. Thomas. *Religions of Africa*. New York: Harper and Row, 1985.
Uses Zulu and Yoruba cultures as examples of diversity in African religions. Notes the presence of the "primitive high god" in both cultures, but questions the meaning.

Mbiti, John S. *Introduction to African Religion*. New York: Praeger Publishers, 1975.
Topical overview of sub-Sahara African religion as a composite. Uses examples of specific practices of different tribes to illustrates generalities. Notes prevalence of Creator God and invisible spirit forces throughout Africa. Denies that African religion is animistic fetish worship or superstition, although he recognizes the role of witchcraft and magic in the cultures.

Parrinder, Geoffrey. *African Mythology*. New York: Peter Bedrick Books, 1986.
Overview of African religion using specific illustrations of overall trends. Begins with the pervading belief in an single original Creator God, although he does not attempt to correlate this foundational belief with the more apparent worship of "lesser spirits."

Satan/Satanism

See Demons and Satan.

Shintoism

Earhart, H. Byron. *Religions of Japan*. San Francisco: Harper and
Row, 1984.
  Survey of key religions in Japanese culture and the social role
  they play. Focus is on the interplay of Shintoism and Buddhism,
  but Christianity (introduced in 1549) is included.

Ichiro, Hori, ed., *Japanese Religion*. Tokyo: Kodansha International,
1989.
  Survey of various religions extent in Japan with observations
  regarding status, sources, and role in Japanese culture. Extensive
  statistical tables at the end.

Ono, Sokyo. *Shinto: The Kami Way*. Tokyo: Charles E. Tuttle Co.,
1989.
  Excellent survey of Shintoism written by a leading Japanese
  scholar.

Varley, H. Paul. *Japanese Culture*. Tokyo: Charles E. Tuttle Co.,
1984.
  Overview of Japanese history and various social factors which
  have produced the modern Japanese culture. Good survey of the
  roles of the various religions, including Shintoism, Buddhism, and
  Christianity.

Sikhism

McLeod, W. H. *Textual Sources for the Study of Sikhism*. Manchester:
University Press, 1984.
  English translation of selected Sikh religious texts, with explana-
  tory remarks.

Rice, Edward. *Ten Religions of the East*. New York: Four Winds
Press, 1978.
  Good section on Sikhism in this survey of Eastern religions.

Taoism

Blofeld, John, translator. *I Ching: The Book of Change*. London Books: Unwin Paperbacks, 1989.
Translation of this basic source book for several Eastern religions. Includes introduction which explains the process used and the history as known.

Blofeld, John. *Taoism: The Road to Immortality*. Boulder: Shambhala Publications, Inc., 1978.
Good summary of teachings of Taoism combined with survey of history of its founding (including background to the legendary beginning of China). Argues for historicity of Lao-Tzu, but maintains that Taoism pre-dates this important teacher.

Kaltenmark, Max. *Lao Tzu and Taoism*. Translated by Roger Greaves. Stanford: Stanford University Press, 1969.
Excellent survey of the history and legends surrounding the man Lao Tzu and the development of Taoism. Argues that historical Lao Tzu founded this religion.

Tzu, Lao. *The Way of Life (Tao Te Ching)*. Trans. by R. B. Blakney. New York: The New American Library, 1955.
Translation of the Tao Te Ching with an extensive introduction relating the background and basic history of the writer and his age.

Witchcraft, Wicca

Gardner, Martin. *The New Age: Notes of a Fringe Watcher*. Buffalo: Prometheus Books, 1988.
Collection of essays from *Skeptical Inquirer*. Writer takes an extremely cynical view of religion in general, and lumps conservative Christianity with the cults and charlatans. Overall tone is caustic. Title is a misnomer since he primarily focuses on purveyors of psychic phenomena with a few essays on Shirley MacLaine.

Hunt, Douglas. *Exploring the Occult*. New York: Ballentine Books, 1964
Overview of various phenomena which come under the general category of occult. Uses anecdotal evidence to support premise

that something transcends materialistic explanation. Some material is background to New Age thinking.

Seabrook, William. *Witchcraft*. New York: Lancer Books, 1968.
Author has explored deeply into various groups which use "magic." Takes view that there is a power behind it, but that it is totally in the realm of psychological suggestion. At the same time records a number of items which he admits fall outside of his definition, and which seem to lie in the spirit realm.

Zoroastrianism

Boyce, Mary. *Zoroastrians: Their Religious Beliefs and Practices*. London: Routledge and Kegan Paul, 1986.
Argues for early date of Zoroaster on the basis of weak evidence. Uses a period of several "unrecorded centuries" to account for discrepancies. Historical portion is a good survey of this religion.

Carnoy, Albert J. *Iranian Mythology*. In "Mythology of All Races." Vol. 6. New York: Cooper Square Publishers, 1964.
A general survey of mythological concepts. Covers various traditions before and during the time of Zoroaster.

Hinnells, John R. *Persian Mythology*. London: Hamlyn Publishing Group, Ltd., 1985.
Good survey of background of Zoroaster and his culture. Also includes Mitraism. Follows Boyce on dating.

Rice, Edward. *Ten Religions of the East*. New York: Four Winds Press, 1978.
A brief overview of Zoroastrianism is included in this survey of a number of eastern religions.

Scripture Index

Scripture references are listed by the page number on which the passage is located, except in the case of endnotes, which include the footnote (fn) number as well as the page. Complete chapter references to a given book are listed prior to chapter and verse references.

Genesis

1-3	13
3	15
4	15
4-6	16
6	16-17, 18, 20, 21 fn4, 22 fn623
11	19, 23 fn15
12	9
16	178 fn4
21	178 fn4
50	203 fn14
1:14-16	36 fn8
1:26	13
1:28	13
2:17	222
3:4	114 fn14, 138 fn15
4:2	36 fn8
4:7	16
4:21	36 fn8
4:23	16
6:1	17
6:4	19
6:14	36 fn8
8:20	16
10:9-12	113 fn13
10:25	23 fn14
11:6	20
11:27	41 fn33

Mark
| 2:1-12 | 232 fn11 |
| 3:22 | 233 fn13 |

Luke
1:26	180 fn9
3:36	19
5:18-26	232 fn11
6:13-16	71, 110 fn4
11:15	233 fn13

John
1:36	61 fn5
2:19-21	220
3:16	182 fn21
4:1-26	53
4:25	64 fn18
8:48	233 fn13
9:13-34	233 fn13
10:20	233 fn13
12:31	14, 227
20:30-32	84 fn2

Acts
1	71
10	71
11	72
13	72
1:15-26	84 fn4
7:2 ff	31
9:7	231 fn4
11:27-29	84 fn5

Romans
1:4	xiii, 84 fn2, 219
1:17	77
2:1-2	8
8:18-23	139 fn18

1 Corinthians
2:4-16	35 fn2
5:7	61 fn5
5:9	86 fn10

SUBJECT INDEX

The following are individuals, items, and subjects mentioned in the text or endnotes. To assist the reader, endnote references are denoted by the note number as indicated by the letters "fn."

Asia	11 fn6, 89 fn25, 129, 130, 135 fn4, 184 fn32
Asia Minor	72, 74, 87 fn16, 111 fn1, 112 fn7, 113 fn13
Assassins	184 fn33
Assyria	30, 31, 111 fn1, 121
Assyrian Empire	34 fn1, 121
Assyrians	52, 63 fn15, 64 fn16
astrology	85 fn9, 146, 157 fn17, 215 fn78
astronomy	34 fn1, 36 fn8
Astyages	156 fn11
Atar	157 fn14
Aten	34, 43 fn43
Athanasius	88 fn20
Atharva Veda	101-102
atheism	xi, xiii fn2, 100
Atisha	134, 142 fn29
Atlanta, Georgia	196
Atman	103-104, 105, 107, 110, 116 fn28, 123, 124
atonement	15, 21 fn1, 73, 86 fn12, 195, 210 fn53, 211 fn56
Atum	42 fn37
Augustine	75, 78, 88 fn22, 88 fn23, 88 fn24, 88 fn37
Aurelius, Marcus	75, 87 fn15
Australia	7, 11 fn9, 11 fn10
authority	11 fn6, 67 fn30, 67 fn33, 73, 78, 79, 90 fn31, 91 fn37, 93 fn45, 204 fn14, 204 fn17, 209 fn46, 211 fn58, 216 fn84, 218-220, 223, 233 fn11
"Authorized Version"	See King James Version
Autobiography of Benjamin Franklin	92 fn42
avatar	114 fn14, 115 fn24, 117 fn32, 117 fn35, 117 fn37, 131
Averroes	76
Avesta	145, 146, 154 fn2
Avetat	156 fn9
Avicenna	76
Ayub, Hassan	180 fn20, 182 fn23, 183 fn25, 183 fn26
Azhi Dahaka	156 fn9
Baal	62 fn9, 63 fn11, 223
Baalism	223
Bab	176-77, 185 fn35, 185 fn36, 185 fn37, 185

Hanukkah	54, 66 fn27
Haran	31, 41 fn34, 61 fn2
Harappa	100-101, 113 fn9, 113 fn10
Harappan culture	100-101, 113 fn8, 113 fn9, 113 fn11, 113 fn12, 130 fn19, 214 fn75
Harbin, Michael A.	23 fn17
Hare Krishnas	110, 119 fn45
Harris, Lucy	202 fn11
Harris, Martin	188, 202 fn11
Harrison, R. K.	63 fn10
Hashim clan	168, 170
Hasidim	69 fn29
Hasidism	58, 59
Hasmonaeans	66 fn 25
Hatcher, William S.	195 fn36, 189 fn38
Hatshepsut	62 fn7
Haurvatat	155 fn7
Haykal, Husayn	178 fn4, 179 fn7, 180 fn8, 180 fn9
healing	192, 193, 194, 207 fn36, 207 fn37, 208 fn39, 208 fn42, 209 fn43, 209 fn49, 220, 233 fn13
heaven/heavens	39 fn20, 100, 133, 140 fn23, 149, 151, 155 fn5, 158 fn22, 165, 188 fn13, 182 fn22, 211 fn59, 227, 235 fn23
heaven god	See sky god
hedonism	122, 123, 126
Hegel	208 fn38
Heidel, Alexander	41 fn36
Hein, Novin	114 fn17, 116 fn28, 116 fn29, 118 fn40
Heliopolis	33
Heliopolis theology	42 fn37
hell	17, 125, 140 fn23, 183 fn24, 192, 202 fn8, 207 fn33
Hellenistic philosophy	See philosophy, Greek
Hellenization	54, 55, 66 fn26, 145
Henry IV (France)	See Henry of Navarre
Henry VIII (England)	79, 80
Henry of Navarre	79
Henschel, Milton G.	196, 213 fn66
The Herald of the Morning	211 fn55
heresy	90 fn29, 92 fn40, 117 fn37
hermeneutics	88 fn23, 91 fn37
hermits	103

Herodotus	156 fn11
Hezekiah	52, 63 fn14, 64 fn16, 64 fn17
The Hierarchy and the Plan	213 fn70
hierarchy (spiritual)	17-19, 22 fn9, 22 fn10, 22 fn11, 25, 26-27, 28-31, 33, 36 fn6, 40 fn27, 40 fn28, 67 fn33, 99-100, 103, 116 fn27, 117 fn35, 125, 140 fn24, 143, 144, 147, 148, 149, 150, 151, 152, 153, 155 fn4, 155 fn7, 156 fn9, 156 fn10, 156 fn12, 158 fn22, 158 fn23, 157 fn26, 160 fn35, 180 fn9, 182 fn22, 187, 197, 198-200, 201 fn7, 213 fn70, 215 fn77, 215 fn80, 218, 221, 222, 223, 224-28, 234 fn17, 235 fn26, 235 fn27
hieroglyphics	202 fn10
high places	63 fn12
higher criticism	38 fn16
Hijira	178 fn1
Hillerbrand, Hans J.	91 fn34
Himalayan Mountains	121, 125, 150 fn21
Hinduism	xiv, 99-119, 121, 123, 124, 125, 129, 130, 131, 134, 137 fn11, 138 fn14, 138 fn15, 141 fn26, 143, 155 fn6, 160 fn38, 197, 198, 214 fn75, 217, 219, 224
Hinduism (Renou)	111 fn1, 116 fn31, 137 fn11
Hinnells, John R.	154 fn2, 155 fn4, 155 fn7, 157 fn14
"hippies"	198
Hislop, Alexander	113 fn13, 235 fn25
The Historical Buddha	135 fn1, 138 fn13
Historical Survey of the Old Testament	23 fn12, 62 fn9
history	xi, xii, 3, 5, 8, 13, 14, 16, 19, 22 fn8, 23 fn14, 25, 27, 29, 34 fn1, 40 fn25, 42 fn38, 42 fn39, 49, 51, 53, 56, 62 fn2, 63 fn12, 65 fn19, 67 fn37, 72, 73, 84, 88 fn21, 91 fn35, 97, 99, 104, 111 fn1, 111 fn2, 121, 128, 134, 136 fn6, 136 fn9, 136 fn13, 136 fn19, 143, 146, 147, 156 fn12, 156 fn13, 158 fn25, 160 fn33, 160 fn35, 161 fn43, 165, 167, 183 fn29, 184 fn34, 187, 194, 199, 200, 200 fn3, 201 fn7, 203 fn11, 204 fn19, 210 fn51, 212 fn64, 215 fn82, 216 fn84, 217, 218-20, 221, 222, 225, 230 fn2, 230 fn3, 232 fn9, 233 fn14, 235 fn25, 235 fn26

Landsberger, Benno	36 fn8, 39 fn24
Lang, Andrew	8, 10 fn5, 12 fn12,
language	
Akkadian	27-28, 34 fn1, 39 fn25, 111 fn2
Arabic	169, 174, 178 fn3, 180 fn9, 180 fn11
Aramaic	54, 60, 65 fn23, 66 fn24, 66 fn29, 68 fn38
Chinese	130, 131, 132, 147, 159 fn29
English	59, 77, 83 fn1, 92 fn38, 180 fn9, 182 fn22, 201 fn7, 203 fn11, 214 fn74
French	59
German	59
Greek	21 fn4, 22 fn9, 66 fn24, 77, 80, 83 fn1, 90 fn31, 90 fn32, 153 fn1, 154 fn2, 180 fn9, 231 fn8
Harappan	100, 113 fn8, 113 fn11
Hebrew	19, 22 fn9, 54, 58, 59, 65 fn23, 66 fn24, 66 fn25, 67 fn31, 77, 83 fn1, 90 fn31, 180 fn9, 190, 202 fn10, 203 fn11, 212 fn65
Indian	113 fn11, 114 fn15
Latin	32, 59, 66 fn24, 231 fn8
Japanese	131, 132
Pali	127, 129
Persian	153 fn1, 154 fn2, 184 fn34
Proto-Dravidian	113 fn11
Proto-Elamite	111 fn2
Proto-Hindu	111 fn1, 138 fn15
Sanskrit	82, 111 fn1, 114 fn15, 123, 130, 141 fn26
Sumerian	27, 28, 32, 34 fn1, 36 fn7, 37 fn12, 111 fn2
Syriac	157 fn17, 231 fn8
Language and Species	35 fn3
"Language Was Created, Not Evolved"	23 fn17
Lao Tan	see Lao Tzu
Lao Tzu	145, 150, 152, 160 fn32
Lao Tzu and Taoism	160 fn33
Laodicea	88 fn21
Laos	131
lapis lazuli	111 fn3
Last of the Giants	235 fn24, 235 fn27
Latourette, Kenneth Scott	67 fn36, 84 fn3, 86 fn14, 87 fn16, 90 fn30, 201 fn5
Latter Day Saints	93 fn45
law, cosmic	100, 116 fn29

Law, Old Testament	21 fn2, 49, 50, 54, 55, 66 fn29, 67 fn30, 72, 85 fn9, 232 fn9
Law, William	206 fn24
"Laws of Manu"	102, 116 fn29, 116 fn31
Layman's Prayer Revival	93 fn48
Lazaris	231 fn5
lead	157 fn16
League of Nations	69 fn44
legal-historical proof	230 fn3
legalism	56, 85 fn9, 199
Lehi	202 fn9, 202 fn10
Lenin, Vladimar	219
leprosy	220
Levi	61 fn1
Levites	65 fn21
Lewis, C. S.	84 fn2, 233 fn12
Lewis, H. Spencer	234 fn19
Lhasa	134
Li Chi	159 fn27
liberal theology	82
Liberty, Missouri	190
Lieber, Francis	208 fn38
The Life of Buddha and the Early History of His Order	136 fn6
The Life of Mary Baker Eddy	207 fn34
The Life of Muhammad	178 fn4
The Life of Mohammed, Prophet of Allah	178 fn3
light, god of	146
literal hermeneutic	88 fn24
Lithuania	59
Little, Paul E.	84 fn2
Logos	88 fn21
"Lord of the Dance"	106
Los Angeles Times	200 fn3
"lost tribes of Israel"	64 fn16, 121, 203 fn13
Louis XIV	79
Loyola, Ignatius	80
Lu	148, 158 fn25, 159 fn27
Lucretius	230 fn2
lusts	222, 225-26
Luther, Martin	78, 79, 90 fn31, 90 fn32, 91 fn36
Lutheran Church	78, 91 fn36

Egyptian	33, 62 fn6
Greek	22 fn9, 22 fn11, 66 fn26, 155 fn7
Hindu	101, 104, 106, 107, 114 fn16, 115 fn25, 116 fn27, 129
Iranian	144, 146, 155 fn7
Persian	112 fn6, 155 fn7
Sumerian	29, 32-33, 39 fn19, 112 fn5
papacy	See popes
papal infallibility	83
papyrus	202 fn10
paradise	183 fn24
Paran	178 fn4
Parfitt, Tudor	135 fn4
Paris	78
Parliament	79
Parrinder, Geoffrey	12 fn 12
Parthian Empire	145
Parvati	117 fn36
Passover	50, 61 fn5, 64 fn16, 64 fn17
Pastor Charles Taze Russell	212 fn60
Pastoral Bible Institute of Brooklyn	212 fn61
Pataliputra	129
Paths of Faith	xv fn1, 12 fn12, 118 fn38
Patna	129, 139 fn17
Patriarch of Constantinople	76
patriarchs	15
Patterson, Daniel	192
Patterson, Mary Baker	See Eddy, Mary Baker
Paul (the Apostle)	xv, 8, 18, 25, 35 fn2, 56-57, 61 fn5, 71, 72, 77, 84 fn2, 84 fn4, 85 fn7, 86 fn10, 180 fn9, 220, 228, 231 fn4, 233 fn12
Paul Johnson Movement	212 fn61
Payne, Robert	179 fn5, 180 fn8, 181 fn14, 181 fn15, 181 fn17, 183 fn29
Peace of Augsburg	78
Peace, Prosperity, and the Coming Holocaust	235 fn26
Pearl of Great Price	202 fn10, 204 fn14, 234 fn18
Pelagianism	75
Pelagius	75, 88 fn22, 88 fn23
Peleg	23 fn15
Pentateuch	See Torah

Ra	33, 42 fn40
Rabi'a	185 fn34
Rabbi/rabbis	54, 55, 59, 72, 167, 170, 175
Rahula	122
rainbow	198
raja	122, 135 fn5
Rajagaha	127
rajanyas	102
Rama, Prince	105, 117 fn32
Ramadan	169, 170, 173, 181 fn16
Ramanuja	107
Ramayana	105, 117 fn32
Ramoth-Gilead	223
Ramses II	62 fn7
rebellion, spiritual	200 fn1
reconciliation	165
Red Hats	134
Red Sea	50, 169
Redating the Exodus and Conquest	42 fn41, 65 fn7
redemption	8, 125, 139 fn18, 179 fn5, 211 fn56, 229
reformation	63 fn14, 77, 123, 134, 176
Reformation, Protestant	75, 77-80, 81, 83, 90 fn30, 90 fn31
Reformed Judaism	60, 68 fn43
Reformed theology	78
Reformed tradition	93 fn45
reformers	77-80, 88 fn23, 90 fn30, 90 fn33, 91 fn34, 92 fn41, 125, 176
Rehoboam	221
Reinach, Salmon	10 fn1, 10 fn5,
re-incarnation	101, 103, 114 fn14, 115 fn24, 123, 124, 125, 134, 138 fn12, 138 fn15, 184 fn30, 213 fn71, 214 fn72, 214 fn75, 214 fn76, 219, 224, 235 fn21
The Religion of the Hindus	117 fn33, 117 fn34
Religions of Ancient Egypt and Babylonia	42 fn37
Religions of Asia	114 fn17, 116 fn28, 119 fn42
Religions of the East	160 fn34
Religions of Japan	200 fn2
The Religious Experience of Mankind	160 fn32, 231 fn4
Remonstrances	90 fn33
Renaissance	76, 90 fn30

	fn33, 91 fn37, 173, 182 fn23, 195, 204 fn14, 206 fn28, 208 fn42, 209 fn46, 222
seals	100
Second Coming	68 fn43, 83, 194-95, 210 fn53, 210 fn55, 211 fn59
Second Reader	194
Secret Doctrine	197
Sects and Separatism During the Second Jewish Commonwealth	67 fn29
secular humanism	xiii, 187
Seeburg, Reinhold	88 fn21
seers	114 fn18, 117 fn35, 122, 199, 214 fn74
Seleucids	54, 157 fn17
semi-pelagianism	88 fn23
Semiramis	113 fn13
Semitic tribes	30, 32, 37 fn10, 41 fn33
separation clause (U.S. Constitution)	93 fn44, 174
Sephardic Jews	58
Septuagint	21 fn4, 22 fn9
serpent	101, 136 fn9, 138 fn15
serpent kings	123, 136 fn9
Seth (channeled being)	198
Seth (Egyptian god)	31
Seth (son of Adam)	16, 19, 21 fn2,
Sethe, K.	42 fn39
"Seveners"	see Isma'ilis
Seventh Day Adventists	93 fn45, 210 fn53
Shabaka	42 fn39
Shafii school	184 fn32
Shafii, Muhammad ibn Idris al	184 fn32
Shah	177
shakti	106-7, 117 fn36
Shaivism	See Shivaism
shaman	7
shamanism	133
Shamesh	40 fn28
Shang Dynasty	158 fn22
Shang Ti	158 fn22
Shar-Kali-Sharri	31
Sharia	174
Sharon, Vermont	188
Shedd, William G. T.	88 fn21

Wycliffe, John	fn19, 159 fn29, 180 fn10 77, 90 fn29

Xavier, Francis	92 fn40
Xemu	233 fn15
Xerxes	145, 154 fn3

Yahweh	181 fn15
Yahweh and the Gods of Canaan	62 fn9
Yahya, Mirza	177
Yajur Veda	101
Yang Chu	149
Yasodhara	122
Yathrib	see Medina
Yazatas	112 fn6, 144
Yazd	157 fn18
Yearbook of American and Canadian Churches	93 fn47
Yellow Hats	134
Yellow River	158 fn21, 158 fn22
Yemen	167, 172, 180 fn8
Yin and Yang	149, 151, 152, 159 fn28, 160 fn38
Yoga	101, 107, 118 fn38, 118 fn40, 141 fn26, 214 fn72, 214 fn75
Yogi, Maharishi Mahesh	110, 119 fn44
Yom Kippur	69 fn45
Young, Brigham	190, 191, 234 fn18

Zadok	67 fn31
Zagros Mountains	99
Zakkai, Jochanan ben	57
Zamzam	178 fn4, 180 fn8
Zarathustra	See Zoroaster
Zaydis	184 fn33
Zealots	57
Zechariah	53, 182 fn23
Zedekiah	63 fn15, 223, 234 fn17
Zen Buddhism	xii, 132, 133, 135, 198
Zeus	22 fn9, 22 fn11, 66 fn26, 112 fn5
Zion	189

About the Author

A graduate of the U.S. Naval Academy, Michael A. Harbin served in the U.S. Navy as a helicopter pilot. While on active duty, he was stationed in Spain, from whence he was given further assignments in Greece and Egypt. After leaving active duty, he joined the Naval Reserves through which he was given assignments around the world. He supported a number of military exercises and special projects, primarily in Japan, Korea, Thailand, and the Philippines. During Operation Desert Shield, he was the Political-Military Officer for the Naval Component Commander of the Coalition Forces, traveling throughout the Persian Gulf region as part of his duties. These travels provided a major foundation for this book. Before retiring at the rank of Captain, he was awarded the Meritorious Service Medal, three Navy Commendation Medals, and the Naval Achievement Medal.

In addition to his BS degree in Engineering and History he has earned graduate degrees from Dallas Theological Seminary (ThM and ThD in Old Testament and Semitic Studies) and California State University at Dominguez Hills (MA in Literature and History). He has taught at Dallas Bible College, El Centro College (Dallas), LeTourneau University's Dallas campus, and is currently Visiting Professor of Biblical Studies at Taylor University.

In addition to his wife Esther, he has three children, Athena, Heidi, and Douglas. Other honors include selection to *Who's Who in Religion* (1992-93), election to the honor society of Phi Kappa Phi, and the receipt of an honorary Black Belt from the Chung Moo Doe Association of Dallas for community service.